MY LORD MAYOR

MY LORD MAYOR

Eight Hundred Years of London's Mayoralty

VALERIE HOPE

WEIDENFELD AND NICOLSON LONDON
IN ASSOCIATION WITH THE CORPORATION OF
LONDON

ILLUSTRATION ACKNOWLEDGEMENTS

The painting of the Thames by Canaletto and the Lord
Mayor's River Procession are reproduced by gracious
permission of Her Majesty the Queen. Other illustrations
were kindly supplied by the author, the Bridgeman Art
Library, the Corporation of London, Sir Peter Gadsden,
the Governor and Company of the Bank of England, Guildhall Library
and Art Gallery, Sir Christopher Leaver, the Worshipful
Company of Goldsmiths and the Worshipful Company of
Mercers.

Published in Great Britain by
George Weidenfeld & Nicolson Limited
91 Clapham High Street
London SW4 7TA

ISBN 0 297 79519 8

Printed and bound in Great Britain by
Butler & Tanner Ltd, Frome and London

800th ANNIVERSARY

CITY OF LONDON
—LORD MAYOR—
1189 – 1989

CONTENTS

FOREWORD

BY SIR CHRISTOPHER COLLETT

The year 1989 marks the 800th Anniversary of the office of Mayor, later Lord Mayor of London, which the Corporation of the City of London is celebrating with a number of special events.

It is highly appropriate that Valerie Hope should write a book which presents a fascinating insight into the evolution of this great public office, while providing with skill and clarity an absorbing account of civic duty and responsibility.

I hope you will find *My Lord Mayor* both informative and entertaining as a book to be opened with expectation and closed with profit.

LORD MAYOR

ACKNOWLEDGEMENTS

My thanks in the first place go to two people who first involved me in the City and its traditions – John Hart, Sheriff 1979–80, a personal friend, and Sir Peter Gadsden, Lord Mayor for that year, who appointed me as his Research Assistant during his year of office. This book has grown out of the interest in the history of the City and its Lord Mayors which that year inspired. Over the years I have received a great deal of help from the staff of the Guildhall Library and the Guildhall Record Office and I should like to thank them all. I am particularly grateful to Miss Betty Masters, former Deputy Keeper of Records, for her guidance in the early stages of my research and for allowing me to see her biographical notes on the City Chamberlains. I am greatly indebted to Mr J.R. Sewell, the City Archivist, who encouraged me to go ahead with the book, has made many valuable suggestions for sources and contacts, and has kindly read the text. His assistants, especially Mrs Vivienne Aldous, have been very helpful.

I am also indebted to Dr Caroline Barron, who lent me her notes on the medieval mayoralty. The librarians and archivists of the Livery Companies whom I consulted have been most helpful – Anne Sutton of the Mercers, Susan Hare of the Goldsmiths, D.E. Wickham of the Clothworkers and Robin Myers of the Stationers. It was only shortage of time that prevented me from talking to many more. The same is true of former Lord Mayors, and I am very grateful to Sir Edward Howard, Sir Peter Gadsden and Sir Greville Spratt for sparing the time to discuss the modern mayoralty with me. Mr Geoffrey Rowley, the Town Clerk, has been extremely kind in reviewing the whole project with me and reading the later chapters. I should like to thank him and the Corporation of London for sponsoring the book.

Tom Graves has given valuable help in researching the pictures and we are both grateful to Ralph Hyde and John Fisher of the Guildhall Print Room for their assistance. I am also indebted to Ian Doolittle's *The City of London and its Livery Companies* for quotations from the *Westminster Review* and *Fraser's Magazine* and W. Carpenter's *The Corporation of London*.

Finally my thanks go to Freda Reavenall who read the proofs with me and to my husband who has throughout been my chief support, critic and first time editor, as well as providing several of the pictures for the book.

Thy famous Mayor by princely governance
With sword of justice thee ruleth prudently
No lord of Paris, Venice or Florence
In dignity or honour goeth to him nigh.
He is exemplar, lode-star and guy [guide]
Principal patron and rose original
Above all mayors as master most worthy
London thou art the flower of cities all.

(William Dunbar, 1465–1530)

Through all the vicissitudes of the City's history from the 1190s to the present day one consistent thread has run: the City's own representative, its leading magistrate, the man who is set between the government of the City and the Kingdom, has been the Mayor, or as he has been called since the 15th century, the Lord Mayor.

(C. N. L. Brooke and Mrs G. I. Keir,
London 800–1216: The Shaping of a City, 1975)

1

⸻ • ◦ • ⸻

INTRODUCTION

It is Michaelmas Day, or thereabouts. While a few leaves, now golden, drift from the trees in the City's tiny gardens, business goes on as usual in the Stock Exchange, the finance houses, the banks and insurance companies, in the Baltic and Metal Exchanges and in Lloyd's. Very few of the army of city workers, typing, telephoning, concentrating on computer screens in their tower block offices, are aware that near by in Guildhall the citizens of London are about to elect their Lord Mayor. But perhaps the odd secretary or bank clerk may take an early lunch-break and wander into Guildhall yard, where a dozen or so police from the City's own force are on duty, ready to control a small crowd of people who seem uncertain what they may be about to see.

Clearly something is going to happen because there is a bustle of photographers juggling with cameras, flash units and tripods. The festive red-and-white-striped canopy is stretched in front of Guildhall's great eighteenth-century Gothic porch. Below it a temporary wooden structure blocks the grand entrance with a series of wicket gates. Over each of these, engraved in gold letters, are the names of the City's ninety-eight Livery Companies in alphabetical order: Actuaries, Air Pilots, Apothecaries, Armourers . . . Haberdashers, Horners, Innholders . . . Wax Chandlers, Wheelwrights and Woolmen. In front, men in long gowns with coloured revers and tassles on their full sleeves stand chatting. These are the Beadles of the Companies, ready to check in their members, because only Liverymen, who for this purpose are the citizens of London, may

I

enter through the wicket gates to take part in the annual election of the Lord Mayor.

Shortly before midday a procession emerges from the church of St Lawrence Jewry on the other side of the square and makes its way diagonally across to Guildhall. These are the Masters, the Prime Wardens and one Upper Bailiff (a Weaver) of the ninety-eight Companies, who have been attending a religious service before the election, following a custom dating back to the year 1406 when Richard Whittington was chosen mayor for the third time. They walk in pairs, middle-aged men with long furred gowns over their business suits, and round their necks chains and badges of office. There may be one or two women, perhaps even a princess. The Princess Royal has been Master of two Companies, the Farriers and the Carmen.

Meanwhile other City dignitaries who have also attended the service have withdrawn to the Aldermen's Court room, a white construction on stilts which projects from the western wing of Guildhall, dating from the 1970s. At the precise moment when all are ready in the Great Hall they start to process solemnly along the modern colonnade and into the hall through the great west door. The Sheriffs' chaplains lead, followed by the Secondary and Under-Sheriff, the Remembrancer, the Comptroller and City Solicitor, the Common Serjeant, the Town Clerk and the Chamberlain, all in black gowns. Several of them – the legal figures – wear wigs, and the Chamberlain is distinctive in a furred robe. The two Sheriffs follow, wearing narrow chains of office from which hang their personal badges. Then come the Aldermen in scarlet robes with fur edging and black braid, accompanied by their Ward Beadles resplendent in black with gold braid, who bear the Ward maces. In their midst is the City Recorder, the senior judge at the Old Bailey. After them walk the City Marshal with a cockade of white plumes, the Lord Mayor's personal chaplain, the Common Cryer and Serjeant-at-Arms shouldering the City's massive gilt Mace, and the Swordbearer wearing an impressive fur hat and bearing aloft the City Sword. Finally the reigning Lord Mayor appears in his scarlet Alderman's robe, wearing his black feathered tricorne hat and his splendid chain of office from which hangs the Lord Mayor's Jewel with the City motto, *Domine Dirige Nos*, in diamonds, sparkling against his white lace jabot. All carry colourful nosegays, specially made by the Worshipful Company of Gardeners, a reminder of the days when posies of herbs offered some protection against the foul odours of medieval city streets.

As they disappear into Guildhall the passer-by may wish he could get in too. But the hall is already packed and the few visitors who have been admitted have been inside for nearly an hour. From the gallery at the back, sitting between the City's giant statues, Gog and Magog, they can look down on some 1,000 gowned Liverymen. The Liverymen constitute the ancient Court of Common Hall, which now meets twice a year, once for the election of the City's two Sheriffs and once for the election of the Lord Mayor. At the far end of the hall there is a low, red-carpeted platform known as the Hustings – an Anglo-Saxon word meaning 'house meeting' and a reminder of the distant origins of the City's government. It is strewn with sweet-smelling herbs. The procession makes its way up the central aisle and all take their places on the Hustings, the Lord Mayor in the centre of a semi-circle with the Aldermen on either side of him. Those who have 'passed the chair' (i.e., been lord mayor) sit on his right and his juniors sit on his left. The Sheriffs position themselves at the ends of the semi-circle and the City officials at a long table in front.

The Common Cryer steps forward and roars 'Silence' at the already hushed throng. He directs that all persons should be uncovered in the Hall and orders 'all those who are not Liverymen to depart the Hall on pain of imprisonment'. He then makes his proclamation. 'Oyez. Oyez. Oyez. You good members of the Livery of the several Companies of this City summoned to appear here this day for the election of a fit and able person to be Lord Mayor of this City for the year ensuing, draw near and give your attendance. God Save the Queen.' Next, the City Recorder comes forward and informs the Liverymen, so their choice may be unfettered, that he, the Lord Mayor, the senior Aldermen and the Town Clerk will retire. This they do, processing out to a hall known as the Livery Hall, preceded by the City Marshal and the Swordbearer.

Now the Sheriffs with the Common Serjeant between them advance to the front of the Hustings and proceed with the election. Each of the remaining Aldermen who has served the office of Sheriff is eligible, and the Liverymen are to nominate two from whom the Aldermen will elect the next Lord Mayor. The names are read out, and held up on a board for all to see, in order of seniority. When the first name is called a forest of hands rises and the combined voices of the Liverymen shout 'all'. The next name is greeted with a few hands and scattered cries of 'next year'. The remaining names provoke an occasional 'another time'. So the first two are declared nominated and the Sheriffs, the Common Serjeant, the Common Cryer and the Aldermen withdraw to the Livery Hall to complete the election. There the Aldermen vote by ballot and the result is declared by the Recorder. The Lord Mayor Elect thanks the Aldermen for the honour done to him and they congratulate him individually.

While this is going on the Deputy Town Clerk entertains the assembly in Guildhall with a paper on some aspect of City history. It is a pause rather like that at a wedding when the choir sings an anthem while the register is being signed, only there is no triumphal tune this time, just a moment of tension before the procession reappears, headed by the Lord Mayor with the Lord Mayor Elect on his left hand. He is greeted by a great burst of applause. For although this election is a formality, as it has been for many years, everyone involved will assure you that the result can never be taken for granted. Speeches of congratulations and thanks follow. When it is all over the Lord Mayor and the Lord Mayor Elect go out under the great porch where they are greeted by a fanfare of trumpets and a clicking of cameras as photographers, professional and amateur, take the first of many thousands of pictures of the man who is to be next year's Lord Mayor.

Who is he? Among those who take part in the City's traditional life and government – the Aldermen, Common Councilmen, City officers, Liverymen and some Corporation staff – he is certain to be well known. He is also known to many of the 6,000-odd people who actually live in the City, and to a wide circle of contacts in the business world. Apart from these, few Londoners and even fewer in the nation at large know his name. During his year of office the Lord Mayor will feature in the press and on television from time to time, but it is unlikely that his name will be remembered, although there are exceptions, such as the incumbent in 1983 – Dame Mary Donaldson – the only woman to achieve the honour, and hailed for this reason. Widely known or not, the Lord Mayor will be king in the City, giving place only to the reigning monarch. He will entertain and be entertained by royalty, visiting heads of state, the law and the church, cabinet ministers and leaders of industry. He will of course star at the Lord Mayor's Show and at the Lord Mayor's Banquet. He will live grandly in the Mansion House, served by the Esquires, the Private Secretary, the Steward, footmen, typists, chauffeurs, doormen and many others. He will attend hundreds of banquets, luncheons and receptions as the guest of honour. He will open all manner of functions, top out new buildings, give prizes at schools and universities, preside at board meetings of hospitals and charitable institutions. He will make hundreds of speeches. He will raise vast sums for special charitable causes. He will represent the

City throughout Britain, and Britain throughout the world when he travels abroad as a roving ambassador. He will be the City's Chief Magistrate, Head of the Lieutenancy, Chancellor of the City University, Clerk of the Markets and Admiral of the Port of London. Only half a dozen regiments may march through the City and they must request his personal permission to do this. He will have the password to the Tower of London. If a new Royal Prince or Princess is born he will be the first to be informed, as he will be if the reigning monarch should die. Everyone, except his immediate family in private, will always address him as 'Lord Mayor' or 'My Lord Mayor'.

Although his title is Lord Mayor of London, his realm is only a tiny fraction of the whole, for the square mile of the City is surrounded by the thirty-two other boroughs and 610 square miles of Greater London. It is not the size which counts, nor the tremendous value of every square foot of that square mile, nor even its commercial importance, because most people who work in the City pay little attention to its traditional and ceremonial activities. It is the past which gives the Lord Mayor his present importance in the life of the nation. For the City, where he reigns, is the historic, essential London. It lies above Roman 'Londinium', to the embarrassment of modern developers who must allow archaeologists months to excavate before the concrete foundations of their office blocks may be sunk. The Saxons gradually took up residence among the ruins of the Roman town and bequeathed to London its road network and the basic structure of City government, wards and parishes, sheriffs and aldermen. In the Middle Ages the Roman walls were repeatedly repaired and strengthened, even though the City boundaries had already extended beyond them to the bars at Holborn and the Temple and north to the Barbican and Moorgate. Royal authority stood east and west of the City: in William the Conqueror's Tower of London, and around Edward the Confessor's Westminster Abbey, where successive monarchs built palaces and held parliaments. The year after the Norman conquest the citizens of London extracted a charter from William in return for acceptance of his rule, which acknowledged their ancient privileges. This gave, and still gives, the City its unique status. It is a Corporation by prescriptive or customary right, since its constitution has been established 'from time immemorial'. This status has been carefully guarded, and partly because of it the City has kept within its ancient boundaries, merely watching the way in which London has grown from the sixteenth century on. It resisted Charles I's attempts at reorganization and extension in the seventeenth century. The Municipal Reform Acts of the nineteenth century passed it by, as did the local government reorganization of the 1960s. The Royal Commission of 1960 stated: 'If we were to be strictly logical we should recommend the amalgamation of the City and Westminster. But logic has its limits and the City lies outside them.' So the City remains separate and elects its lord mayor from among its aldermen as it has done for centuries, the only local authority in the country to remain 'unreformed'.

London had its first mayor in 1189 and has had the right to elect him since 1215. Some 660 men (and one woman) have filled the post over the past 800 years, for in the early days some mayors lasted for several years and others were re-elected at intervals. It is now over 100 years since anyone has served as lord mayor for more than one year.

In theory any British citizen can become Lord Mayor of London. The essential qualifications remain the same as they have always been. The aspirant must be a liveryman; he must have been elected, as their alderman, by the voters of one of the City's twenty-five wards (and must have been approved by the rest of the aldermen, who have the right, which has been exercised in recent years, to veto him); and he must have been elected by the liverymen in Common Hall as one of the two sheriffs and have served that office for one year. This, as an ordinance of the Common Council of 1385 put it, is 'so that he may be tried as to his governance and bounty before he attains to the estate of Mayor'. Nowadays it is a useful way for him to get to know the ropes. Finally he must be nominated by the liverymen in Common Hall and elected lord mayor by the aldermen.

It takes between ten and twenty years for a would-be lord mayor to work his way to acceptance by the traditional establishment. He needs to be able to devote a great deal of time and money (by way of charitable giving and hospitality) to the project. As an alderman his duties will include sitting as a City magistrate, and when he serves his year as sheriff he will have to take leave from his business or profession. The same will apply when he is lord mayor. Then there is the question of his 'bounty'. It is impossible to quote a figure, for the extent of the hospitality offered varies with individuals, but there is no doubt that he must be wealthy by any normal standards.

A variety of men have filled the post, some men of great ability, a few who have become famous, many who have done a great deal of good, one or two who have come to a sticky end. They have been champions of liberty and instruments of oppression. Some have been royal nominees, others leaders of the opposition. In the past many have been members of parliament and played an active part in politics, but today the City is determinedly non-party-political. Most of them have been new blood, that is non-Londoners in origin. Schools, almshouses and mansions, monuments in churches and parks all over England remain as evidence of their munificence to their native homes. They have come from all walks of life – very few from the aristocracy, although many have founded aristocratic families. On several occasions men have followed their fathers, grandfathers or even more distant ancestors to the mayoralty, but the preferred image is of the self-made man. The legend of Dick Whittington as the poor boy who made good – cat or no cat – has been the inspiration of many. With such a limited term of office it is hardly surprising that most past lord mayors have sunk into obscurity. Fewer than one fifth of the total number rate a mention in the *Dictionary of National Biography*, for example. But the stories of those who have made a mark one way or another have an extraordinary variety and often real significance in the life of the nation.

2

EARLY STRUGGLES

Eight hundred years ago the City of London was already an impressive sight, rising above a River Thames much wider than it is today. The old Roman walls encircled it on the north, with six double gates and fortified towers at intervals. Within these walls more than 100 churches raised towers and spires to the sky. There were thirteen great religious houses with all their outbuildings and gardens. There were hospitals, convents and priories. Great houses of the wealthy were surrounded by the huddled wooden shacks of the poor. In the east the White Tower dominated the river and in the west were two more castles, Baynards and Montfichet, built by the Conqueror 'against the restlessness of the vast and fierce populace'. Beyond them and outside the wall great houses and palaces lined the curve of the river westwards towards the Royal Palace of Westminster and the Abbey of St Peter. Building was unceasing, for the early medieval town suffered from frequent fires, the most disastrous of which had destroyed the greater part of London, including the old cathedral of St Paul and the wooden bridge across the river. From 1087 men were at work on a huge new cathedral, while in 1176 Peter of Colechurch had begun building the magnificent stone bridge which was to become one of the wonders of the medieval world. It would not be finished until 1209, four years after his death.

The river which it spanned was a busy thoroughfare, with craft of all sizes making for the city quays to unload their merchandise of wine, silks and velvets, and take on cargoes of wool and hides. London was already a major trading centre with a population of about 40,000, including many foreigners – Frenchmen, Italians and Jews. William Fitzstephen in his *Description of London* pictures for us the vitality of the people with their carnivals, tournaments and horse racing. He describes them trading, practising archery and wrestling, competing at leaping and javelin-throwing. In the winter they would skate on the great marsh north of the Moorgate. In summer there would be mock battles on the Thames where the spectators could enjoy a good laugh at the expense of those who fell in. Writing about the government of this teeming population, Fitzstephen compares London with ancient Rome. He mentions the wards into which the city is divided, the sheriffs whom he compares with consuls and a senatorial order, which must mean the aldermen. He proudly claims that the inhabitants are called barons, rather than mere citizens (but this too must surely refer to the aldermen). These wealthy and influential merchants had controlled the wards since Anglo-Saxon times and were the real power in the City.

The City's official ruler was a royal servant, the portreeve, who was mentioned in the 1067 charter. The sheriffs were royal law officers and tax gatherers. The mass of the citizens would attend the Folkmoot, which also dated from Anglo-Saxon times, on three annual occasions: at Michaelmas to acknowledge the new sheriffs, at Christmas for keeping order in the wards and at midsummer to remind the citizens of the fire precautions.

However, during the later years of Henry II's reign the Londoners began to form a 'commune'. This was a sworn association of citizens such as had been already established in several continental towns. One of the first was in Rouen, and it is interesting that around the port of Dowgate in the City was a flourishing community of merchants from that town. The leader of the commune was known as the 'maior'. Although the Londoners' commune was not officially recognized until 1191, by Prince John, it was clearly in existence before then. There is no conclusive evidence for the exact date when London's first mayor took office. The thirteenth-century chronicler Alderman Arnald FitzThedmar placed the beginning of London's mayoralty in the first year of Richard I's reign. So the year 1189 was considered the first year of the mayoralty and as such was painted on the Lord Mayor's coach in 1757. The 700th anniversary was celebrated in 1889 by a special Lord Mayor's Show. Twentieth-century historians have disputed the choice of this date on the grounds that the commune was not officially granted until 1191 and that the first recorded use of the title was in 1193. Therefore in recent years the accepted date has been 1192, estimated between the two. The evidence for this is of a negative character and mainly based on supposition. In the absence of firm evidence to the contrary it seems logical that the traditional date of 1189 should be accepted as the year when London's first mayor, Henry FitzAilwyn, first took office.

Henry FitzAilwyn was not only the first mayor but also the longest serving. He must have been a man of considerable standing and authority. He had been an alderman already in 1168, so he will have been quite old by the end of his mayoralty, which lasted until his death in September 1212. One of his earliest actions was to make a collection in London for the ransom of Richard Coeur de Lion, captured on his way home from the Third Crusade. This first known example of London's rulers coming to the aid of the monarch probably helped to make the new title, mayor, more acceptable. Among the Londoners themselves his status can be assessed from the allegation made in 1194 by William FitzOsbert, that the rebel Robert Brand had said, 'come what may, Londoners will have no king but their mayor'. These contradictory forces – the mayors as allies and supporters of the Crown, but also the personification of the citizens' desire for independence from royal despotism – lay behind the stormy history of the thirteenth and fourteenth centuries. Little is known of FitzAilwyn's work in establishing the new office. The only other recorded event concerning his mayoralty was the assize held after a particularly disastrous fire in 1212 at which he was credited with having ordered that London should be rebuilt in stone. He remains a shadowy figure, though we can picture him living somewhere near the present Cannon Street, since the phrase 'of London Stone' follows his name in early chronicles: a large stone dating from Roman times and known as 'London Stone' can still be seen behind a grating opposite Cannon Street Station.

The office of mayor became firmly established and the idea spread to other English towns, so that by 1200 Winchester had a mayor, Exeter by 1205 and Lincoln by 1206. The next Mayor of London was Roger FitzAlan, probably not a relation of FitzAilwyn, but a close friend and associate who held the office for two years. He was followed by Serlo le Mercer, who was Mayor of London during the crisis of King John's reign. Threatened by the rebellious barons, John attempted to win the support of Londoners by formally granting them the right to elect their mayor. The right to elect their own sheriffs had already been granted in 1199, but the office of mayor soon became more important. Since the citizens could choose a new mayor annually it became easier for them to control him and harder for the King to do so. This significant concession by the King was however made too late to win over the Londoners and the barons entered the City, where they had many supporters. John's charter to the City was dated May 1215. A month later, having taken refuge in Windsor Castle, he was forced to meet the barons on open ground at Runnymede and seal Magna Carta. William Hardel, who succeeded Serlo as mayor, was one of the committee of twenty-five barons appointed to see that the provisions of the charter were carried out. Clause 13 deals with London and other towns, stating 'That the City of London shall have all its ancient liberties by land as well as by water' and that 'all other cities, boroughs, towns and ports shall have all their liberties and free customs'.

John died in 1216 and his nine-year-old son succeeded as Henry III. His first charter to the City confirmed his father's concessions, but during the fifty-six years of his reign there were frequent clashes between the City's rulers and the King, and struggles between these rulers and the mass of the citizens. It is not at all clear in these early years how elections to the mayoralty were held, or indeed if they were held. Some mayors remained in office for three or four years at a time, others were deposed in mid-office. Their names give an indication of varied origins, with Normans like Serlo le Mercer and Richard Renger, and Italians like Andrew Buckerel (anglicized from Bokerell) after whom Bucklersbury is named – London was already a cosmopolitan city. But in reality all the mayors came from a close-knit oligarchical group who frequently intermarried. It is estimated that during the thirteenth century sixteen families controlled the City government. They were all wealthy merchants, owning land in the city and the surrounding countryside. They often owned ships and traded in wine, wool and hides with Europe. They supplied the Court with clothing, wine and foodstuffs. They held high office under the king, serving as Royal Chamberlain and Keeper of the Exchange. They loaned large sums of money to the Crown. William Joynier had to be rescued from prison in 1216, where he lay, ruined by the enormous debts owed to him by King John. Subsequently he recovered his fortunes, made himself into a city magnate and became mayor in 1239. Sometimes, rather than make a loan or a gift the mayors would pay the salaries of royal servants. Andrew Buckerel paid the expenses of the Coronation of Queen Eleanor when she married Henry III in 1236. In return for such services they received gifts of deer from the Royal Forests, were granted safe conduct for their ships and exempted from certain taxes.

Despite these mutual advantages the relationship between Crown and City rulers was far from smooth. On several occasions during these early years there were difficulties over the formal acceptance of the new mayor. John's charter had stipulated that the newly elected mayor must present himself to the king, a formality which was the origin of the Lord Mayor's Show. But medieval kings were constantly on the move and early mayors would travel to, say, Woodstock Palace, only to discover that the king was in Wales – or that, because of some dispute, the king refused to admit them. For example, because of a quarrel over the demotion of one Simon Fitzmary from his sheriffwick by the citizens, Henry III at first refused to admit the new mayor, Gerard Bat, on his election in October 1240. A few months later he grudgingly agreed to receive him but ordered that the usual payment of £40 on the assumption of the office be withheld. When a disappointed Gerard Bat protested: 'Alas my Lord, out of this I might have found a marriage portion to give my daughter,' there was an angry scene and Bat resigned.

The problem of locating the king was eased when in 1252 Henry gave the citizens a new charter (in return for 500 marks) which allowed them to present their mayor to the Barons of the Exchequer at Westminster 'in case the King should not be in London at the time when the Mayor was elected'. However the king was still free to dispense with the mayoralty if he wished, and whenever he was dissatisfied with the Londoners over taxes, wills, assizes, franchises or whatever, he simply took the City into his own hands. Recognizing the underlying discontent of many of the citizens with their rulers he sometimes mobilized this to attack mayors with whom he was displeased. In 1257 a major scandal broke when Ralph Hardel (son of William, mayor in 1215) was mayor. A parchment roll sealed with green wax was mysteriously discovered in the Wardrobe at Windsor, in which the Mayor and Aldermen were accused of fraud over taxes. Henry summoned the Folkmoot where he heard the complaints of the citizens, and the Mayor and Aldermen were deposed. Most of the Aldermen were re-elected the following October, but the new mayor, William FitzRichard, was a royal nominee.

Troubles between Henry III and his barons were now coming to a head, and in London there was strong support for the rebels, led by Simon de Montfort. However, Thomas FitzThomas, elected in 1261, seemed a safe mayor from the royal point of view. He was a nephew of William FitzRichard, had been sheriff under Ralph Hardel and had been one of the few aldermen to emerge from the tax enquiry of 1257 with credit. So in

1262, confident of his control of the City, Henry left to campaign in France. But by 1263 de Montfort was in open rebellion. In the City, FitzThomas put himself at the head of the popular movement, which not only supported de Montfort but was also protesting against the aristocratic control of City government and demanding greater influence for the craft guilds. He rejuvenated the Folkmoot which had declined. The citizens formed their own militia and vented their fury against overpowerful magnates like Adam de Basing, who had been mayor in 1251, by tearing down his house which had recently been extended, blocking a street. (Basinghall Street reminds us of this family.) London was in an uproar and the Pope sent a rebuke to the Bishop of London saying England was in 'a boiling whirlpool of universal disruption'. There was no doubt of FitzThomas's ascendancy. In October 1263 he was re-elected by mass acclamation. Henry III refused to admit him, but by now London was committed to de Montfort. In 1264 a strong force of London militia fought with the rebel barons at the Battle of Lewes. There they were routed by royalists under Prince Edward, the King's eldest son, but de Montfort won the day.

Later that year, at a public reconciliation between the King and the barons in St Paul's, FitzThomas did somewhat equivocal homage to Henry, saying 'My Lord, so long as you are willing to be to us a good king and lord we will be faithful to you and true.' The royalist chronicler FitzThedmar was shocked by the 'unheard of conduct of this most wretched mayor'. It looked as if the popular party was in the ascendant, but a change in the fortunes of war turned the tables on them. In August 1265 de Montfort was defeated and killed at the Battle of Evesham, and Henry regained control. That October FitzThomas and forty leading citizens were summoned to Windsor Castle, under 'safe' conduct, and imprisoned. Henry entered the City in triumph and retribution fell on the hapless citizens. According to a Suffolk plea roll, being a Londoner could be regarded as an offence in itself. The following year the King issued a formal pardon to the citizens and ordered a fine of 20,000 marks, which was still in arrears years later, with many of the citizens ruined. Their civic liberties were not restored, and the City was governed by a succession of royal wardens until 1270, when John Adrien was formally elected mayor. As for FitzThomas, he disappeared from public view and it was thought that he died in prison, but the records show that he bought his release in 1269 and died a few years later.

The movement for a more democratic city government was still alive.

In 1272 Walter Hervey was elected mayor. He had been appointed by Henry III to act as bailiff under the Constable of the Tower after the Battle of Evesham and since 1267 had been Royal Escheator. But as mayor he too favoured the craft guilds and was very popular with the commons – so much so that in 1272 the Aldermen tried to choose another, Philip le Taillour, as mayor but the people protested noisily 'Nay, nay, we will have no-one for Mayor but Walter Hervey'. Both sides set off for Westminster to appeal to the King, the commons insisting that the election of the mayor was their right while the Aldermen stated that they were the head and the people merely the limbs of the body politic. The King was mortally ill and the hideous tumult which went on for days forced the Council to temporize so that he could have some peace. They appointed Henry Frowicke warden for a few weeks. After Henry III's death an agreement was patched up and Hervey's election was allowed for that year. Under the next mayor Hervey continued to support popular causes, defending the butchers and fishmongers whose stalls had been removed in Cheapside to clean up the City for the return of the new King, Edward I, from France. Finally Hervey was summoned to Guildhall where he faced a long list of charges including bearing false witness, misappropriation and taking of bribes. He was degraded from his aldermanry and no more was heard of him. Like FitzThomas he seems a man ahead of his time, but he could be regarded as a dangerous demagogue and troublemaker.

The government of the City was bound to be influenced by Edward I, a strong monarch who needed a well-organized and prosperous city to help finance his aggressive wars against the Welsh, the Scots and the French. For much of his reign the office of mayor was held alternately by two powerful and influential men: Henry le Waleys and Gregory de Rokesley, who served together as sheriffs in 1270. During their term of office a new pillory was erected in Cheapside to punish offending bakers. When even they failed to provide the control he needed, Edward I too took the City into his own hands and for thirteen years from 1285 to 1298 royal wardens ruled in place of the mayor.

Little is known either of le Waleys's origins or of the source of his wealth, but his name indicates that he may have come from Wales. Apparently his chief business was as a vintner. From his first mayoralty in 1273 he was high in the royal favour and in May 1274, together with de Rokesley and two others, he was summoned to meet the new King in Paris to confer about his forthcoming Coronation. Le Waleys's interests in France were considerable, for in 1275 he was Mayor of Bordeaux. In

1282 he was one of six citizens, as was Rokesley, summoned to the Parliament at Shrewsbury, the first known members for the City. Le Waleys was an important royal servant, spending much time abroad on the King's business in Scotland, Rouen and Gascony. Together with de Rokesley he was consulted by the King on the planning of Berwick-upon-Tweed and on the new town of Ilam, built 'for the barons of Winchelsea as that town is already submerged by the sea'.

As Mayor of London in 1273, 1281-3 and 1298, le Waleys was busy drawing up ordinances for the safe keeping of the City gates, where sergeants 'fluent of speech' were posted to question suspicious strangers. Every night the curfew was to be rung simultaneously in the City churches to signal the closing of gates and taverns. He was the mayor who dealt with Hervey and cleared the stalls from Cheapside for the reception of Edward I. Later he erected new houses and stalls for the tradesmen near Wool Church Haw, where Mansion House now stands. He built the Tun prison on Cornhill, incorporating 'a fair conduit of sweet waters' in the building. He was so vigorous in punishing lawless citizens and maintaining order that he aroused some hostility in the people, for the King issued a mandate ordering justices at the Tower not to molest him for his activity 'for the quiet of the said city'.

In 1274 Gregory de Rokesley succeeded le Waleys as mayor and served until 1281 and again in 1284. He came from Rokesley in Kent, where he held extensive lands. He was the richest goldsmith of his day, but also a great wool merchant. In 1285 he and le Waleys were considered by the men of the Cinque Ports as the leading wine merchants in England. He too was a royal servant, acting officially as royal butler and as the Master of the Exchange in charge of the Royal Mint, in which capacity he called in clipped coinage and issued new coins. He was closely involved with the Lombard bankers and made substantial loans to the King. It is possible that his control in the City was too lenient for the King's liking, and that his fall was partly caused by maladministration. The actual event was set off by a scandal over a murder in Bow Church. The King appointed John de Kirkeby, the Lord Treasurer, to hold an inquiry, having already expressed dissatisfaction with the state of public order, describing the area of the Folkmoot at St Paul's as 'a den of thieves'. De Kirkeby issued a peremptory summons to the Mayor to attend him at the Tower. Offended by the failure to be given the customary forty days notice, de Rokesley stripped himself of his insignia and attended as a private citizen. Whether or not he intended to resign, it was the end of his mayoralty and Edward installed Ralph de Sandwich as warden. So from 1285 until 1298, when le Waleys was re-elected, the City was ruled by royal wardens. They probably did keep firmer control over law and order, and there is no record of public protest at this lengthy suspension of the mayoralty. The urge of Londoners to have their own rulers did not die out, but it is noticeable that le Waleys, restored in 1298, was particularly strict, and clearly many substantial citizens appreciated stronger control. In 1303, during the mayoralty of John le Blund, a citizen said he wished to God the royal warden was still in charge because under him business was dealt with speedily.

Le Blund, mayor from 1301 to 1307 was a wealthy Draper and the last mayor to come from the ranks of the old ruling oligarchy. He was distinguished by being the first Mayor of London to be knighted during office. In 1306, together with many courtiers and noblemen and the Prince of Wales, he received the accolade before the seventy-year-old Edward set off for Scotland to take the field against Robert Bruce – a journey from which he would never return.

The reign of Edward I had given the City a period of stable government and enabled the rising middle class to get a foothold in the City government. The administration of the City became more professional, and in 1298 the first Recorder, (the senior law officer) of the City, Geoffrey de Norton, took office. The craft guilds grew in importance and influence. The commonalty became more active, pressing complaints about corruption and the activities of alien merchants. In the City, as in the whole country, the confused and bloody reign of Edward II was a testing time. Inevitably the citizens were involved in the struggles between Edward and his favourite, Piers Gaveston, against the barons and Queen Isabella. Nicholas de Farndone, a Goldsmith, was mayor four times and served as Member of Parliament for London. The Farringdon Wards are named after him. Richer de Refham was mayor only in 1310, but his career is of interest because he was a newcomer from Norfolk who made a fortune as a mercer and became a great landowner in London. As mayor he kept order and destroyed encroachments on the city streets (these 'purprestures' were a constant nuisance in the narrow medieval streets). Also he caused ancient customs and liberties of the City to be recorded. He had them read to the aldermen and got their confirmation that they wished them maintained. Unfortunately his career was cut short when he quarrelled with his fellow Mercers and was deposed. He was succeeded by John de Gisors, whose grandfather had been mayor in 1246. He introduced constitutional reforms giving the commonalty greater control and making all officers stand for election annually. The mayor and aldermen were obliged to get the consent of a citizen assembly before setting the common seal on any document of importance. This particular arrangement did not last but the commonalty were beginning to win recognition as a permanent part of the government of the City. There was a period of reaction when John de Wengrave, who was the Recorder and Deputy Coroner and therefore a royal nominee, was mayor from 1316 to 1318.

In 1319 Hamo de Chigwell was the first Fishmonger to become mayor. Like Refham and Gisors he was a reforming mayor, but they had the support of their fellow aldermen (unlike the rebels FitzThomas and Hervey). Like so many medieval mayors, de Chigwell had many business interests and was a prominent wine merchant as well as a Fishmonger. He was a man of commanding personality with great political talents. He managed to keep the support of the middle class to which he owed his rise to power, and yet retain the King's favour for most of the time. The great achievement of his first mayoralty was the charter of 1319, which settled the City's constitutional issues, establishing the part of the commons in the City government and their share in the control of finance, and regulating the powers of officials. As the French *Chronicle of London* put it, 'at this time many of the people of the trades of London were arrayed in livery and a good time was about to begin'. Certainly the guilds were growing in influence and had established their sole right to grant the Freedom of the City. De Chigwell was elected mayor three times and served six years in all. As a supporter of the unpopular Edward II, he had enemies, and was described by one of them, John de Cotun, as 'the vilest worm that has been in the city for twenty years'. In the final crisis of Edward II's reign, de Chigwell could no longer control the rebellious element in London. The mob in the streets rose against the King in 1326, murdered John le Marshall, a royal counsellor, and Bishop Stapleton, the Treasurer, hacking off the latter's head in Cheapside. They looted treasure in St Paul's, then seized de Chigwell and dragged him to Guildhall, where they made him swear allegiance to the barons and Queen Isabella. In October the citizens refused to re-elect him and there was a gap until the Queen permitted a free election and her candidate, Richard de Betoyne, was chosen. He sent a letter from the commonalty to Westminster demanding Parliament's support for the City in deposing Edward II. In January 1327 a stream of barons, knights and bishops came to Guildhall to swear loyalty to the Queen and the fourteen-year-old Prince Edward. Edward II was forced to resign the crown, kept a prisoner, and finally in September was hideously murdered in Berkeley Castle.

Edward III formally pardoned the City for their part in the rebellion against his father and granted them a new charter which was read in English at Guildhall. This confirmed their liberties yet again and guaranteed London would be free from interference by the Crown. In 1327 de Chigwell was mayor again, but by now he was a discredited man. The following year the Aldermen chose him, but the citizens would not have him, and in 1329 he was tried on charges of corruption and condemned to death. He avoided this penalty by claiming benefit of clergy and died in bed in 1332 – an inglorious end to the life of one of the outstanding early mayors.

Edward III reigned for fifty years, during which time London was finally established as the capital of the kingdom. Had Edward II succeeded in pursuing his father's aim of conquering Scotland it is quite possible that York might have become the capital of the kingdom. But with the abandonment of the Scottish wars and the opening of the English campaigns in France, which were to be known to posterity as the Hundred Years War, London became the headquarters of the government. For the City the proximity of Westminster was vital, since it was the regular meeting-place for Parliament, and the Exchequer was moved there from York. Co-operation between the King and the citizens of London was to their mutual benefit. The financial support of the London merchants was essential for a warring monarch, while for those same merchants success against the French must help trade, which was booming. Like Chaucer's Merchant in the Canterbury Tales, they 'wolde the sea were kept for anything, Betwixt Middleburgh and Orewell'. As control of capital passed into their hands they became a power in the realm. When Edward I had expelled the Jews in 1290, largely because of the citizens' hostility to them, Italians, whose expertise in banking had developed in city states like Florence, moved in to take their place as moneylenders to the Crown. Lombard Street, still a banking centre today, is named after them. But by the mid fourteenth century the Lombards were ruined by the demands of Edward III's campaigns and the London magnates took over merchant banking. They also took a great interest in the affairs of Parliament, with four members regularly sitting for the City. These were usually aldermen and therefore often mayors or ex-mayors. With their knowledge of civic affairs and of the vital wool trade they had much to contribute to discussions in Parliament. For their own part they could look to the sessions of Parliament at Westminster to bring more people to London and so bring business to the City, and they could take the opportunity to protest against any infringements of the City's liberties. It is an indication of the importance they attached to becoming a member of parliament that if they could not win a City seat, they would sometimes look for seats outside – to Middlesex or Southwark.

The aldermen were no longer drawn from a handful of families. New blood came in with immigrant families from the provinces. Gradually the craft guilds grew in strength and influence and the citizens began to take a greater part in the civic government through the Common Council. During the years of civic peace London's government developed the durability which was to serve it well in the chaotic years of Richard II's reign.

During most of Edward III's reign city life was comparatively peaceful. John de Pulteney was mayor in 1330–1, 1333 and 1336. He was a prosperous Draper who sat as Member of Parliament for the City in 1327 and 1337. He served as the King's Butler and Coroner from 1325 to 1326 and was knighted by Edward in 1337 – a rare honour in those days. He was the only alderman to be knighted between 1314 and 1381. His wealth can be judged from his properties. He had two mansions in London. One was the Manor of the Rose in Pountney Lane, which subsequently became the London residence of the Black Prince. Here he had wall hangings spangled with butterflies and stars, and red and green curtains and coverlets ornamented with lions, fleur-de-lis, popinjays and apple blossom. The other was Coldharbour in Thames Street which had the largest garden in the City and was later inhabited by the Earl of Salisbury. Neither of these houses has survived, but his great mansion of Penshurst in Kent, with its splendid great hall and for which he received a licence to crenellate in 1341, gives an idea of his importance. He left to the Bishop of London 'his finest ring with a red stone called a ruby' and to the Earl of Huntingdon 'a beautiful ring with two stones called diamonds' on condition they 'see after the establishment of chantries in St. Paul's, which the Mayor, Recorder, Sheriffs, Common Pleader and servants to be rewarded for attending ... and the endowment of St. Lawrence Pountney as a collegiate church'.

In the fourteenth century it was characteristic of wealthy men, and certainly of mayors, to donate money for chapels and chantries, where Masses would be said for their souls, and to make other charitable bequests. Stow lists some of Sir John's chapels, relief for prisoners in Newgate and the Fleet (who without charitable help would starve, since there was no proper provision for their keep), money to St Giles Hospital – and then gives up with 'and other legacies too long to rehearse'. Sir John died in 1349, a victim of the Black Death. Mayor of London during the year the Black Death rampaged throughout England was John Lovekyn, Fishmonger. There is practically no information on what happened in London during the Black Death so, unlike the heroic Sir John Lawrence during the Great Plague of 1665, we cannot describe the Mayor's work during that disaster, when it is estimated about one third of the inhabitants of the City died. John Lovekyn was a good example of a successful immigrant to London. Coming from an ancient Surrey family in Kingston, he became a wealthy fishmonger and lived first in a house near St Mary at Hill, and then in a large mansion in Thames Street, which looked out on to the river and the bridge. He was Member of Parliament for the City several times, made a large personal contribution towards the King's wars and served again as mayor in 1358 and in 1366 when he was appointed by the King to take over from Adam de Bury who had been disgraced. Clearly the appointment was approved by the citizens for he was re-elected the following October. He not only rebuilt his parish church, St Michael's, Crooked Lane, where he was buried in 1368 under a fine alabaster monument, but also built and endowed a hospital in Kingston. His house in Thames Street he left to one of his apprentices, William Walworth.

Another wealthy and influential mayor in Edward III's reign was Henry Picard. A Vintner, he was elected mayor in 1356, the year of the Black Prince's great victory over the French at Poitiers. John, King of France, was captured and brought back in triumph to London the following spring. There was a splendid procession through the City, and Henry Picard provided a great banquet for the Black Prince and his royal prisoner. John was kept in the Tower awaiting the collection of his ransom. He was allowed to return to France in 1360 when his son took his place as hostage, but when the Prince broke his parole in 1363 John returned, and so was one of the four kings entertained, according to legend, by Henry Picard at Vintners' Hall, the others being Edward III, David II of Scotland and Pierre de Lusignan of Cyprus. The Mayor 'kept the bank' at gaming and luck was on his side, but when the King of Cyprus lost badly Picard munificently offered to return all his winnings. (In fact these four could not have been present together on that occasion, but it is a popular story and the subject of a Vintners' Company toast.)

In London the situation deteriorated during the last years of

Edward III's reign. The King's health was failing, and his eldest son, the Black Prince, was mortally ill. The latter died before his father in the summer of 1376, leaving his young son Richard as heir to the throne. The wars in France were going badly and finances were strained. The heretical views of John Wycliffe were spreading among the people, and he had a strong following in London. In the City there were deep rivalries between the guilds which frequently broke out in violent fights in the streets. The autonomy of the City government was threatened by the over-ambitious John of Gaunt, Duke of Lancaster. In the summer of 1376 a Parliament was called to raise money needed for the wars. It was known as the Good Parliament because of the reforming zeal of its members, who attacked corruption among the nobles, in the church and in the City. Among those impeached were two former mayors, John Pecche and Adam de Bury. Following this, an assembly of City dignitaries and representatives from the guilds degraded the impeached citizens from their rank of alderman and changed the system of electing the Common Council from the wards to the guilds. Later that year it was decided that aldermen must be elected annually.

John of Gaunt had failed to dominate that Parliament but a new Parliament which met in January 1377 was packed by him. Determined to control the City, he and his ally, the Earl Marshal, introduced a bill which would have given control of the City government to the latter. While this was being debated the church leaders decided to move against Wycliffe and summoned him to appear before them in St Paul's. The great Cathedral was packed with Londoners, many of them sympathetic to Wycliffe's views but violently hostile to the Duke of Lancaster, who chose to support Wycliffe, and now strode up the nave by his side. There followed a noisy quarrel between the Duke and the Bishop of London. The mob joined in and the meeting broke up in disarray. The day after this disgraceful scene in St Paul's the Londoners heard that the Earl Marshal, anticipating the magisterial powers he would receive under the new Act, had already imprisoned a citizen in his house. City leaders took up arms, marched round to the house and released the prisoner. The mob who followed them were soon out of control and shouting for the blood of the Earl Marshal and the Duke of Lancaster. These two were dining together at the Duke's house. Stow tells us how one of the Duke's knights came to warn him that 'without the gate were infinite numbers of armed men, and unless he tooke great heede that day would be his last: with which wordes the Duke leapt so hastily from his Oisters, that hee hurt both his legges against the forme'. The two of them escaped across the river to Kennington. Thwarted, the rioters turned towards the Duke's great palace of the Savoy and were only prevented from burning it down by the Bishop of London. They satisfied themselves by reversing the Duke of Lancaster's arms hung up over a shop in Cheapside – seemingly trivial, but a serious insult. All this demonstrated the danger of the London mob when roused to fury. The obnoxious bill to control the City was heard of no more, but for insulting the Duke the citizens had to make a solemn procession to St Paul's with wax tapers bearing the Duke's arms (the right way up!), and the Mayor, Adam Stable, and the Sheriffs were dismissed by the King. Very soon after this new elections were held and Nicholas Brembre became mayor, in March 1377. Edward III died in June and was succeeded by the ten-year-old son of the Black Prince, Richard of Bordeaux.

3

THE MAYORALTY ESTABLISHED

Richard II's reign was to become one of the most tumultuous in the City's history. Much can be ascribed to the King's youth on his Accession, to the ambitions of his overbearing uncle, John of Gaunt, and to the bubbling discontent among the people, stirred up by the ideas of Wycliffe and his followers, known as Lollards. But the City had its own special problems with the intense rivalries among the guilds. On one side were aligned the victualling guilds – notably the Fishmongers, who with their control of a staple food were in a particularly strong position. Several of their number served as mayor, notably William Walworth. With them were the Grocers, of whom Nicholas Brembre, John Philipot, William Venour and John Hadle were all mayor at some time. Ranged against these were the clothing guilds led by Nicholas Twyford and John de Northampton – both to become mayor in due course.

Richard II was the first king to lodge in the Tower the night before his Coronation and ride in state through the City to Westminster. Wine flowed from the water conduits, and as the young King passed under the arch of a decorated castle with four towers, virgins dressed as queens cast flowers and gold leaves on his head. There were many splendid pageants, but one made a neat political point. Under a triumphal arch in Cheapside Richard saw a grotesque effigy of a man vomiting. It was immediately recognizable as Sir Robert Belknap, Chief Justice of Common Pleas, who had attempted to deny the Mayor and Aldermen their traditional privilege of serving as royal cupbearers at the Coronation banquet.

The early years of Richard's reign found the City leaders strongly on the King's side. Nicholas Brembre was extremely wealthy, owner of extensive property in the City, in Middlesex and in Kent. He was connected with leading City families by marriage. Having first become mayor in March 1377 he was re-elected the following October. The next year he was followed in office by a fellow Grocer, with whom he had served as sheriff in 1372, John Philipot. This man was an outstanding mayor, for he not only served frequently as member of parliament and made considerable loans to the Crown, but he fitted out a fleet of ships and provided 1,000 men at his own expense to deal with French pirates who had captured the Isle of Wight and seized several English merchant ships. This fleet recovered the ships and captured John Mercer, a Scottish pirate in league with the French. Philipot was an immensely popular mayor who enforced justice fairly, had the city ditch cleaned out, and paid for one of two great towers below London Bridge from which a chain was suspended to protect the City from invaders by river. In his will he was a substantial benefactor to the poor and to the City government. Philpot Lane in the City still reminds us of him.

Then in 1380 the Fishmonger William Walworth became mayor for the second time. He had begun his career as apprentice to John Lovekyn, had inherited his house and succeeded him as Alderman of Bridge Ward. That year the new Poll Tax, widely regarded as unfair and onerous, was introduced. It was to bring the growing ferment among the ordinary people to a head in the Peasants' Revolt. By mid-June the men of Essex were gathered on the northern boundaries of the City, while south of the Thames the men of Kent gathered on Blackheath. They were determined to march on London and force their demands for fair treatment on the King. Richard, now fourteen, had taken refuge in the Tower with his chief ministers and several leading citizens including the Mayor. The City gates on the north and the great drawbridge at the south end of the bridge could have kept the rebels out, but some of the Londoners were sympathetic to their cause. The drawbridge was lowered, Aldgate was opened and the hungry and desperate hordes poured into the City. Murder and pillage followed. Richard rode out to Mile End with a band of supporters to meet the rebel leaders where he promised wide-ranging concessions to their demands. Some of the mob dispersed after this but many remained still unsatisfied. The next day there was another meeting, in Smithfield. William Walworth rode at the King's side as he came up to the rebels. The Mayor was keyed up to deal with any trouble and as the

City records recount, 'most manfully, by himself, rushed upon the captain of the said multitude, Walter Tyler by name, and as he was altercating with the King and the nobles, first wounded him in the neck with his sword, and then hurled him from his horse mortally pierced in the breast'. It was a perilous moment, but Richard showed astonishing presence of mind and calmly rode up to the horrified rebels, told them he was their leader and they meekly followed him away from the scene. Walworth rode into the City for reinforcements and the situation was soon under control. The King showed his appreciation of the City's support by knighting William Walworth, Nicholas Brembre, John Philipot, Nicholas Twyford and another Alderman, Robert Lande. It was a very unusual mark of royal honour at that time, and Stow tells us that Walworth demurred, saying 'he was niether worthie nor able to take such state upon him for he was but a merchant'. But he had certainly earned his place in history. Two hundred years later the fishmongers were celebrating the event in their pageant for lord mayor Sir John Leman. To this day Walworth's dagger is preserved in Fishmongers' Hall and Mansion House has a nineteenth-century stained glass window in the Egyptian Hall depicting the scene at Smithfield.

In October 1381 John de Northampton, a Draper, was elected mayor, breaking the long ascendancy of the victualling guilds. There was a popular reaction against the over-powerful Fishmongers. Northampton, with far less wealth than his predecessors, set about a reformist policy. In some ways he seems more like a modern politician, for he set up a party organization, removed officials who opposed him, such as the Recorder, Chamberlain and Common Clerk, and set about attacking the privileges of the Fishmongers. They were forced to slash their prices, and the King extinguished their monopoly in the fish trade. An Act of Parliament was passed saying no Fishmonger or victualler could be mayor. Northampton forced several of them to resign their aldermanry, even the distinguished and popular ex-mayor John Philipot. He then began a programme of moral reforms turning on quacks, cheats, slanderers and prostitutes. He marched across London Bridge and raided the notorious stews on the south bank, several of which were owned by Sir William Walworth. Northampton was re-elected after his first year in office, but by the end of his second the City (and the King) had had enough. His Acts were cancelled and he fell from power. His real support had come from the weaker section of the citizenry, 'mochel smale people that konne non skyl of governance ne of gode conseyl'. As the chronicler Thomas Walsingham put it in *Historia Anglicana*, he was 'so proud that he could neither get on with his inferiors nor be deterred by the suggestions or warnings of his superiors from striving to carry out his drastic ideas to the bitter end'.

In October 1383 Nicholas Brembre was back in office – with royal support. Northampton refused to accept his election and attempted to have it quashed. Failing that, he raised up a band of 500 followers and marched through Cheapside, where he was stopped and arrested by Brembre. In August 1384 he was tried for corruption and insurrection by the King's Council at Reading. His demand that he should not be tried while his lord, John of Gaunt, was out of the country threw Richard into a fury. Northampton was sentenced to death but this was commuted to imprisonment. He spent the next six years incarcerated in Tintagel Castle until Gaunt returned and secured his pardon and release. Meanwhile Brembre was elected for a second year, having made sure of the result by concealing armed men in Guildhall, thus defeating the Goldsmith Sir Nicholas Twyford. The following year the victuallers were still in the ascendant with the Fishmonger Nicholas Exton as mayor. Brembre had however made many enemies and relied too much on force and on the support of the King. He was attacked in the Merciless Parliament of 1388 and accused of treason by the Lords Appellant. These Lords 'appealed' against five leading men. The others, the Archbishop of York, De Vere, Tresilian and de la Pole fled, but Brembre stood his trial at Westminster. At first he claimed trial by battle, but was refused. The King tried to defend him but his enemies were too determined. Nicholas Exton – the Mayor – and the Aldermen who might have stood by him were afraid of the Lords Appellant, so he was condemned to death and executed at Tyburn on 20 February, the only one of London's mayors to meet such a fate.

That October Sir Nicholas Twyford stood for the mayoralty a second time and was elected. He was followed by William Venour, Grocer, to whom Brembre had made over his property when he was summoned for trial. In 1390 Adam Bamme, Goldsmith, was mayor. It was during the mayoralty of John Heende, Draper, the following year that the King's displeasure turned upon the City. It was said that there was a lack of order, but an exorbitant royal demand for money, which the citizens refused, was the real cause of trouble. An offended Richard moved against the City, first by removing the Court of Common Pleas, the Chancery and the Exchequer (plus the inmates of the Fleet prison) to York. Such a removal of business spelt ruin for City merchants. The Mayor, Sheriffs and Aldermen were summoned to York where the Mayor and Sheriffs were removed from office and sent to prison because of 'intolerable damages and perils'. A warden was appointed to rule the City: Sir Edward Dalyngrigge, the builder of Bodiam Castle in Sussex. Two months later he was replaced by Sir Baldwin Radyington, possibly because Dalyngrigge was too sympathetic to the Londoners. The situation became unbearable to both sides and by autumn peace was made, with the City paying a heavy fine and giving a splendid reception for the King and Queen. The offending Mayor and Sheriffs were pardoned, and the citizens were allowed to elect new sheriffs on the Feast of St Matthew, 21 September. On 13 October William Staundon was chosen mayor in the customary way at Guildhall. New statues of the King and Queen were erected on London Bridge. The City's liberties were restored 'until the King shall otherwise ordain', but in effect this was the last time the mayoralty was suspended in the Middle Ages.

In 1396 Adam Bamme became mayor for the second time. The antagonisms of the 1380s must still have been simmering because he found it necessary to issue an ordinance forbidding anyone to express opinions about Nicholas Brembre or John de Northampton: 'The men of the City are to be of one accord and to be silent on the late controversy'. Shortly after this, in June 1397, he died and the King appointed Richard Whittington (of whom more later) to take his place. As for Richard II, he had begun his reign with City support which continued for much of the time. But the troubles of the later years told on the relationship between him and the citizens of London. When in 1399 Henry Bolingbroke, the son of John of Gaunt, Duke of Lancaster, was poised to seize power the majority of Londoners supported him. As Henry approached the City in the early morning of 4 July, the Mayor, then Drew Barentyn, was roused from his bed. With 500 citizens he rode out to meet the Lancastrian and escorted him into the City. When Richard was brought back to London by his captors he especially asked to be protected from the Londoners, and was taken to the Tower at night. Subsequently he was deposed and removed to Pontefract Castle where he met his death the following year. Henry Bolingbroke claimed the throne through conquest and the acclaim of the people of London. Five years later a man was accused of saying that Henry IV had been elected 'by the London rabble'. The chronicler Froissart believed the Londoners had directly invited Henry to return from France and take the throne. His comment on the Londoners was that they were 'the most dangerous branch of a proud and dangerous people'.

At the election of the sheriffs in 1401 a horde of apprentices and serving-men thronged into Guildhall and made such a clamour that the Mayor, William Askham, and the Aldermen were unable to make out what the trouble was or to proceed in an orderly manner with the election. It was clear that there must be some control over which of the citizens should be allowed to attend. For the mayoral election of 1406 it was agreed that the Mayor and Aldermen and 'as many as possible of the wealthier and more substantial commoners of the said City ought to meet at the Guildhall as the usage is to elect a new Mayor for the coming year'. Furthermore:

> A Mass of the Holy Spirit should be celebrated, with solemn music, in the Chapel annexed to the said Guildhall: to the end that the same Commonalty, by the grace of the Holy Spirit, might be able peacefully and amicably to nominate two able and proper persons to be Mayor of the said City for the ensuing year, by favour of the clemency of Our Saviour, according to the customs of the said City.

The commonalty duly 'peacefully and amicably, without any clamour or discussion, did becomingly nominate Richard Whittington, Mercer, and Drew Barentyn, Goldsmith', whereupon the Mayor and Aldermen 'with closed doors' chose Richard Whittington, 'by guidance of the Holy Spirit'.

Thus began Richard Whittington's second full term as Mayor of London. More than a mere royal protégé, Whittington had popular support and was elected mayor in October 1397 as well as in 1406 and 1419. He was, of course, destined to become London's most famous mayor and during his time a new era began in the City government. The violence of faction died down and the City entered a period of prosperity. As we have seen, he was first chosen as a royal nominee in June 1397 and duly elected the following October. His name has since become a legend and it is reasonable to ask why this particular mayor achieved lasting fame and attracted so many myths. The first of these myths is that he was a poor boy who arrived penniless in London and acquired a cat which subsequently made his fortune as a prize rat-catcher on ships trading abroad. It was bought for a vast sum by the King of the Moors after it caught the rats which were eating a banquet he intended for his guests. In fact Whittington's father was Sir William Whittington, a wealthy knight of Pauntley in Gloucestershire. Richard, his third son, was never knighted, contrary to popular belief. However, like all younger sons he had to make his own way in the world and, as many had before him, he came to

London. There he became apprenticed to a Mercer (possibly his uncle, Sir William Warren). He did very well, for by the time he was twenty-one he was capable of contributing five marks to a city loan and soon became a highly successful supplier of cloth of gold, velvet and damask to the royal household. Clearly he decided early on to take an interest in City politics for in 1384 he became a Common Councilman for Coleman Street. In March 1393 he was elected Alderman for Broad Street and later that year was elected sheriff, while still in his mid-thirties. He was a far more impressive figure than the legendary Dick, pathetically making his despondent way out of London, only to be summoned back from Highgate by Bow Bells to be made lord mayor. Whittington was a genuinely self-made man, even if his origins were not romantically poverty-stricken. He knew how to make money work for him, moved into the area of royal finance and was involved in the wool trade, exporting wool from London and Chichester. His appointment as Collector of the Wool Subsidy in London was not only lucrative, but gave him security for his loans to successive kings. Another favourite story, that he cast bonds owed by Henry V on to the fire, is most unlikely, for Whittington was a man who saw to it that his loans were repaid. His work for the Crown was extensive. He was custodian of royal goods and manors. He sat on Commissions of Oyer and Terminer, dealing with cases of profits and plunder in war. He sat on various special commissions like that set up to sort out captured Spanish and French merchandise, and one to search out and seize Lollards in the City. He served as Mayor of the Westminster and Calais staples. As would be expected, he was Master of the Mercers' Company three times. Many private individuals turned to him for advice on financial matters and asked him to act as arbiter in disputes. In 1419, when he must have been about sixty, which was old for those days, he was elected mayor for the third time.

He was one of the most highly regarded of London's many wealthy merchants, but was not involved in any dramatic political events, only sat once as a member of parliament and was not mentioned in contemporary annals. *Gregory's Chronicle*, written some years after his death, does refer to 'that famous merchant and mercer, Richard Whytyndone'. It was written by William Gregory, himself mayor in 1451. There is no doubt that Richard Whittington's subsequent fame rested on his legacies. Although married to Alice Fitzwaryn, she died before him and he had no heirs. He had invested in property in London, but he had not made extensive purchases of land elsewhere in the country, preferring to keep his money fluid in cash, jewels and plate. He died on 8 March 1423, leaving his executors a vast fortune to administer. His munificence was visible all over the City. There were the almshouses for thirteen poor men and women (later moved to Highgate and now Whittington College at East Grinstead, where they still bear his name and arms). There was the college for secular priests attached to St Michael, Paternoster Royal, remembered in the name of College Hill today. He rebuilt Newgate prison and contributed to repairs at St Bartholomew. The new Guildhall, begun in his lifetime, received from his executors the paved floor and newly glazed windows – with his name on them. He gave libraries to Guildhall and to Greyfriars. An unusual and practical provision was a very early public toilet, known as Whittington's longhouse, in Vintry Ward. This provided two long rows each with sixty-four seats, one row for men and one for women, built over a gully which flushed into the Thames on every tide. There were five or six rooms above for almsfolk. (The longhouse was known to be still in use in the seventeenth century because there were complaints that the Lord Mayor and Aldermen were failing to provide lanthorns and candles 'whereby many inconveniences have happened'.)

So Whittington's name was constantly before Londoners' eyes and traditional stories were attributed to him. (A cat story appears frequently in European folklore.) In the sixteenth century persistent rumours that such a rich man must have valuables buried with him led to the opening of his tomb in St Michael, Paternoster Royal. Disappointed to find no gold or jewels, the plunderers stripped the tomb of its lead and reburied the remains. Later the parishioners opened the tomb to replace the lead and buried him again, for the third time. Whittington's beneficence was considerable, but by no means unique for the fifteenth century. It was part of the established 'custom of London' for wealthy men to divide their fortunes, leaving a third to their wives, a third to their children and a third to charity. Whittington was unusual in having all of it to leave to charity.

William Sevenoke, mayor in 1418, was named after the town in which, according to Lambert's *Perambulation of Kent*, written in the sixteenth century, he was found as a baby lying in the streets. In the City records he is given as the son of William Rumschedde, possibly his foster father, an official of Sevenoaks. William Sevenoke was apprenticed to an Ironmonger in London, but at the end of his apprenticeship he applied to the Grocers' Company, saying that his master had used the trade of Grocer and was accepted in that Company. He sat as member of parliament in

1417. He became a very wealthy merchant and was able to leave his home town enough money to found almshouses for twenty poor people and for a free school, which flourishes today as Sevenoaks School.

John Reynwell, Fishmonger, mayor in 1426, was an outstanding benefactor to the City's own funds, City Lands. He owned property all over the City, and lands and tenements in Calais, all of which he left to the City. From the funds the City derived from these properties, £10 per annum was granted to Southwark, thus removing the need to collect tolls there. The sheriffs were given £8 per annum to free Englishmen from paying tolls on London Bridge. And the inhabitants of the wards of Billingsgate, Dowgate and Aldgate were given certain relief from taxes. Provision was made for grain supplies in time of need and for clearing the Thames of obstructions. Reynwell died in 1445 and was buried in St Botolph's, Billingsgate, a church which no longer exists, but Stow recorded his epitaph:

> Citizens of London, call to your remembrance, The famous John
> Rainwell, sometime your Maior, of the Staple of Callis, so was his
> chance. Here lieth now his corps, his soule so bright and faire, Is taken
> to heavens blisse thereof is no dispaire. His acts beare witnes, by matters
> of recorde, how charitable he was, and of what occorde, no man hat
> beene so beneficiall as hee, unto the Citie in giving liberallie.

The Grocer, John Welles, mayor in 1431, must have been an extraordinarily active man. He sat as Member of Parliament for London six times and for Southwark three times. The King appointed him Warden of Norwich in 1437 to deal with riots there. He was one of the earliest mayors to introduce pageantry in his procession to Westminster, with three fountains (or 'wells', as puns on names were very popular at this time) which ran with wine at the Cheapside conduit, and also three virgins representing Mercy, Grace and Pity. John Welles's legacies rival Whittington's. He rebuilt the standards for water at Cheapside and Fleet Bridge, repaired the highway from the City to Westminster, and made a major contribution to the Guildhall Chapel, where his tomb was. He gave a Sword of State to Bristol engraved 'John Wellis of London Grocer Mair Gave to Bristol this Sword Fair'.

Simon Eyre, mayor in 1445, came from Brandon in Suffolk. He was originally apprenticed to an Upholsterer and served his term believing he was a Draper. Later he had to transfer at some expense to another master in order to become a Draper. A story about him tells how at first he refused office on grounds of poverty. He said he had a table at home for which he would not accept £1,000. This, an enquirer discovered when he went with Eyre to see it, was his wife's lap! He must have done well for, as Weever put it in his Memorials, 'Hee built Leaden Hall for a common granary for the City. He gave £5,000 and above to poore Maid's marriages'. Simon Eyre is unusual in that he appears in literature as the Lord Mayor in Thomas Dekker's *The Shoemaker's Holiday*, and he is one of the earliest mayors of whom a full-length picture exists.

Geoffrey Boleyn, mayor in 1457, came from Norfolk, and much of his charity went to provide for poor householders in London and Norfolk. However, his most remarkable legacy was his posterity. It would be possible to devote a book to the subject of the descendants of lord mayors. Here it is only possible to mention the most noteworthy, of which Boleyn's were indeed outstanding. Through his second marriage to the daughter of Lord Hoo and Hastings he was great-grandfather to Mary and Anne Boleyn and thus through Mary ancestor of Lord Nelson, and through Anne ancestor of Queen Elizabeth I. He also owned two great houses which still stand, Blickling in Norfolk and Hever Castle in Kent, where Henry VIII courted Anne Boleyn.

The fifteenth century was a more stable period in London's history than any previously. The dynastic struggles between the royal houses of York and Lancaster, known as the Wars of the Roses, were disruptive in the country as a whole, but for London's merchants this was a prosperous time. The comparative insecurity of the kings and their great need for financial support from the City meant that there was no more royal interference in the City government. London played an important part in the fluctuations of the power game, but the citizens managed to stay with the winning side. Timothy Baker, in his book *Medieval London*, commented that the City might have played a more heroic part in national politics:

> Time and time again the Mayor and Aldermen waited on events before trooping out in ceremonial scarlet to greet the victor. After they had escorted him amid ringing bells to the usual Te Deum at St. Paul's they gave thanks less for one man's triumph than for a decision which should once more allow them to get on with their own business.

That may seem a cynical view, but considering the attacks made on the City's rights during the fourteenth century and the immense value of the City's contributions to the national coffers, their attitude was practical and sensible. They managed to ride out the dynastic storms and emerge into the comparative calm of the Tudor period with the City's liberties intact and the City government secure.

Henry IV, having won his throne with the aid of the Londoners, drew upon them for major contributions to his wars against the French. He appointed five special treasurers for a new war tax in 1404, including John Hadle, mayor in 1379 and 1393, Richard Merlawe, mayor in 1409 and 1417, and Thomas Knolles, mayor in 1399 and 1410. Robert Chichele, mayor in 1411 and 1421, brother of Bishop Chichele, had property in the City worth double that of Richard Whittington, from which he made large individual payments towards the war expenses.

Henry V had a particularly happy relationship with the City merchants and was careful to take counsel with them before he left for France in March 1415. They granted him a loan for which he pledged jewels worth 10,000 marks. Thomas Fauconer, mayor, with the Aldermen and civic dignitaries, rode with him to Blackheath to speed him on his way. Letters came to the City from the King reporting on his campaigns. News of his great victory of Agincourt on 25 October arrived in London just before the new mayor, Nicholas Wotton, was sworn in. The City dignitaries made a special pilgrimage to Westminster on foot, to give thanks for the victory and to present the new mayor to the Exchequer lords. Four weeks later, on 23 November, the triumphant King returned to London to be greeted by the loyal citizens with a splendid reception. In 1420 there was a grand procession to St Paul's in honour of Henry's marriage to the French princess, Catherine, and in February 1421 the King and Queen stayed in the Tower before riding in state through London for the Queen's Coronation at Westminster. Sadly, the following year the streets of London were lined with citizens, all in white mourning, to receive the body of their King who had died in France.

He left a nine-month-old baby to inherit the throne as Henry VI, and the administration of affairs fell into the hands of the baby's uncles: John, Duke of Bedford and Humphrey, Duke of Gloucester. They were soon bitter rivals competing for control of the young King. As the opposing parties struggled for power the City's rulers were sometimes in an awkward position. Stow comments on how John Coventre, mayor in 1425 was commended in the chronicles 'for his discreet carriage in the debate betwixt Humphrey Duke of Gloucester and Henry Beaufort, that wealthy Bishop of Winchester'. In Shakespeare's *Henry VI, Part 1* (Act III, scene i) he is portrayed entreating the two magnates to stop their followers throwing stones in the City streets. When Henry VI was crowned at the age of eight,

William Estfeld, as mayor, received the customary gold cup and ewer for his services as butler at the Coronation banquet. Two years later, when Henry returned from his Coronation in France, he was greeted by the Londoners, led by their Mayor, John Welles:

> in Crimson velvet, a great velvet hat furred, a girdle of golde about his middle, and a Bawdrike of gold about his necke trilling down behind him, his three Henzmen, on three great coursers following him, in one sute of red, all spangled in silver, then the Aldermen in Gownes of scarlet, with sanguine hoodes and all the comminaltie of the citty cloathed in white gownes and scarlet hoods with divers cognizances embrodered on the sleeves. [Stow]

In 1445 Henry married Margaret of Anjou, who was to prove as disastrously aggressive as he was hopelessly weak. England's fortunes in France declined and the returning disgruntled soldiers were bound to be a source of trouble. Discontent with maladministration led to rebellion. In an isolated episode in 1450 London again experienced sacking and looting, when the Kentish rebels, led by Jack Cade who had intended to control them, stormed over London Bridge. Cade had cut the ropes of the drawbridge so it could not be raised against them. They retired to Southwark for the night, but the next day they were back, holding mock trials in Guildhall and carrying out executions. Jack Cade struck his sword against London Stone and declared himself Lord of the City. All this was too much for the Londoners, who had had some sympathy with Cade's disgust with the Government. They rallied and, led by Lord Scales and the Mayor, Thomas Chalton, set upon the rebels in Southwark. Cade was later captured in Sussex, executed and his head impaled on London Bridge.

During the next decade the mental feebleness of the King laid the way open for his ambitious rivals. The dynastic struggles later known as the Wars of the Roses began. The birth of a son and heir to Margaret did not stop the Yorkists, nor did the King's occasional returns to sanity. London had remained Lancastrian, but by 1460 the citizens were tired of the Government's weakness and allowed the Yorkist earls to enter the City. In March 1461 they officially recognized Edward of York's title to the throne. The acclaim of the Londoners was vitally important to the new King Edward IV and he took great pains to win their affection and loyalty. He was a merchant prince, himself an active trader, and in 1464 he married Elizabeth Woodville, the widow of one of his subjects. At her Coronation in 1465 the King made Ralph Josselyn, the Mayor, and three others

Knights of the Bath, 'a great worship to alle the city'. One of these was Thomas Cooke, who as Stow put it 'had great troubles after'.

Cooke was the only Mayor of London to suffer personally through the vicissitudes of fifteenth-century politics. He was a very wealthy draper from Lavenham in Suffolk who served as mayor in 1462. He had a fine country house at Gidea Park as well as his London house, both mansions well furnished with valuable plate and fine tapestries, in particular an arras 'wrought in most richest wise with gold of the whole story of the siege of Jerusalem', as Fabyan, who was apprenticed to Cooke, relates in his chronicle. This tapestry was much coveted by the Duchess of Bedford but Cooke refused to sell it to her for the price she offered. In 1467 Cooke was arrested on the evidence of a servant and accused of conspiring in a Lancastrian plot against the King. At his trial the chief judge was the Mayor, Thomas Oulegreave, 'a replete and lumpish man' as Fabyan described him, who fell asleep, much to the amusement of the Duke of Clarence. Cooke was acquitted of treason but found guilty of misprision (knowledge of the plot). He was removed from his aldermanry and heavily fined. Both his houses were ransacked and woollen cloths, jewels, plate and the tapestry were seized. (It is not known whether the Duchess got the tapestry in the end.)

Edward IV's treatment of Sir Thomas Cooke soured his relations with the Londoners, and as the fortunes of war turned against the King their loyalty to him wavered. In October 1470 they welcomed the return of Henry VI who was restored to the throne. Edward fled to France. Cooke was reinstated as an alderman, replacing Oulegreave who resigned because of age and died two years later. In November Sir Thomas presented a bill in Parliament for the restoration of certain lands which according to Fabyan 'he had good comfort to have been allowed of King Henry if he had prospered. And the rather for Yt he was of the Common House and therewith a man of great boldnesse in speech and well spoken and singularly witted and well reasoned.' Unfortunately for Cooke, Henry did not prosper. Edward was gathering forces for an invasion, and by March 1471 he was in the north of England. As he advanced towards London John Stockton, the mayor, announced he was ill and took to his bed, whether diplomatically or not is a matter of dispute. Cooke assumed the mayoralty, but when in April Edward reached the City he took flight for France. Ralph Verney, mayor in 1465, took over for the time being. He and the Recorder opened the gates to Edward who was soon back in power. Cooke was captured at sea, brought back and again heavily fined. In spite of all these misfortunes his connections and his wealth were such that when he died in 1478 he was still able to leave his sons a considerable inheritance. Through his great-grandson, Sir Anthony Cooke, he was ancestor of Sir Francis Bacon and Sir Robert Cecil.

Edward IV pursued the forces supporting Henry VI and defeated them at Barnet. Queen Margaret fought on for a few weeks but was defeated at the Battle of Tewkesbury, where her son was killed, so there was no immediate Lancastrian heir. There was one last spurt of defiance. The 'Bastard' Fauconberg mustered the men of Kent and sent word to the City that he was supporting Henry VI against the usurper Edward. The Mayor, John Stockton, now restored to health, and the Aldermen refused him passage. He made assaults on the bridge, at Aldgate and at Bishopsgate, but was repulsed. He was eventually captured, executed and his head joined Jack Cade's on London Bridge. Henry VI met his end in the Tower.

Edward IV was now firmly established on the throne and his mutually profitable relationship with London's rulers was resumed. In 1471 he knighted the Mayor John Stockton, the Recorder Urswick and eleven Aldermen including Mayors Richard Lee (1460 and 1469), Mathew Philip (1463), Ralph Verney (1465), John Yonge (1466), William Taillour (1468), William Hampton (1472), Bartholomew James (1479), William Stokker (1485) and John Crosby, sheriff in 1470. He rewarded the City for its support with new charters and occasional special entertainments. In 1482 the Mayor, William Haryot, was knighted, and he and the Aldermen were invited by the King to a hunting party in Waltham Forest. This showed the King's appreciation of 'a merchant of wondrous adventures into many sundry lands by reason whereof the King had yearly of him notable sums of money for his customs besides other pleasure that he had shown to the King before times'. A fine repast was prepared for them and a 'pleasant lodge of green boughs erected for their dining place'. The King also took special thought for their wives, with some of whom he was rumoured to be particularly friendly. Two harts and six butts and a tun of wine were sent to the Mayoress and the Aldermen's wives 'to make them merry with' in the Drapers' Hall.

During this period of Edward's reign William Caxton, who had been apprenticed to the Mercer Robert Large, mayor in 1439, set up the first printing press by Westminster Abbey. Trade prospered and London flourished. So confident were the citizens that they could not be persuaded to take much interest in projects for repairing the city walls, which were in a ruinous condition. Sir Ralph Josselyn, who had been knighted during his first mayoralty, was keen during his second term of office in 1476 to undertake this task but had to pay for much of the building material himself, and even went around with a collecting box to raise money for bricks and lime. He did so well that large stretches of the walls were repaired during that year and plenty of materials remained for his successors to continue the good work. However, as the *Great Chronicle of London* commented, 'much of the said brick was lost and bribed away and in the end such as was preserved from the danger of the weather was occupied about reparations of such housing and other things appertaining to the City'. As the chronicler cynically explained 'they be of such minds that when a good act is begun by any of them, the successor of that mayor will not perform his predecessor deed, because he thinketh the honour thereof shall be ascribed unto his predecessor and not unto him.'

The citizens' sense of security must have been shaken when in April 1483 Edward, not yet forty years old, suddenly died. His brother Richard of Gloucester moved to seize the throne, shutting up Edward's two young sons in the Tower. Richard knew the importance of getting the City on his side. He made use of Dr Ralph Shaa, (the brother of the Mayor, Edmund Shaa) who preached at Paul's Cross before a large assembly of citizens to whom he denounced Edward IV as illegitimate (some accounts say the accusation was against Edward's sons). Shortly afterwards Richard harangued the citizens in Guildhall, which was packed with his supporters. There was little real enthusiasm for Richard in the City, but the Londoners gave in to pressure and a deputation waited on Richard the next day and petitioned him to take the throne. In Shakespeare's play the Mayor plays an equivocal part in the affair, accepting the dubious story of treachery put about by Richard and his ally Buckingham to explain Hastings' murder:

> . . . your Grace's word shall serve
> As well as I had seen and heard him speak.
> And do not doubt, right noble princes both,
> But I'll acquaint our duteous citizens
> With all your just proceedings in this cause.

Later he is a willing stooge when Richard pretends he does not want to accept the throne and has to be entreated.

When Richard III's short reign ended at Bosworth Field in August 1485 the citizens were ready to greet Henry Tudor, whom they met with a special deputation at Shoreditch as he approached London. The Mayor and Aldermen were arrayed in scarlet, and every guild was represented in the procession of over 400 which conducted the new King to St Paul's. Henry VII spent much of his reign dealing with Yorkist plots, but in fact the Wars of the Roses were over. The King who 'could not bear to see trade sick' was a ruler after the City merchants' hearts. The basic understanding that a good relationship between the City and the Crown was to their mutual advantage continued throughout the Tudor period.

4

INTERLUDE: FROM MAYOR
TO LORD MAYOR

By the end of the fifteenth century the mayoralty was securely established at the head of a powerful City hierarchy. Many of the guilds had achieved the status of Livery Companies and the richest and most powerful of these had begun to accumulate great wealth and to build themselves halls. The Mayor was acknowledged as the Master of all the Companies and from 1437 all their charters had to be submitted to the Mayor and Aldermen for approval. All the Aldermen came from one of the twelve great Companies whose order of precedence was finally confirmed by the Court of Aldermen in 1516. Even by the end of the sixteenth century this limitation on the field of choice was regarded as quite normal, and Stow remarked that 'those of inferior rank are not capable of such dignitie'. During the seventeenth century it was gradually accepted that an alderman could come from a lesser Company but anyone elected mayor had to translate to a great Company until the mid-eighteenth century.

The centre of city activity was Guildhall. The early medieval Guildhall, of which the present West crypt was the undercroft, lay a little to the west of the present building. By the beginning of the fifteenth century it was no longer adequate so, as the chronicler Fabyan quaintly put it, 'the Guylde Halle began to be new edyfied and of an olde and lytell cotage made into a fayre and goodly house as it nowe apperyth'. Building began in 1411 during the mayoralty of Thomas Knolles. Money was raised from the Livery Companies, and fines and extraordinary fees were allotted for the work. Henry V allowed the free passage of stone 'by land or water'.

Even so the work dragged and it was nearly thirty years before it was finished, with paving donated by Whittington's executors and glazed windows bearing his coat of arms. In this great hall the City's courts would meet: the Court of Aldermen, the Court of Common Council, the Court of Husting, and the Court of Common Hall, at which elections were held.

The actual date for the election of the Mayor was established in 1346 on the Feast of the Translation of St Edward the King (13 October). The Mayor-Elect then had two weeks to set his affairs in order before taking his oath on the Feast of the Apostles St Simon and St Jude (28 October). In 1546 the date of election was altered to Michaelmas Day (29 September). The form of the election as described in the *Liber Albus* (written in the fifteenth century) differs hardly at all from that used nowadays. Earlier disputes between the commonalty and the Aldermen had resulted in the custom whereby the commonalty (which by the late fifteenth century meant the liverymen meeting in Guildhall) nominated two aldermen 'each of whom had been sheriff and was a fit and proper person for the office of Mayor'. The Mayor and Aldermen left the Hall and ascended into the Upper Chamber where they elected one of the two by a plurality of votes. They would then return to the Hall, the Mayor holding the new Mayor by the hand. The Recorder announced the election of the new Mayor and told the people to be ready to accompany him on horseback to Westminster 'on the morrow of the Feast of the Apostles then ensuing and so uphold the honour of the City'. On 28 October the Mayor, Aldermen and commoners, arrayed in cloaks of violet, met in Guildhall to witness the oath-taking. After the new Mayor had complimented the old Mayor, the latter would vacate his seat so that the new Mayor could take his place. After he had taken his oath on the Book the old Mayor delivered the Seal of the Statute Merchant and the Seal of the Mayoralty. However, the old Mayor continued to serve until the new Mayor had been accepted by the King. The next day, unless it were a Sunday, the procession, accompanied by bands of minstrels, would set forth 'along Cheapside, through the gate of Newgate and along Fleet Street and so to Westminster into the room of the Exchequer'. There the Recorder presented the Mayor to the Barons of the Exchequer who charged the Mayor to preserve peace and tranquillity in the City and to control prices. The Mayor swore an oath of loyalty to the King, who on most occasions in the fifteenth century was present. The procession then returned to the City where the Mayor held his feast, either in his own house or in his livery hall. Guildhall was not used for this until the sixteenth century, Sir John Shaa, who added kitchens, being the first to hold his feast there in 1501. After dinner everyone went in procession to St Thomas of Acon (just off Cheapside) and thence to St Paul's to pray for Bishop William, who by his entreaties obtained the City's charter from William I in 1067. Then they returned by torchlight to St Thomas of Acon for prayers, then all went home. During the fifteenth century the custom of making the journey to Westminster by water was first introduced.

Even in the more settled fifteenth century the election was not always a peaceable affair. In 1441 Robert Clopton, Draper, was only chosen after a noisy protest by the Tailors, who were rooting for Ralph Holland. The retiring mayor, John Paddesle, was unable to command silence, and eventually the Sheriffs had to arrest the offenders. After this a Royal Writ was proclaimed confirming the limitation of the franchise to those who had been summoned to attend, and in 1444 as a further precaution the door of Guildhall was to be shut. There were fines for refusing to undertake the office of mayor if elected, but by now it was recognized that the burden was too great to expect a man to do it repeatedly as mayors had in the past. In 1424 the Court of Aldermen ordered that seven years should elapse before a man could be asked to serve again and that no one who had served twice could be asked to serve a third time. This was finally enacted by the Court of Common Council in 1435. Thus Richard Whittington in 1419 was the last Mayor to have a third full term of office.

The honour of the post was great and there were privileges. The Mayor officiated as butler at the coronation banquet and received the gold cup and ewer he used in that office as a gift. He received presents of bucks from the Royal Forests and casks of red wine. He could enrol his apprentices free and had his water supplied free. He could if he wished, and at this period many did because some wards were wealthier and some easier to run than others, remove to any aldermanry which fell vacant during his year of office. He had considerable patronage at his disposal and could request lucrative offices for his friends and relations. He got the profits from the sale of appointments which were his to make, and received income from rent farms and market leases. All this helped, but in no way covered his expenses, which were very great. He had to entertain lavishly and keep great state. That this was a matter of some pride is illustrated by the story of Matthew Philip, mayor in 1463. He had been invited to a banquet at Ely House by the King's Serjeants-at-Law, but left in high dudgeon when he saw that the Earl of Worcester was given precedence over him. He returned with the Aldermen who had accompanied him to his own house. The messengers sent hot-foot after him with apologies from his hosts were astounded to see the Mayor and his guests sitting down to a feast far more magnificent than that which they had left.

The Mayor had an official entourage headed by the Swordbearer, who ruled the household and walked or rode before him in processions bearing the civic sword aloft. His distinctive fur hat marked his rank. The Swordbearer's office dates from the fourteenth century although the first written reference to it was in 1419, when it was recorded that the mayor should have an esquire to bear his sword before him 'to support the honour of his Lord and of the City'. The Mayor also had various serjeants in attendance and in the fifteenth century the Common Cryer and Serjeant-at-Arms was established as one of the mayor's esquires. The third of the present esquires, the City Marshal, was first appointed in 1589, to apprehend rogues and vagabonds, but he did not join the other two as one of the mayor's household officers until the mid nineteenth century. In the fifteenth century two important officials were the Common Hunt and the Water Bailiff. The citizens of London claimed ancient hunting rights in the Chilterns, Middlesex and Surrey and the Common Hunt had 'to do all things touching hunting and fishing that pertain to that office'. Among other things he had to keep the City's hounds, whose kennels near Moorgate were often a cause of complaint. In 1512 a new 'Dogge Hous' was built on the Moorfield, as can be seen on maps of the sixteenth century, but even that was too near for comfort and in 1570 the Doghouse was moved to the northern part of Finsbury fields. The office of Common Hunt was abolished in 1807, The citizens were conservators of the Thames, and the Water Bailiff had to enforce regulations about fish weirs and the size of nets. He dealt with unlawful fishing and supervised the weighing of eels, which were a very popular food, as can be seen from the number of eel ships shown in old pictures of the City. The office of Water Bailiff ended in 1857 when the Thames Conservancy Act ended the City's conservancy of the Thames. An indication of the size of the mayor's household at the end of the fifteenth century can be seen from a list of 1517 which gives as well as the officers already mentioned three serjeant carvers, three serjeants of the chamber, a serjeant of the market, two yeomen of the chamber, four yeomen of the waterside, one serjeant of the market's yeoman and one yeoman of the fishmarket. All of these were fed at the mayor's expense.

The mayor's house would be one of the City's grander mansions, like that of Sir John Crosby, the hall of which can still be seen, now removed to Chelsea. Sir John, Sheriff and Alderman, never in fact served as mayor, but it is an indication of the esteem with which the office was regarded that Thomas Heywood made him mayor in his play *Edward IV*, assuming that such an important and wealthy man must have been mayor. Crosby Hall, then in Bishopsgate, was leased by Richard III when he was in London before he assumed the Crown, and three lord mayors in the sixteenth century – Bartholomew Rede, John Rest and John Spencer – kept their mayoralty there.

The duties of office were onerous and time-consuming. As first citizen, the preservation of peace and maintenance of law and order in the City were his responsibility. In March 1458 the King ordered a council of reconciliation between the rival nobility in St Paul's. During the month it took for all the protagonists to arrive the Mayor, Geoffrey Boleyn, in full armour patrolled the streets by day while 3,000 armed men were kept in readiness at night. The Mayor had to supervise the work of all civic officials. The Chamberlain who dealt with finance, the Common Clerk for secretarial matters, the Recorder and the Common Serjeants all looked to him. He would preside at all meetings of the City's administrative courts. As chief magistrate he had to act as judge, dealing with anything from law breakers to complicated commercial cases. It was his business to supervise the conduct of trade in the City and see that it was carried out in accordance with civic ordinances. Richard Whittington made himself very unpopular with the Brewers over the issue of standard sizes for barrels and his attempt to regulate the price of beer. The Brewers protested that this was governed by the cost of malt. John Reynwell, mayor in 1426, caught the Lombard merchants adulterating wine and ordered 150 butts to be thrown into the Thames whence 'there issued a most loathsome savour'. The Mayor was arbiter in the various disputes which arose between the guilds. Probably the most famous of these decisions was when Robert Billesden in 1484 settled a long standing quarrel between the Skinners and the Merchant Taylors over their position in processions by ordering that they should take it in turn over sixth and seventh place, and that they should entertain each other as a sign of friendship. This is probably the origin of the phrase 'at sixes and sevens'. The tradition between the two Companies continues to this day, the only exception on precedence being that if the Lord Mayor comes from one of these Companies it will take sixth place for that year.

The welfare of the citizens was the mayor's concern. In times of grain shortage he would order stocks to be laid in. Stephen Broun, mayor in 1438, was a Grocer who owned a wharf on the Thames with large granaries. He was also a corn factor, and when in 1439 there was a dearth of grain he sent to Prussia to buy quantities of grain, which he stored in his granaries, thus not only providing for the immediate need but also driving down prices. Many mayors undertook some public works. Ralph Josselyn, as already mentioned, repaired the walls; William Estfeld provided a new conduit for drinking water in Aldermanbury; Thomas Fauconer in 1414 made a new gate at Moorgate 'for the ease of the citizens that way to pass upon causeys [causeways – Moorfields was very marshy] into the field for their recreation'; Stephen Forster in 1454 'enlarged Ludgate for the ease of prisoners there'. There is a story that as a young man he was confined to the debtors' prison in Ludgate and stood at the grille, begging passers-by for food. A rich widow took to him and paid £20 to free him. She employed him and later married him. They amassed a fortune and constructed an extension to the prison with an exercise ground. They endowed the building:

> ... so that for lodging and water prisoners here nought pay
> As their keepers shall answer at dreadful doom's day.

After Stephen's death in 1458 Agnes, his wife, maintained her interest in the welfare of the prisoners and suggested reforms which were carried out by the Court of Aldermen.

One of the mayor's most important functions was as the City's link with the Crown. He served as Royal Escheator (dealing with reversion of property to the Crown in the absence of legal heirs). He was the channel through which royal commands and proclamations were conveyed to the citizens. It was his job to see to the raising of money and soldiers from the City Companies when the King required them. He played the leading role on all great royal ceremonial visits to the City. As an alderman he would very likely serve as one of the City's Members of Parliament, although in this period it was rare for him to do so during his mayoralty.

As an alderman the Mayor was accustomed to a prestigious position in London society. He was used to being hailed by others as 'worshipful' and 'sovereign lord' or even 'your high wisdom'. He was entitled to wear scarlet robes trimmed with fur. In the fifteenth century sumptuary laws (which regulated the dress of subjects) classed mayors and former mayors with knights for wearing gold and fine fur. An alderman's wife was accorded the title of 'lady'. When men hesitated to take office because of the expense, their wives would egg them on, for as Chaucer put it:

> They had the capital and revenue.
> Besides their wives declared it was their due.
> And if they did not think so, then they ought.
> To be called 'madam' is a glorious thought.
> And so is going to church and being seen
> Having your mantle carried like a queen.

Wives were valued, particularly when, as so often, they came from wealthy families. John Mathewe in 1490 was said by Stow to have been the first bachelor mayor and was thus disadvantaged. Fuller, in his book *The History of the Worthies of England*, 1811, commented 'It seemeth that a Lady Mayoress is something more than ornamental to a Lord Mayor, their wives' great portions or good providence much advantaging their estates to be capable of so high a dignity.' The Mayor ranked as an earl 'as well in the King's presence as elsewhere'. His importance in the City was emphasized by his right to precedence over all save the King. This was established in 1415 when Thomas Fauconer was given the centre seat at a meeting in Guildhall before Henry V crossed to France. The Primate and the Bishop of Winchester sat on his right and the Duke of York and the King's brothers on his left. It may be noted that the King had raised a particularly large loan from the City on this occasion.

It was still a rare honour for a Mayor of London to be knighted and very unusual indeed for him to be a knight in his own right. But Edward IV made much of the City merchants. During his reign many mayors were knighted and Henry VII continued the habit, knighting amongst others Henry Colet, father of the founder of St Paul's school, and Bartholomew Rede, who spent his mayoralty in Crosby Hall, where he entertained Katherine of Aragon a few days before her marriage to Prince Arthur. Ralp(sic) Astry, mayor in 1493, was knighted at a court dinner during his year of office. He was delighted and went home 'by breking of day ... and kissed his wife as a dowble lady'. The title 'Lord Mayor' was never officially conferred. The phrase 'Dominus Maior' did appear in a document in 1283, but the first recorded English version appeared in a petition of 1414 addressed to 'our worshipful Lord Mair of the Citie of London'. During the fifteenth century the title 'Lord Mayor' gradually crept into use and by the sixteenth century was the regular form of address as it has been ever since. With the exception of York the lord mayors of other English cities have had their titles granted by royal letters patent, whereas the title of 'Lord Mayor of London' is enjoyed by virtue of long usage.

5

THE FLOWER OF
CITIES ALL

During the Tudor period the population of London multiplied five times, from under 50,000 when Henry VII became King in 1485 to about 250,000 when Elizabeth I died in 1603. This reflected a general rise in the population of the kingdom, but the City's growth was out of proportion to national trends. London was now firmly established as the economic, financial and political capital, and as such it acted as a powerful magnet, drawing in immigrants from all over the country and from Europe. It was a place of exciting opportunities for men of ability and determination.

The Court was based nearby at Westminster, as was Parliament. In times of plague the monarch might retreat to Hampton Court, Windsor or Greenwich, and if displeased with the citizens he or she might even threaten the City with the Court's absence. By now, so confident were Londoners that they could respond as one alderman did when Mary Tudor threatened to remove Parliament to Oxford. Stow tells how he asked if the Queen meant to divert the course of the Thames also, for if not 'by God's grace wee shall do well enough at London whatsoever become of the (legal) terme and parliament'. These were brave words considering how important the presence of the Government and the law courts was to the citizens. London's control over the nation's trade was however not to be shifted, much though other towns, like Bristol, Southampton and Norwich might complain. Its position on the Thames was unrivalled for trade with Europe. Ships sailed up to the wharves below the bridge and crowded the pool of London with a forest of masts. Lighters carried goods to the quays of Billingsgate, and through the arches of the bridge to Dowgate and Queenhithe. They took away the wool and cloth which were England's staple exports and brought in a growing variety of goods: furs, hemp, oil, timber, silks, spices, wines. As world horizons expanded in the sixteenth century, goods came from the New World, from the Far East, from Muscovy and the Levant.

London merchants who dealt in this trade made fortunes. Their wealth made them pre-eminent in the City and the City's wealth made it invaluable to the Crown. So, although the sixteenth century saw major upheavals – violent changes in religious belief in the Reformation; a revolution in the government of the Church; significant economic and social changes in consequence of the Dissolution of the Monasteries; and an unprecedented inflation in prices – it was nonetheless a stable time in relations between the Crown and the City government. The City's rulers, secure in their alliance with the Crown, had no desire to meddle in the political or religious ferment. Their chief concern was the City's prosperity and the orderly management of its administration.

It could be said that the prestige of London's rulers was not as high as it had been in the Middle Ages. The mayor, although still a man of consequence, lacked the standing he had in earlier reigns as a frequent counsellor and right-hand man of the king. But his greater distance from the monarch meant that he was no longer in the precarious position of his predecessors. Instead he exerted considerable influence as the Crown's ally in the City. It is not without significance that he was now called 'Lord Mayor', nor that from 1519 when James Yarford was knighted by Henry VIII, until 1641, just before the outbreak of the Civil War, all the lord mayors not already knighted were so honoured during their year of office. As the Elizabethan William Harrison wrote in his *Description of England*: 'of a subject there is no public officer of any city in Europe that may compare in port and countenance with the Lord Mayor of London'.

The majority of London's mayors, as before, were not themselves Londoners by birth. Each had to make his own way. Some married into the merchant class, a close-knit group who intermarried frequently. Any chart of the inter-relationships of sixteenth-century lord mayors would be a tangled web indeed. Others depended on a Livery Company for their start in life. Those who began with apprenticeship in a minor Company had, of course, to translate to one of the great Companies if they wished to win City honours. Not all were willing to do this. Ralph Dodmer, lord mayor in 1529, had to be arrested by the Sheriffs before he agreed to translate to the Mercers from the Brewers, and Thomas Curtes, lord mayor in 1557, was committed to Newgate prison for wilful 'stiffness and disobedience' before he would translate from the Pewterers to the Fishmongers. It is not surprising that a man felt a strong tie with his parent Company, especially if he had started life in London as a young apprentice coming from distant parts – Pickering, Yorkshire, in the case of Curtes.

Through his Livery Company a man would learn his trade and make the social and business connections which would sustain him throughout his career. When he eventually reached high office he could turn to his Company for help. This might take the form of a grant of money 'towards the trimming of his house', grants for clothing, loan of the Company plate, the use of the Company hall, 'divers persons to attend upon him' and when the Lord Mayor's Show reached its zenith in late Elizabethan and early Stuart times, the provision of a lavish pageant.

Most of the men who reached the mayoral chair in this period owed the achievement to their own determination and hard work. They came from all over the country. Although more were from the home counties there were several from Yorkshire, Staffordshire, Lancashire, Lincolnshire and even Westmorland. Some came from the west, especially from Shropshire, some from East Anglia. One, Stephen Pecocke, was from Dublin. Often they came from prosperous families but nearly all were, like Richard Whittington, younger sons who did not expect to inherit the family estate and knew they had to make their own way. Of all the Tudor lord mayors a few followed relations. Sir John Browne, lord mayor in 1480, was followed by his nephew, William in 1507 and his son, also William, in 1513. George Barne, lord mayor in 1586, followed his father, George (1552). John Garrarde (1601) followed his father William (1555). John Gresham (1547) followed his brother Richard (1537) and the Rowe family provided Thomas (1568), a Merchant Taylor whose Ironmonger cousin William became lord mayor in 1592 and whose Mercer son, Henry, was mayor in 1607. It was more common for a man to follow his father-in-law, as Edward Osborne (1583) followed William Hewet (1559). Nicholas Woodruffe (1579), Wolstan Dixie (1585) and William Webbe (1591) were all sons-in-law of Christopher Draper (1566). On Draper's death his widow married Henry Billingsley (1596). The widow of Ralph Warren (1536 and 1544) married Thomas Whyte (1553). John Milborne (1521) married the widowed mother of William Chester, then a young child, who was brought up in Milborne's house and became lord mayor in 1560. A very few lord mayors remained bachelors like John Mathewe and Hugh Clopton in the late fifteenth century. Rowland Hill (1549) was unmarried, but Thomas Leigh married his niece and ward, Alice, and became lord mayor in 1558.

What combination of abilities and circumstances brought a man into the élite circle of aldermen in this period, and thus within reach of the mayoralty? Connections, as we have seen, were important. But most of all he would need ambition, luck, good health and sheer ability to enable him to acquire the necessary wealth, because living in the lavish style of the rulers of London was a very expensive business. There were literally dozens of men elected to the aldermanry who refused office and paid the fine, reckoned in the seventeenth century to be the equivalent of about one third of the cost of taking office. The office of sheriff was sometimes deliberately foisted on unwilling recipients in order to collect the fine, which then augmented the resources of the City Chamber. Traditionally the lord mayor had the privilege of nominating one of the sheriffs by drinking to him at a feast. In 1513 no fewer than thirteen nominated sheriffs turned down the office and paid the fines. Several of those who subsequently became distinguished lord mayors tried to avoid office at first, like Henry Amcotts, Fishmonger, who when chosen Alderman for Billingsgate refused the office, was fined, had his shop closed and his goods sequestered, and suffered imprisonment in Newgate for a week. He subsequently served as sheriff in 1542 and mayor in 1548. Thomas Whyte, too, had to be imprisoned in Newgate before he would become Alderman of Cornhill. William Hewet, an alderman since 1550, begged to be discharged 'of his cloke and room' in 1556 but was prevailed upon to stay by a committee of aldermen. He then managed to delay his term as sheriff for two years and finally became lord mayor in 1559. John Branche had attempted to avoid becoming an alderman, but failed. When he became lord mayor in 1580 he refused to give the usual feast, 'not on account of any sparing,' he averred, 'but lest, through the feeble state of his health he should not be able to bear the pain requisite'. However, since he also complained of a lapse of the usual mayoral hunting privilege of yearly warrants for bucks from the Royal Forests, it looks as if expense was part of the problem. Thomas Blanke, lord mayor in 1582, spent five days imprisoned in the sheriff's house until he would accept his election as an alderman. Thomas Curtes, who had resisted translation to a great Company, tried to avoid becoming sheriff 'by reason of his insufficiency of goods'. He eventually submitted 'with an evil will' and 'kept it at his house and would not paint his house nor change it'.

Aldermen had to pay for their robes and for dinners for ward officers and their livery brethren. It was essential to keep up appearances (maintain their 'port' as William Harrison would have put it). Their duties were onerous, with the Court of Aldermen meeting two to four times a week to supervise orphans, aliens, apprentices, craftsmen, liverymen, merchants and civic officers. The aldermen also had to regulate markets, poorhouses and hospitals, to control public order and private morals. A Common Council ordinance of 1545 stated that 'noe Blasphemous song in Latin, Italian, French or English shall be sung by musicians of this citie. No Latin, Italian or French songs whatever till it be first read in English to the Lord Mayor and by him allowed'. All this came on top of committee work, ordering of justice, administration of ward affairs and keeping the peace. It was time-consuming enough without having to devote a year to the job of sheriff and another year as lord mayor. But the expense was the most serious problem. The cost of being lord mayor grew and grew. Stow wrote that 'all men fly and refuse to serve the honourable City'. In 1545 it was agreed that no man should serve more than one year, and with a few exceptions this was observed. In 1554, while Thomas Whyte was lord mayor, sumptuary laws were passed limiting the number of dishes to be served and the number of people to be invited to City feasts. These laws also put a stop to the medieval practice of having a Lord of Misrule and the tradition of having a Fool at feasts who would leap into a huge bowl of custard, which as Ben Jonson wrote:

> Shall make my Lady Mayoress and her sisters
> Laugh all their hoods over their shoulders.

In spite of these attempts to limit mayoral expenditure, accounts of foreign visitors indicate that the lord mayor was expected to keep open house and receive all comers. Paul Hentzner, visiting London in Elizabeth's reign, wrote (in his *Itinerary*) of the lord mayor that: 'During the year of his magistracy, he is obliged to live so magnificently that foreigner or native, without any expense is free, if he can find a chair empty, to dine at his table where there is always the greatest plenty'.

It is surprising that so few of them landed in financial straits. At the beginning of the period some were unfortunate enough to fall into the hands of Henry VII's notorious tax collectors, Empson and Dudley. Sir William Capel, having been lord mayor in 1503, had to pay a huge fine and spent several years in prison, from which he was released only on Henry VII's death in 1509. Nevertheless he served again as lord mayor in

1510, taking over from Thomas Bradbury who died in January of that year, and still managed to add an extra chapel to St Bartholomew's and leave a considerable estate. Thomas Kneseworth, lord mayor in 1505, was also imprisoned by Empson and Dudley, but managed to leave his company, the Fishmongers, £1,600 for the support of thirteen poor men and women. Sir Lawrence Aylmer, lord mayor in 1508, did less well. He too had been fined and imprisoned by Empson and Dudley. But he was 'undone by the expenses of the mayoralty although he kept no feast' (since he only took over in March from William Browne who died in office). In 1524 he was dismissed from his aldermanry, heavily in debt, and imprisoned in Ludgate. Thomas Whyte died a poor man, but then his charitable expenditure had been extraordinary, including the founding of St John's College, Oxford. Lionel Duckett, lord mayor in 1572, a very wealthy man, chief executor and partner of Sir Thomas Gresham (the founder of the Royal Exchange) and chief officer of the Mines Royal for many years, was able to leave respectable sums to charity, but his estate was greatly diminished at his death. Richard Martin, Goldsmith, who served twice as lord mayor in 1589 and 1594, on both occasions taking over from mayors who had died in office, had a very successful business career, being Governor of the Society of Mineral and Battery Works and Master of the Mint. He was, however, removed from his aldermanry in 1602 for poverty and imprisoned for debt.

The most unfortunate case was that of Thomas Lodge, son-in-law of William Laxton, lord mayor in 1544, and father of the well-known Elizabethan dramatist, Thomas Lodge. During his mayoralty in 1562 one Edward Skeggs, purveyor for the Queen, seized twelve capons from the mayor's table. Lodge, affronted, threatened him with 'the biggest pair of bolts in Newgate'. Skeggs complained to the Earl of Arundel who swore to punish the Lord Mayor. Lodge wrote to Robert Dudley and William Cecil urging that Skegg's word should not be taken against his, for 'he had not seen for his time that the Mayor of London had been so dealt with'. All the same he was fined and four years later was forced to resign his aldermanry. This was mainly because of financial problems caused by the loss of one of his ships, pillaged by the French in a trade war, and a crisis of credit in the City during a plague year. Later, considerable efforts were made by the City and the Queen herself to help him, which indicates a concern for the dignity of the office of lord mayor.

Financial failures were the exceptions. Most sixteenth-century lord mayors were very successful merchants and financiers. Indeed the wealth

William I's 1067 Charter to the citizens of London.

King John's 1215 Charter granting the citizens of London the right to elect their mayor.

Henry FitzAilwyn, first Mayor of London – a sixteenth-century portrayal.

Matthew Paris – View of London c. 1292.

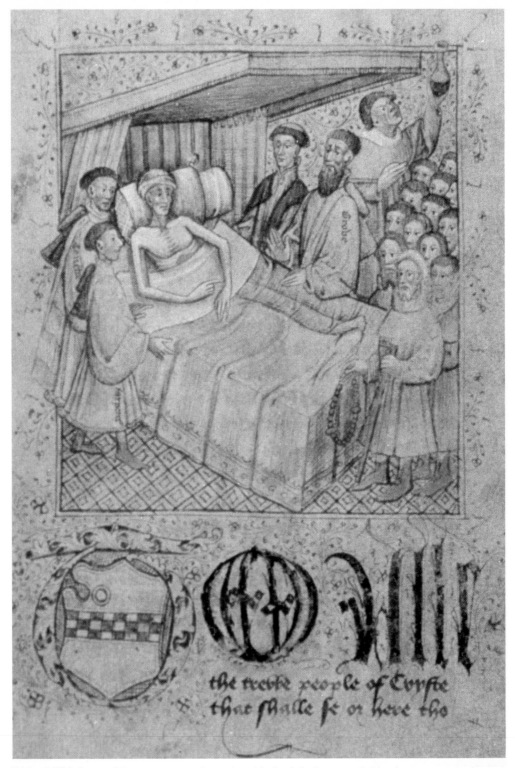

the trewe people of Cryste
that shalle se or here tho

Richard Whittington (Mercer, 1397, 1406, 1419) on his death-bed surrounded by the executors and inmates of his almshouse.

Simon Eyre (Draper, 1445) in the robes of a City alderman. A sixteenth-century portrayal.

The Tower with London Bridge in the background from a fifteenth-century manuscript.

of the lord mayors was legendary. The story was told of Bartholomew Rede (lord mayor in 1502, who kept his mayoralty in Crosby Hall) that at a banquet an Italian merchant showed him a jewel worth 1,000 marks and said that it was beyond the purse of the King. Rede had it ground to dust and drank it with his wine. 'Speak honourably of the King of England,' he said to the Italian, 'for thou hast now seen one of his subjects drink 1,000 marks at a draft.' A more down-to-earth comment on the wealth of the City's chief citizen was that of John Stow. His brother Thomas attempted to cut him out of their mother's will because he had called Thomas's wife a harlot. In the event John got £5 when each of the other children got £10. Stow bitterly remarked that 'if he could so punish all men that will more openly say so much then he would soon be richer than any Mayor of London'. A few of them were fortunate in inheriting considerable wealth. William Chester's father was a successful Draper who had died when William was four years old. His mother had then married Sir John Milborne, lord mayor in 1521, also a Draper, and William followed them into the Company. He did well, but was fortunate to receive a fortune on the death of his mother in 1545. This tided him over an embargo placed by the Emperor Charles V on English merchandise (probably because of Henry VIII's break with the Pope) which brought him serious trade losses. At about that time he went in for the new art of sugar refining, and set up two sugar bakeries which were very profitable. His trading activities involved him in expeditions to the coast of Africa. He became governor of the Muscovy Company and was very successful in the eastern trade. Elizabeth I referred to him in a despatch as one of her greatest and best merchants trading with the Shah of Persia. He retired from active business life in 1572 and retreated to Cambridge where he had been as a young man, although he had left without taking a degree (as many did in those days). Here he devoted himself to classical learning until his death in 1595. Although his fortunes had declined he left capital worth £600 to provide for six poor women patients at St Bartholomew's Hospital.

Martin Bowes was born in York at the end of the fifteenth century. He told his story to his fellow aldermen in 1549 when presenting a ceremonial sword to the City, and described how he lived in York until he was fourteen 'and then came hither up to London, young and with small substance and so have continued here these thirty-eight years ever since'. He was apprenticed to Robert Amadas, a noted goldsmith, and became prosperous. He was lord mayor in 1545, and during his year of office was responsible for the examination and punishment of many heretics, including Anne Askew, who was tortured and executed. This was no reflection of Bowes's humanity, but shows how the lord mayor had to carry out royal policy. He worked hard to improve the City's water supply. He sat as a Member of Parliament for London six times. As Treasurer for St Bartholomew's he played a major part in the negotiations for its purchase as a hospital for the City after the Dissolution of the Monasteries. He was Master of the Mint and Prime Warden of the Goldsmiths' Company from 1559 to 1562. He was very active as a Justice of the Peace in Kent and Middlesex. He remembered his home and gave the City of York a civic sword, which they still have. He also repaired the church in which he was baptised, and rebuilt a bridge. The City received its first Lord Mayor's Jewel from him, a cross of gold set with rich stones and pearls. The Goldsmiths' Bowes Cup was presented to them by Sir Martin, and they believe it is the cup which was used for Elizabeth I's Coronation. Martin Bowes had eighteen children, seven of whom survived and had to be provided for, but he was still able to leave over £2,500 for charity. He left lands to discharge his ward of Langbourn 'of all 15ths (taxes) to be granted to the King in Parliament'. He established a yearly sermon on St Martin's day at St Mary Woolnoth, which is still preached although now it is the service of St Dunstan (the Goldsmiths' patron saint) and is held in May instead of on St Martin's Day in November. Sir Martin was buried in St Mary Woolnoth, where his reconstructed monument can be seen.

The Greshams were an ancient family from the village of Gresham in Norfolk. Richard, the third of four brothers, was born at Holt in 1485 and was apprenticed to John Middleton, a London Mercer. Richard was admitted to the Freedom when he reached the age of twenty-one and was soon successful on his own account. In 1511, when he was about twenty-five, he advanced money to the King. In 1516 he was appointed Gentleman Usher Extraordinary in the royal household. In 1520 he was supplying tapestries to Cardinal Wolsey at Hampton Court. He remained closely involved with Wolsey and was loyal to him to the end, but Wolsey's fall from power did not disturb Gresham's career. During his mayoralty in 1537, the year after the beginning of the Dissolution of the Monasteries, he was closely involved in negotiations with the King over the future of St Mary's Spital, St Bartholomew's and St Thomas's, and his recommendations that their future use should be for the relief of the poor were carried out by Henry VIII and Edward VI. He was one of the major city purchasers of monastic lands, the greatest of his acquisitions being Fountains Abbey. Richard Gresham was the originator of the idea for an Exchange in London but he was unable to muster support to carry it through, so it was his son Thomas who did so. His younger brother John followed in his footsteps and was sheriff during his brother's mayoralty. As lord mayor in 1547, John revived the procession of the Midsummer Marching Watch (described in the next chapter) which Henry VIII had suspended in 1524 because of the expense and a fear of disorder. He bought the family home in Holt from his elder brother William and converted it into a free grammar school which he entrusted to the Fishmongers' Company. During his lifetime he gave £2,000 for poor clothiers in Bristol. His funeral in 1556 was particularly magnificent.

The lord mayors were answerable to the king for the behaviour of their citizens. John Rest, lord mayor in 1516, who kept his mayoralty in Crosby Hall, had to deal with a violent outbreak of hostility to foreign workers which broke out in London in May 1517, known as Evil May Day. A mob of apprentices, armed with clubs, rioted all night. The next morning they were met by a large force collected by the Mayor, and 300 prisoners were taken. Gallows were raised at the Cross in Cheapside and elsewhere to hang thirteen of the rioters and the situation was brought under control. It had been a very unfortunate episode, and a deputation of Aldermen set forth clothed in black to ask the King's forgiveness at Greenwich. Later there was a formal pardon in Westminster Hall which the Mayor and Aldermen attended in their best liveries. The remaining prisoners were brought in with ropes round their necks and officially pardoned. Since the riots had begun with the May Day celebrations, the custom of annually erecting a maypole by St Andrew Undershaft (so named because of the maypole) was ended.

On occasion the lord mayor would have to act as pacifier between the king and the Londoners. Henry VIII's marriage to Anne Boleyn in 1533 was very unpopular in the City. The King was furious when he heard that the congregation had left a church when prayers for the Queen were asked for. The Mayor, Stephen Pecocke, had to summon the guilds and order them to cease murmuring against the King's marriage and see that their journeymen and servants 'and a still more difficult task, their wives' also refrained. After that there was a splendid river procession to convey the King and Queen from Greenwich for the Queen's Coronation, which was described by Archbishop Cranmer in a letter to the English Ambassador at the Court of the Holy Roman Empire.

All the Crafts of London thereunto well appointed, in several barges decked after the most gorgeous and sumptuous manner, with divers pageants thereunto belonging, repaired and waited all together upon the Mayor of London; and so, well furnished, came all unto Greenwich where they tarried and waited for the Queen's coming to her barge; which so done they brought her unto the Tower, trumpets, shawms, and other divers instruments playing and making great melody, which as is reported was as comely done as never was like in any time nigh to our remembrance.

Thus an episode which might have soured relations between the King and the City was smoothed over. They were allies and had a mutual interest in the good government of London. The Privy Council kept in close touch with the lord mayor, and the royal wishes were expressed by a stream of orders, precepts and requests. These might be anything from a request to raise troops, or for a loan, to a query about an important lost document. In 1524 the records of the Court of Aldermen show that the mayor had to issue a proclamation on the king's behalf for the recovery of some rather sensitive papers about the formation of a league against France. Apparently 'a hat with certeyn letters and other billes and writings' had been lost, and a reward was offered for their recovery. (They do not seem to have been found.)

After his marriage to Anne Boleyn, Henry set about cutting the English Church off from Rome (since the Pope had refused to grant him a divorce from Katherine of Aragon). All leading citizens had to swear the Oaths of Supremacy and Succession, accepting Henry as the Head of the Church and Anne's expected child as his rightful heir. Then Henry began to dissolve the monasteries. It was a tense time and perhaps for that reason the King took a close interest in who was lord mayor. In 1535 Sir John Aleyn was elected, against his own wish, to serve a second time at the King's express request. Aleyn was a leading Mercer and had been made a member of the Privy Council. To this day the City remembers him as the donor of the Lord Mayor's Collar composed of twenty-eight gold and enamel SS links. The following year Ralph Warren, who together with the Greshams had extensive financial dealings with the King, was chosen mayor at Henry's personal request. He had to keep the City calm during the agitation over the northern rebellion in protest against the Dissolution of the Monasteries, known as the Pilgrimage of Grace, which at one time seemed to threaten the capital. The year after that the King specially asked for Richard Gresham to be elected mayor although this meant that eleven aldermen senior to him had to be passed over, since he had only been an alderman for two years.

In 1547 Henry VIII died and the Mayor, Henry Huberthorn, attended the King's Council where the young Edward VI presented him and the Aldermen with black livery for the old King's funeral. Later they rode in Edward's Coronation procession from the Tower to Westminster. Although Henry VIII broke with Rome, he was not a Protestant. But his son, the young prince, had been brought up by Protestant tutors and now with his uncle, Protector Somerset, and after his fall from power, with his other uncle, the Duke of Northumberland, Edward set about changing the country's religion. In the City, churches were whitewashed and statues broken and the new English service introduced. Sir Rowland Hill, lord mayor in 1549, was the first Protestant to hold the office. As sheriff in 1541 he had been involved in a controversial case over parliamentary privilege in the course of which he had imprisoned George Ferrers, a member of parliament. He was himself imprisoned for two days because of this, and it is possible that his knighthood conferred in 1542 was compensation for the indignity. A bachelor, he was a noted public benefactor who endowed a grammar school at Drayton in his home county of Shropshire.

Edward VI died at the age of sixteen in 1553 and there was an immediate crisis. On his deathbed he had been persuaded by his uncle, the Duke of Northumberland, to bypass his Catholic sister Mary (daughter of Katherine of Aragon) and to leave the throne to his Protestant cousin, Lady Jane Grey, who was married to Northumberland's son, Guildford Dudley. The Lord Mayor, George Barne, was summoned with several Aldermen, including John Gresham, Andrew Judde (both ex-mayors), Thomas Offley, William Garrarde, William Hewet and Thomas Lodge (all to become mayor). These countersigned a document accepting Lady Jane Grey as Queen. A few days later the tables were turned. Northumberland unwisely set off to confront Mary in Suffolk, where she had raised supporters. His forces, unenthusiastic for his cause, melted away and Mary advanced towards London. The Lords of the Council met the Lord Mayor when he was out riding and told him to bring the Sheriffs and Aldermen to a meeting at Castle Baynard. There they all agreed to proclaim Mary as the rightful Queen and rode together to Cheapside to do so. When Mary entered London in triumph through Aldgate Bars the Mayor and Aldermen met her and presented the Civic Sword. In October Thomas

Whyte was elected mayor, and Mary's Coronation procession through the City took place the next day.

During his mayoralty Thomas Whyte had to act on the Queen's behalf to impose the Catholic religion. He was obliged to follow Government policy, but in fact the Imperial Ambassador wrote to his master that the Lord Mayor was a good Catholic. He presided over the trials of state prisoners – Cranmer, Lady Jane Grey and Lord Guildford Dudley – in Guildhall. He received the Spanish envoys who came to negotiate the Queen's extremely unpopular marriage to Philip of Spain. When Thomas Wyatt led a rebellion intended to dethrone Mary and place her sister Elizabeth on the throne instead, Whyte had to use all his authority to keep the City loyal to the Queen, who came herself to Guildhall where she made a courageous speech to the citizens defending her position. Subsequently he ordered the Aldermen to urge residents of their wards to follow the Catholic religion. None of this accorded with the sympathies of the majority of the citizens and it is possible that the antagonism he aroused led to an assassination attempt. One day, as he was attending a sermon at St Paul's, a shot fell near him, which may have been an accident but was possibly more serious. After the royal marriage, which took place in Winchester, Whyte made preparations for the reception of Philip and Mary in the City, ordering that the gibbets be cleared away, that the Cross in Cheapside be regilded and that two aldermen should be on duty at night for fear of disturbances.

Any affection that Londoners might have had for Mary Tudor was stifled by her fanatical Catholic policy which culminated in the horrifying fires of Smithfield. Antagonism was increased by the requirement to provide contingents to fight in Philip's wars in France. When Mary died on 17 November 1558 the City prepared to receive Elizabeth, herself descended from one of their mayors, Geoffrey Boleyn. Thomas Leigh, the newly elected lord mayor, led the City's welcome and a joyful reception of the Queen's splendid Coronation procession. The Recorder presented her with a crimson satin purse richly wrought with gold and containing 1,000 marks in gold. 'I thank my lord mayor, his brethren and you all', replied the new Queen, 'And whereas your request is that I should continue your good lady and queen, be ye assured that I will be as good to you as ever queen was to her people'.

William Hewet followed Thomas Leigh in the mayoral chair, the first mayor from the Clothworkers' Company. He came to London from Yorkshire, did well in commerce and was joined in business by members of his family. He lived in Philpot Lane and owned a country house at Highgate. There is no proof that he lived on London Bridge, but the romantic story told by Stow places him firmly there. It tells how one day a careless nurse dropped his baby daughter Anne into the Thames. His young apprentice Edward Osborne leapt into the river and rescued her. When she grew up Hewet gave her in marriage to Osborne with a large dowry. Osborne, son of a minor country gentleman from Ashford in Kent, became a very successful merchant and financial agent. He travelled widely on business and resided abroad for long periods. He traded with Spain and Turkey and was the first Governor of the Levant Company. Together with Richard Staper he financed John Newby and Ralph Fitch's epic land journey which opened up communications with India. He became lord mayor in 1583.

Elizabeth cemented the alliance with the City which her predecessors had begun. Her reign was not an easy time. She had to make a settlement of religion which inevitably, although it was a compromise, could never please all the people. Some disappointed Catholics turned to Mary Queen of Scots, and there were several serious plots against Elizabeth. In none of these was there any City involvement. From 1585 England was at war with Spain and the City played a vital part in providing money and men for that war. In 1586 John Harte, a very wealthy Grocer who was to be lord mayor in 1589, personally helped to finance the Earl of Leicester's expedition to the Netherlands. George Bonde was lord mayor when the Armada sailed against England in 1588, and the City joined with the whole nation in providing men and ships to combat the danger. When in the 1590s the strain of repeated demands for money began to tell, the City tried to resist a request for a loan. The royal reply was that the Livery could cut down on their feasting. A precept from the Court of Aldermen went out accordingly.

At the other religious extreme the Puritans were really more of a problem to Elizabeth than the Catholics. Puritan feeling was strong in the City. Two eminent Elizabethan lord mayors, Wolstan Dixie and Henry Billingsley, were noted Puritans. Wolstan Dixie came from Huntingdon-shire and was lord mayor in 1585. During his year of office he took measures to suppress a conspiracy of apprentices to attack foreigners in London. In 1588 he was appointed by the Court of Aldermen to ensure that innholders, butchers, brewers and bakers did not put up their prices to soldiers stationed in the City for defence against the Armada. He gave money for divinity scholarships at Cambridge and supported the Puritan colleges of Emmanuel and Sidney Sussex. He endowed a grammar school at Market Bosworth and assisted with the building of Peterhouse College, Cambridge. Henry Billingsley was unusual as lord mayor, in being a scholar in his own right. He was the first translator of Euclid's *Elements of Geometry* into English. His translation was prefaced by a noted scholar, John Dee, who was the Queen's personal astrologer. Some people thought that Dee must have done the work but he stated that he had only contributed annotations. In spite of Billingsley's scholarly distinction Elizabeth disliked his Puritanism and ordered that he be passed over for the mayoral chair in 1596 and Thomas Skinner be elected in his place. The Aldermen complied, but when Skinner died in office after two months Billingsley was elected, and the Court of Aldermen entered a formal protest at the Queen's interference with 'ancient coustoom'. Nevertheless, loyalty to Elizabeth remained strong, even though her popularity waned towards the end of her reign. When in 1601 the Earl of Essex, the Queen's former favourite, rode through the City streets trying to raise a rebellion he found no support. William Ryder, the lord mayor, refused to help him and kept the City loyal to the Queen.

The wealthiest of all the Elizabethan lord mayors was Sir John Spencer, a Clothworker from Suffolk, who was elected in 1594. He was known in the City as 'rich Spencer' and was reckoned by contemporaries to be worth £500,000 to £800,000, having made his fortune from building up landed estate and from moneylending. He bought Crosby Hall and restored it at enormous cost for use during his mayoralty, which he kept in great state. Otherwise he lived in his country house at Canonbury. As lord mayor he was noted for asserting the right of the City to freely elect the Recorder. His reputation had suffered from the stories about his harsh treatment of his daughter Elizabeth. This was a time when aristocrats in financial difficulties were looking for wealthy wives. One of them, Lord Compton, was an attractive young man and a favourite with the Queen. He laid passionate suit to Elizabeth Spencer who was dazzled by his charm and nobility, but her father considered such a match would be imprudent. He shut her up and beat her. For this he was thrown into the Fleet prison. Legend has it that Elizabeth escaped from Canonbury Tower in a bread basket, but actually Lord Compton had her removed to the care of another Alderman and then married her. The young couple lived extravagantly but Sir John held aloof from them and threatened to leave his fortune elsewhere. A son was born and was christened Spencer, but the story that the Queen persuaded Sir John to stand godfather to a mystery child who was his own grandson is fiction. It was in fact some years before Sir John became reconciled to his daughter. He died intestate at a great age in 1610, so his full estate went to Lord Compton anyway, since his daughter was his only heir. It was said that Lord Compton's brain was temporarily turned by such luck. Or was it luck? As the historian Lawrence Stone pointed out in an article on the subject (*History Today*, 1961) it was very strange that such a prudent man as Sir John should fail to make a will, thus ensuring that his entire fortune went to his profligate son-in-law. It is also hard to believe that such a man would want to be remembered as the only rich Elizabethan lord mayor who left nothing to charity or to his Livery Company. His nephews strongly believed he intended to leave £5,000 to the Clothworkers to set poor craftsmen up in business. So perhaps his will was suppressed by Lord Compton, who then had a temporary mental breakdown from the strain. Sir John had a lavish funeral at St Helen's Bishopsgate, where his tomb is, and baskets of bread were distributed to the poor. Lord and Lady Compton lived on, still extravagantly, in their beautiful house of Castle Ashby, and in 1618 Lord Compton became the first Earl of Northampton.

The most outstanding and worthy Elizabethan lord mayor was Sir Rowland Heyward, also a Clothworker, from Shropshire. He was an active and successful merchant and financier, who loaned money to the Queen, sat as a member of parliament between 1572 and 1583 and was very active on parliamentary committees. He served for no less than thirty-three years as an alderman, was sheriff in 1563, Master of the Clothworkers in 1559 and lord mayor in 1570–1, the year in which Gresham's Royal Exchange was opened, and again in 1591 when he took over on the early death of John Allot. He was at various times governor of the Muscovy Company, governor of the Mineral and Battery Works, Justice of the Peace for Shropshire and Middlesex, president of Bridewell and Bethlem hospitals, president of St Bartholomew's, Surveyor General and Comptroller General of Hospitals. His most valuable work was in dealing with visitations of the plague, especially in the epidemic of 1563. Disease was one of the most serious problems the City authorities had to cope with in the Tudor period. At the very beginning, in 1485, Thomas Hill, lord mayor, died in office and was followed by Sir William Stokker who died four days later. Four other aldermen died in the same week. Plague recurred frequently in the sixteenth century and was particularly bad in 1556 when seven aldermen died during two months. In 1563 and in 1569 no mayoral feast was held because of plague. The authorities made all sorts of attempts to control it, quarantining sufferers in their houses, burning herbs in the street, killing dogs. In the outbreak of 1593–4 the Mayor, Cuthbert Buckle, and two ex-mayors, Wolstan Dixie and Rowland Heyward himself, were all victims.

Sir Rowland's career epitomized all that was best in the sixteenth-century lord mayors. Most worked incredibly hard, not only during their year of office but throughout their lives as presidents and surveyors of hospitals, members of parliament, collectors of customs, treasurers, arbitrators. Their expert knowledge on commercial and financial affairs was invaluable to the Government. In 1588, the year of the Armada, for example, Richard Saltonstall, who had lived in the Netherlands and would become lord mayor in 1597, was consulted by Lord Burleigh on means of raising money in the continental market to finance defence measures against the threatened Spanish invasion. Their active promotion of trade and exploration and their spirit of adventure in these matters made them instrumental in the founding of the British Empire. Through their legacies they made a huge contribution to the care of the poor and sick and with the founding of schools they influenced the development of education all over the country. They rebuilt chapels and churches. They provided for road and bridge repairs, for the provision of water, for the cleansing of ditches. They founded hospitals and almshouses.

Many of their good works have already been mentioned. To catalogue them all would fill several chapters, but there remain some which cannot be left out. We must go back to the reign of Henry VII to look at Hugh Clopton from Stratford-upon-Avon. About 100 years before Shakespeare was working in London, Hugh Clopton, Mercer, was elected lord mayor, in 1491. He was the third son of an established local family, and was born at the family home, Clopton Manor House. Like Shakespeare, he left home to seek his fortune in London. He did well, never married, and devoted a great part of his wealth to endowing his home town. He built for himself 'a pretty house of brick and timber' which was later bought by Shakespeare, and the site is visited today by millions of tourists as New Place. Tourists cross the River Avon by Clopton Bridge, mostly unaware that this fine stone bridge was built for the town by Hugh Clopton in the years before he became Lord Mayor of London. In his will he left money for the bridge and for the chapel adjacent to the school where he, and later on, Shakespeare, were educated, for rebuilding the cross aisle of the Parish Church, where there is a monument to him, and for Exhibitions for poor scholars at Oxford and Cambridge.

Stephen Jenyns, Merchant Taylor, came from Wolverhampton, where he founded the grammar school. He also built a great part of St Andrew Undershaft in London. Jenyns was lord mayor in 1508 so he attended the funeral of Henry VII and the Coronation of the eighteen-year-old Henry VIII, who knighted him before he sat down to his Coronation banquet. Jenyns served the King according to tradition 'with ipocras in a cup of gold which cuppe, after his Grace had drunken thereof, was with the cover give unto Sir Stephen, like as other his predecessors, Mayors of the City were wont to have at the coronacion of the King'.

George Monoux, Draper, began his career in Bristol, of which town he was mayor in 1501. He came to London where he exported cloth to Bordeaux and Lisbon, and imported wine, oil, salt and sugar. He made considerable purchases of property around London, particularly in Walthamstow, where he founded an almshouse and a free school. Another Draper, John Milborne (1521) also founded almshouses.

William Laxton, Grocer, lord mayor in 1544, endowed a school in his home town of Oundle. It is a now a famous public school. The Latin inscription over the door reads:

Oundellae natus Londini parta labore
Laxtonus posuit senibus puerisque levamen.

Another great public school owes its origin to the Skinner, Andrew Judde, lord mayor in 1550. He came from Tonbridge, where he founded in 1553 'The Free Grammar School in the town of Tonbridge'. In his will he left property to the school and the management to the Skinners' Company, whose Court of Assistants form the Board of Governors. Judde was followed as lord mayor by another Skinner, Richard Dobbis, who played a major part in setting up Christ's Hospital as a school for the City. Andrew Judde was a close friend of Thomas Whyte and was associated with him in the founding of St John's College, Oxford. In recognition of this, Whyte endowed a fellowship at St John's for Tonbridge School. Whyte was the son of a poor clothier in Reading. He was apprenticed at the age of twelve to a tailor, who left him £100 in his will, thus giving him a good start in life. Remembering this, Thomas Whyte gave money to towns all over the country to help young men to make a start. There are statues to him in Coventry and Leicester, and his portrait can be found in fifteen towns, apart from Oxford and London. He also played a major part in the founding of the Merchant Taylors' School.

Another Merchant Taylor, Thomas Offley, lord mayor in 1556, bequeathed half of his estate to the poor, including the poor of Chester, whence his father came, and the poor of Stafford, where he was born. He went to Jesus School in St Paul's churchyard, where he studied under the famous Greek scholar, William Lily, and was apprenticed to a Merchant Taylor friend of Lily's. He was known as the Zaccheus of London, not as Fuller said 'for his low stature but for his high charity'. He lived very frugally himself. A popular rhyme went:

> Offley three dishes had of daily rost
> An egge, an apple and (the third) a toast.

Isaac Walton dedicated *The Compleat Angler* to his son, Sir John Offley of Madeley.

William Harper, lord mayor in 1561, came from Bedford where he refounded the grammar school after the Dissolution of the Monasteries. He endowed the foundation with thirteen acres of what was then hunting land in Holborn, and is now part of Bloomsbury. There is a description of how he and the Aldermen went on an expedition to visit the conduit heads west of the City. They dined at a banqueting house at the head of the conduit (which was known as the Lord Mayor's Banqueting House from 1585 until it fell into decay in the eighteenth century. It is marked on old maps where Stratford Place, Oxford Street, now is). Then they went hunting. The hounds killed the fox at the end of St Giles's after which 'so rode through London, my Lord Mayor Harper with ys compone home to ys own place in Lombard Street' (Henry Machyn's *Diary*). The property in Bloomsbury still belongs to Bedford Corporation and Bedford Row is named after the town, and not after the Dukes of Bedford, like other Bloomsbury property such as Bedford Square.

Rowland Heyward endowed a school at his home town of Bridgnorth in Shropshire. Stephen Soame, Grocer, lord mayor in 1598, came from Norfolk and was a successful cloth trader, who as his wealth increased turned to moneylending and investment in land. He became a leading Eastland merchant and chaired the first meeting that was held to discuss the formation of the East India Company. He wainscotted and re-roofed the Grocers' Hall, re-edified and glazed the great north window of old St Paul's, and at Little Thurlow in Suffolk founded and endowed an alms-house and a school.

The attitude of social responsibility which inspired these men continued well into the seventeenth century. The creation of wealth was not an end in itself for them. Their aim was an orderly and stable society, a prosperous and well-governed City, and they were prepared to direct much of their wealth to social purposes and much of their energy and time to the responsibilities of government. Their relationship with the Tudor monarchs was based on recognition of the mutual benefits which co-operation brought. Under the Stuarts this co-operation was to break down.

6

INTERLUDE:
THE LORD MAYOR'S SHOW

'Ridings', that is processions, were an essential part of City life. They were naturally a popular entertainment for the people, and an important way of impressing upon them the dignity and power of their rulers. As we have seen, in the Middle Ages the most splendid processions were those on royal occasions, especially at coronations and to celebrate victorious returns from the wars. A particular feature of these was the pageant: a static display, mounted on a platform, featuring a castle or elaborate fountain, with actors, often children, dressed as angels, knights, symbolic virtues, etc. There were many simpler processions, as for example the annual attendance by the Livery Companies at church on their saint's days. For many years the lord mayor's journey to Westminster to be presented to the king was a straightforward, though long and lavishly dressed procession, with the aldermen, sheriffs, City officers and leading liverymen mounted and wearing their finest gowns.

A new feature was added in the fifteenth century when the custom of making part of the journey by water began. The first time the mayor actually went to Westminster along the Thames was in 1422, after the death of Henry V, when first the sheriffs after their election, and then the Mayor on succeeding to the chair, were requested not to ride through the streets but to go by barge. But it is generally accepted that the water procession really started in 1453 when Sir John Norman was rowed up the river in a fine barge with silver oars.

The Lord Mayor's procession thus became a combination of land and water show. When he took office the new lord mayor would tour his own ward and then proceed to the nearest stairs where he would embark and be rowed up to Westminster to take his oath. Afterwards he would return by barge to Blackfriars and from there process to St Paul's for a service of thanksgiving, thence to Guildhall for his feast. The diarist Henry Machyn described Sir Thomas Whyte's procession in 1553:

First were two tall men bearing two great streamers of the Merchant Taylors' arms, then came one with a drum and a flute playing, and another with a great fife, all they in blue silk, and then came two great 'wodyn' armed with two great clubs all in green and with squibs burning, with great beards and side hair, and two targets upon their backs, and then came sixteen trumpeters blowing, and then came men in blue gowns and caps and hose and blue silk sleeves, and every man having a target and a javelin to the number of seventy, and then came a devil, and after that came the bachelors all in livery and scarlet hoods, and then came the pageant of St. John Baptist gorgeously with goodly speeches, and then came all the king's trumpeters blowing and every trumpeter having scarlet caps, and the waits caps and goodly banners, and then the crafts, and then the waits playing, and then my Lord Mayor's officers, and then my Lord Mayor and two good henchmen.

It was at about this time that the Lord Mayor's Show began to take over from the earlier Midsummer Marching Watch as the most important civic annual parade. Stow gives a poetic description of the Midsummer Marching Watch, in which all the Livery Companies and the City dignitaries took part every summer:

On the vigil of St. John the Baptist and on St. Peter and Paul the Apostles, every man's door being shadowed with green birch, long fennel, St. John's wort, orpin, white lilies, and such like garnished upon with garlands and beautiful flowers, had also lamps of glass with oil burning in them all the night; some hung out branches of iron curiously wrought, containing hundreds of lamps alight at once, which made a goodly show, namely in New Fish Street, Thames Street etc. Then had ye beside the standing watches all in bright harness, every ward and street of this city and suburbs, a marching watch, that passed through the principal streets thereof, to wit, from the little conduit by Paul's Gate to West Cheap, by the Stocks through Cornhill, by

Leadenhall to Aldgate, then back down Fenchurch Street into Cornhill, and through it into West Cheap again.

There were hundreds of lights carried in cressets, with 2,000 participants, soldiers, whifflers (to sweep the road),

> drummers and fifes, standard and ensign bearers, sword players, trumpeters on horseback, demi-lances on great horses, gunners with hand guns or half-hakes, archers in coats of white fustian signed on the breast and back with the arms of the city, their bows bent in their hands with sheaves of arrows by their sides, pikemen in bright corslets, burganets, etc.

There were morris dancers and minstrels and then 'the mayor himself well mounted on horseback, the sword bearer before him in fair armour well mounted also, the mayor's footmen, and the like torchbearers about him henchmen twain upon great stirring horses following him.' Stow's account was nostalgic, for by the time he wrote the midsummer procession had been abandoned for many years. It was stopped by Henry VIII ostensibly because of the expense, but probably also because of its religious nature during the period when the King was breaking with Rome. From time to time it was revived, as for example by Sir John Gresham in 1547, but in Elizabeth's reign the Lord Mayor's Show took its place as London's great annual parade.

Now the Lord Mayor's Show began to incorporate the pageantry formerly associated with royal processions and to include the pageants in the procession, so that they moved along the streets for all to see (as the pageants did in the medieval mystery plays). With royal processions the aim was to impress the monarch with a static pageant as he or she passed by, and this continued for royalty. When Elizabeth I was carried through the City to her Coronation on a flower-strewn litter she was greeted by elaborately staged pageants, with children speaking specially composed verses to celebrate her Accession.

As the Show became more complicated and pageants were introduced it was necessary to put someone in charge of the work and in 1566 the first Pageantmaster, Richard Baker, a Painter Stainer, was appointed 'for the making of the pageant'. Theatre in all its aspects – poetry, music, spectacle – blossomed in the reign of Elizabeth, and all these were absorbed into the Lord Mayor's Show, making it a work of art. The great Livery Companies rivalled each other to produce the best possible show for their mayor. The pageants themselves were enormously expensive constructions, but could often be re-used. The Fishmonger's Ship, which first appeared to greet Edward I on his return after a Scottish victory, was used for Sir John Leman in 1616. The Goldsmith's Castle, produced for the Coronation of Richard II reappeared several times, as did the Mercers' great Maiden Chariot. This pageant was a 22 foot high Roman chariot with sides of embossed silver and surmounted by a golden canopy above which sat Fame blowing her trumpet. In it sat the Mercer's Maiden, a young and beautiful gentlewoman with flowing hair surmounted by a gold and jewelled coronet. At the Lord Mayor's feast she dined royally at a separate table.

The outstanding feature of the late Elizabethan Shows was the introduction of poetry and drama, for which the talents of many leading writers were engaged. The first full printed text was that which George Peele wrote for Sir Wolstan Dixie in 1585. He used verse to salute the Lord Mayor and glorify the City.

> This now remains right honorable Lord
> That carefully you do attend and keep
> This lovely lady, rich and beautiful
> The jewel wherewithal your sovereign Queen
> Hath put your honour lovingly in trust
> That you may add to London's dignity
> And London's dignity may add to yours.

Peele introduced abstract virtues and characters: Magnanimity and Loyalty, the Country and the Thames, the Soldier, the Sailor and Science. The verses were declaimed by children who featured in most of the pageants. In 1591 Peele's pageant *Decensus Astraea* for William Webb concentrated on glorifying the Queen but included a neat punning compliment to the Lord Mayor through the symbolic character Time.

> I wind the web that kind so well begins
> And Fortune doth enrich what nature spins.

During the last years of Elizabeth's reign the show declined because of the strains of war and outbreaks of plague. The great welcome that the City planned for James I with pageants by Ben Jonson had to be postponed because of the plague. But early in James's reign the show revived and entered its golden age. For thirty years noted dramatists wrote for the Lord Mayor's Show as the Companies vied with each other in spectacle and expenditure. The Court entertainment of the day was the masque, a combination of drama and moral instruction, with poetry, music and ingenious scenic devices. All of these also found a place in the Lord Mayor's Shows, which were often written and staged by the same artists.

Sometimes there were hitches. In 1605 the Merchant Taylors employed Anthony Munday to put on Sir Leonard Halliday's Show. It included the City's giants, Corinaeus and Gogmagog drawing 'Britain's Mount' with golden chains. However the Company's records noted that 'by reason of the great rain and fowle weather hap'ning and falling upon the morrow after Syman and Jude's day, being the day my Lord Mayor went to Westminster, the great costs the Company bestowed upon their pageant and other shows were in manner cast away and defaced'. It was a pity for the Lord Mayor, but the pageants were repaired and used later by the Company on All Saints' Day. In 1609 Munday was invited to do the Ironmongers' show for Sir Thomas Cambell, but they were far from pleased at the result, considering it 'very imperfect and unsatisfactory'. They complained 'that the children weare not instructed in their speeches which was a spetiall judgement of the consideration, then that the Musick and singinge weare wanting, the apparrell most of it old and borrowed, with other defects'. Munday's excuse was that 'our time for preparation hath bene so short', but in any case he was not a gifted writer and was singled out for criticism by Thomas Middleton, the playwright who was employed by the Grocers to write the show for his namesake (but no relation) Sir Thomas Middleton. This was a truly dramatic presentation. As the Lord Mayor rode along Soper Lane towards the river he came upon a Senate House where musicians were playing. Then a Grave Feminine Shape stepped forward representing London, with a model of steeples and turrets on her head, and welcomed him in blank verse. After this he embarked on the river 'on whose crystal bosom float five islands artfully garnished with all manner of Indian fruits, trees, drugs and spiceries'. On his return from Westminster the Lord Mayor found himself in the midst of a conflict between Truth clad in white silk, and Error in ash coloured robes, with a mist hanging over her eyes. Truth drove Error before her down Cheapside where, at the Great Conduit, they came upon a mountain covered with clouds and guarded by Error's monsters. Truth's Angel dispersed the clouds to reveal London surrounded by the cardinal virtues, seated at the feet of Religion. Zeal, Truth's ally in all this, completed the drama by shooting a flame from his head which destroyed Error's chariot, and the day ended with fireworks.

Anthony Munday recovered his reputation with a truly splendid show for the Fishmonger, Sir John Leman, in 1616. Moving in the procession were several colourful pageants. The first was the Fishing Busse (ship) from which fishermen cast from their nets live fish to the crowd. It sailed grandly on wheels hidden by curtains. This was followed by the dolphin from the Company's arms, with Arion on his back. The third pageant was the King of the Moors (a recognized allusion to trade). He was mounted on a golden leopard 'hurling gold and silver every way about him'. This symbolized the friendship between the Fishmongers and the Goldsmiths which had taken the place of earlier violent rivalry. Then came the Lemon Tree, part of the Lord Mayor's crest and a pun on his name. Under the tree sat a pelican feeding her young with her blood, showing 'the cherishing love borne by the Mayor to the Citizens.' The fourth pageant glorified the Fishmongers' history. In Walworth's Bower the hero was seen as a marble statue on his tomb in St Paul's. A youth portraying London's Genius touched the statue with his wand and Sir William Walworth came alive and addressed his successor as Lord Mayor and Prime Warden of the Fishmongers:

> And see my Lord this bower relates
> How many famous magistrates
> From the Fishmongers ancient name
> Successively to honour came.

John Webster produced a fine literary pageant for Sir John Gore, Merchant Taylor, in 1624, which took a world view, portraying 'a fair Terrestrial Globe, circled about in convenient seats, with seven of our most famous navigators: as Sir Francis Drake, Sir John Hawkins, Sir Martin Frobisher, Sir Humphrey Gilbert, Captain Thomas Cavendish, Captain Christopher Carlisle and Captain John Davis'. It then turned to history, presenting the famous knight Sir John Hawkwood, who fought as a mercenary in the wars between Italian cities, and eight kings of England who had been Merchant Taylors. To symbolize trade and travel there was a Lion ridden by a Moor and a Camel ridden by a Turk. Then followed the Monument of Charity, showing a beautiful garden in the middle of which sat Sir Thomas Whyte 'who had a dream that he should build a college where two bodies of an elm sprang from one root ... and riding one day at the North Gate at Oxford he spied upon his right side the self same elms ... and in the same place built the College of St. John the Baptist'.

Probably the finest literary Lord Mayor's Show was Thomas Dekker's *London's Tempe*, written in 1629 for the Ironmonger, Sir James Cambell (who thus did much better than his father twenty years earlier). In his introduction the author wrote:

> Were it possible for a man, in the compass of a day, to behold (as the sunne does) all the cities in the world, as if he went with walking beames about him, that man should never see in any part of the yeare, any city so magnificently adorned with all sorts of triumphes, variety of musicke, of bravery, of bewty, of feastings, of civill (yet rich) ceremonies, with gallant lords and ladies, and thronges of people, as London is enriched with, on the first day that her great lord (or Lord Maior, for 'tis all one) takes that office upon him.

The last four shows during Charles I's reign were written by another dramatist, Thomas Heywood, who ended Sir Henry Garraway's, in 1639, with a prophetic couplet:

> Lest that too late (having stern war accited)
> We wish that peace which (whilst we had) we slighted.

It was the last proper Lord Mayor's Show for nearly twenty years. With the coming into power of the Puritans the theatres were closed and the Lord Mayor's Show ceased to contain any pageantry. It was not until the last few years of Cromwell's rule that it began to revive. In 1656 Cromwell himself watched the water pageant from a balcony in Whitehall. With the Restoration of Charles II the Show came back with full spectacle, but the standard of writing and composition never recovered its earlier level. John Evelyn reported on the first Lord Mayor's Show in Charles II's reign, 'one of ye pageants represented one greate wood, with ye royal oak and historie of his Majesty's miraculous escape at Boscobel'. Samuel Pepys saw it too and was unimpressed. 'Had a very good place to see the pageants which were many and I believe good for such kind of things, but in themselves poor and absurd'. Nevertheless the Show continued to be a popular and lavish entertainment until the end of the seventeenth century, although there was a gap of several years because of the Great Plague and the Fire of London. However, by the eighteenth century the pageants had disappeared from the Show although the procession continued to be very grand, particularly that on the river with the barges of the lord mayor and all the Livery Companies, flags and banners streaming in the wind as they rowed up to Westminster.

Celia Fiennes described a Lord Mayor's Show in William and Mary's day in her diary:

Ye Lord Major has his Sword bearer wch walkes before him with the Sword in an Embroyder'd Sheath he weares a Great velvet Cap of Crimson, the bottom and ye top of furr or such Like standing up Like a turbant or Great bowle in forme of a Great open Pye, this is Called ye Cap of Maintenance. This is ye Lord Majors Chiefe officer.... He thus walkes before the Lord Major with ye water Bayliff beareing a Gold Mace &c. At Fleete ditch they Enter ye Barges wch are all very Curiously adorned and thus he is Conducted ye river being full of Barges belonging to ye severall Companyes of London, adorned with streamers and their armes and fine musick, and have sack to drinke and Little Cakes as bigg as a Crown piece. They Come to Westminster staires where they Land and are Conducted, the Lord Majors traines being borne up as well ye old as new Lord Major, they Enter Westminster Hall and are Conducted to ye severall Courts of justice where there is severall Ceremonyes perform'd. The new Lord Major is presented to ye King or those deputed to act under him and then is sworne, all which being over they are Conducted back to their Barges and soe to ye staires they took barge, where they are received by some of ye nobility deputed by the King who made some Little speech of Compliment and Give ye Lord Major and aldermen a treate of wine and sweet meates passant. They mount on horseback and returne only ye new Lord Major takes ye right hand and haveing by ye sheriffs invited ye King and Court to dinner, wch sometymes they accept but mostly refuse, because it puts the Citty to a vast Charge; they being then Conducted through ye Citty with Greate acclamations their own habits and trappings of their horses being very fine, and they haveing all the Severall Companyes of ye Citty wch walke in their order and gowns with pageants to most or many of their Companyes, wch are a sort of Stages Covered and Carryed by men and on ye top many men and boys acting ye respective trades of Employments of Each Company, some in shipps for ye Merchants, and whatever Company the new Lord Major is of his pageant is ye finest and yt Company has ye precedency that yeare of all ye Companyes Except ye mercers Company, wch allwayes is the first and Esteemed ye Greatest, and when there is a Lord Major of yt Company their pageant is a maiden queen on a throne Crowned and with Royal Robes and scepter and most richly dressed, with Severall Ladyes dressed, her attendants, all on ye same pageant and wth a Cannopy over her head and drawn in an open chariot with 9 horses very finely accouter'd and pages that Ride them all, with plumes of feathers. After being drawn through ye Citty she is invited by ye Lord Major to a dinner provided on purpose for her, and soe many Rich Batchelors are appointed to Entertaine her that is a ranck among ye freemen. She has her traine bore up and is presented to Lady Majoris that salutes her as doth the aldermens Ladyes, all wch are Conducted in their Coaches to Guildhall.

7

REVOLUTION AND RESTORATION

In 1603 John Stow dedicated his great *Survey of London* to the Lord Mayor, Sir Robert Lee. 'I am not doubtful where to seeke my Patrone,' he wrote, 'since you be a politique estate of the Citty, as the walls and buildinges be the materiall parts of the same.' Lee was in office when Queen Elizabeth I died on 24 March 1603. As was customary the Mayor and Aldermen were provided by the Court with black cloth to attend her funeral. It was a splendid affair, but already everyone was looking forward to the new reign. The road to Scotland had been busy during the last weeks of the old Queen's illness with courtiers making their way to meet King James VI of Scotland, now to become James I of England. The Lord Mayor of course remained in London, secure in his constitutional position. Heading the list of signatories of the proclamation of the King's Accession was Robert Lee, Lord Mayor, 'before all the great officers of state and all the nobility, being said upon the death of the King the prime person of England'. As the new King rode south through his domain, plague broke out in London, so the splendid welcome the City had prepared for him had to be postponed. Instead the Mayor and Aldermen met the King at Greenwich, where Robert Lee was knighted. The rest of the Aldermen were knighted later at Whitehall, so for many years every lord mayor was already a knight before his election.

Sir Thomas Bennett accompanied the King and Queen through London's cheering crowds the next year. Everyone was in an optimistic mood about the new reign. Elizabeth's later years had been hard for the people, with poor harvests, outbreaks of plague and the strains of war with Spain and rebellion in Ireland. There were underlying discontents over religious differences, which Elizabeth had tried to settle by making a church which both extremes could accept. It was only partially successful. Catholics were hard pressed by severe laws against them, while the Puritans regarded the settlement as far too sympathetic to Catholic principles. Both these groups anticipated a better deal from James, and both were to be disappointed. The Catholics relied on the religion of his mother, Mary Stuart, while the Puritans believed that his upbringing by Scottish Protestants (Presbyterians) would incline him to their point of view.

Catholic hopes that the recusancy laws, which penalized them for failure to attend Church of England services, would be relaxed were soon dashed. The Gunpowder Plot of 1605 which attempted to blow up Parliament at the State Opening, and so destroy the existing Government, was the desperate reaction of a small group. The danger had been great, and from then on for over two centuries English Catholics were regarded with suspicion and debarred from public office. In London the Lord Mayor, Sir Leonard Halliday, ordered bonfires to be lit in the City streets to express the people's joy at their deliverance 'from this most horrible treason'.

Londoners tended to be Puritan and, as we have seen, some leading Elizabethan mayors supported the Puritan cause. This continued in the seventeenth century. Sir William Craven provided for Puritan lectures at St Antholin, and Martin Lumley left money in his will for a lecturer at St Helen's, Bishopsgate. Nicholas Rainton, lord mayor in 1632, was a member of the Puritan society of feoffees for the purchase of impropriations (i.e. trustees of funds to purchase ecclesiastical property in the hands of laymen and use the proceeds to promote Puritan teaching.) One of the Puritan causes was the strict observation of the Sabbath. On a Sunday in 1617 the Lord Mayor, George Bolles, stopped the royal carriages from progressing through the City during divine service. More astonished than angry, James commented that he had thought there was no king in England but himself. However, he was furious in August 1618 when there was an attack on the Spanish ambassador, Gondomar. James was attempting to bring about a *rapprochement* with Spain, but the citizens of London regarded the Catholic Spaniards as their enemies. Driving through London, the Ambassador's coach had accidentally injured a child, whereupon an angry mob gathered, hurling stones and cursing Spain. George Bolles was probably in sympathy with the citizens' antagonism to Spain, but as was his duty he quieted the crowds and ordered the rioters to be punished. Later that year, in pursuance of his pro-Spanish policy, James ordered the execution of Sir Walter Raleigh who was a prisoner in the Tower. Anticipating a hostile reaction from the Londoners the execution was carried out on 29 October, the day of Sir Sebastian Harvey's Lord Mayor's Show, 'that the pageants and fine shows might draw away the people'.

Apart from these early indications of trouble over religion, the alliance between the King and the City merchants remained strong. James was made a freeman of the Clothworkers' Company when the Lord Mayor, Sir John Watts, entertained the King at his house next to Clothworkers' Hall. The King's eldest son, Prince Henry, was made a Merchant Taylor. When urged to invest in colonizing ventures by the Government the Liverymen co-operated. The Virginia Company was formed to set up a colony across the Atlantic with the aim of 'propagating all Christian religion to such people as yet live in Darkness'. For the overcrowded City it was suggested that this could be a practical way of disposing of surplus population. In 1609 the Lord Mayor, Sir Humphrey Weld, a Grocer, ventured seven ships, and other Companies followed his example. The colony got off to a shaky start, and without the contribution from the City would never have got going at all. The City was also persuaded to set up settlements in Ulster, and in 1613 the Irish Society was formed. The twelve great Livery Companies took part and induced minor Companies to join them. The town of Derry was built up, fortified and renamed Londonderry, and lands were allotted to the Companies who undertook to develop them. The venture did not prosper, the plantations were a financial drain on the Companies and Government dissatisfaction with the way they were managed led to serious friction in Charles I's reign.

The lord mayors were involved with these commercial ventures and many more. Some of them were successful merchants trading overseas, members of the East India Company, the Levant Company and the Merchant Adventurers, and often served on these companies' committees, sometimes as governor. Others concentrated on domestic trade and industry.

Sir John Swynnerton, lord mayor in 1612, came from Shropshire. His fortune was derived from the trade in French and Rhenish wines, and he was one of the founder members of the East India Company in 1599. He was master of the Merchant Taylors in 1606 when they entertained the King and Queen at a reception which cost over £1,000. The music for the occasion was written by John Bull, and included a tune which later became the national anthem. Swynnerton's Lord Mayor's pageant was *Troia Nova Triomphans* by Thomas Dekker. Here he entertained the Count Palatine, who was soon to become the husband of James's favourite daughter, Princess Elizabeth (the Winter Queen of Bohemia). One of the last official engagements of his mayoral year was the opening of the City's first proper fresh water system at New River Head, Islington. The originator of the scheme was Hugh Middleton, brother of the lord mayor elected that very day, Sir Thomas Middleton. (Thomas had set his brother up in business in the City as a Goldsmith.) The New River scheme showed the co-operation between King and City at its best, for Hugh Middleton had great difficulty in raising sufficient funds and in getting the necessary authority to cut through public rights of way. The King, who had watched the scheme with interest from his house nearby in Theobalds Park, agreed to take half a share in the project, and so it went ahead. Sir Thomas celebrated the opening in style and followed it the next month with his magnificent Lord Mayor's Show.

Thomas Middleton was one of the outstanding lord mayors in this period. He was born in 1560, the fourth son of a Denbighshire family of sixteen children. He went up to London to seek his fortune and was apprenticed to Ferdinand Poyntz, a Grocer, dealing amongst other things in sugar. Thomas set up a sugar refinery in Mincing Lane which did well. He extended his trade to dealing in cloths, fustians and kerseys, as he was entitled to do under the Custom of London. (A freeman of one retailing trade could deal in the goods of any other in the City.) He also tried farming, mining and the production of metal goods, and for a while was involved in exporting fish. He invested in Elizabethan trading ventures and 'reprisals' against Spain, and was connected with Sir John Hawkins. When the captured Portuguese treasure ship *Madre de Dios* was brought in to Plymouth, Middleton was one of the officials sent down to supervise its unloading. He invested in the East India Company and the Virginia Company and went in for moneylending, sometimes at 10 per cent interest, sometimes against securities of gold and jewels. He never lost interest in his origins, and when he inherited the family estate of Galch Hill he set about establishing himself as a Denbighshire landowner. He served as Member of Parliament for Merioneth in 1597 and was Custos Rotulorum for the county two years later. (He also bought Chirk Castle.) Like many others, Middleton accepted civic office with reluctance, at first refusing to serve as an alderman. For this he was committed to Newgate, and although the King, valuing his services as Surveyor of Customs, ordered his immediate release, the wish of the City prevailed and he had to accept the office. He served as Member of Parliament for the City in 1624, 1625 and 1626, and was President of Bridewell and Bethlem hospitals. He died in 1631, leaving money for the London hospitals and for the relief of the poor.

The career of John Leman makes an interesting contrast. His origins were even more distant from London than Middleton's, since his grandfather, John Le Mans, was a refugee from Spanish persecution in the Netherlands. The family settled in Norfolk where his father was a wealthy tanner. John Leman, born in 1544, moved to London and joined the Fishmongers' Company. He built up an extensive business in dairy produce from East Anglia, dominated the coastal trade supplying London, and made a considerable fortune. Leman Street is still there to remind us that he was one of London's richest citizens. His Lord Mayor's Show, as we have seen, was one of the grandest in a splendid period. The following February he was very ill, as the French Ambassador who dined at his house reported that he 'poor man hath been at death's door this six or seven weeks'. He recovered sufficiently to be knighted in March, and lived on until 1632 when he died aged eighty-eight and still working hard. Leman was one of the very few bachelor lord mayors and he left considerable bequests. He left £2,000 to Christ's Hospital, of which he was president for twenty-four years. There was money for a school for forty-eight boys in Beccles, Suffolk, where his father had a business. He left an annuity to the Fishmongers for coal for the Company almshouse. Finally he left £1,000 for preachers at Paul's Cross, and for a weekly sermon in the Fishmongers' church of St Mary at Hill. (Here we see the Puritan leanings again.) His portrait is at Hampton Court, the only picture there of an ordinary citizen.

The affairs of Sir William Cokayne, lord mayor in 1619, illustrate another aspect of co-operation between the King and the city merchants. Cokayne was a Skinner and a very active merchant. He came from Warwickshire, a second son who was apprenticed to his father. He became a governor of the Eastland Company, helped to establish Londonderry, and was the first governor of the Irish Society. He was Purveyor to the Army in Ireland, exported cloth to the Baltic and lent money to the King. Probably this brought him to the King's notice, so he was able to interest him in a scheme to break the Dutch monopoly of finished and dyed cloth. Previously, unfinished cloth was exported to Holland by the Merchant Adventurers and there it was finished and dyed and then sent on to

Germany and the Baltic states. Cokayne proposed a project to dye and dress the cloth in England before export. James granted him a patent, prohibited the export of white cloth to Holland, and seized the charter of the Merchant Adventurers, setting up a new company, the King's Merchant Adventurers, in its stead. Unfortunately the venture failed because the Dutch hit back with a trade embargo, and anyway the English finishing process was unsatisfactory. This was a commercial disaster, causing damage to the cloth trade, and unemployment. But even though the King had to withdraw the whole deal, restore their charter to the Merchant Adventurers and impose a new tax on exported cloth to recoup his losses, William Cokayne did not appear to lose favour. He was knighted when the King dined with him at Cokayne House in 1616, and was elected lord mayor three years later. He left each of his six daughters £10,000 and they all married into the peerage. He left his son £12,000. He was the ancestor of the Earl of Pomfret and a member of his family, Francis Cockayne, was lord mayor in 1751. Sir William died in 1626 and was buried in St Paul's where there was a monument to him. His funeral sermon was preached by John Donne.

All of these apparently made their own way with no family civic connections to help them, although Middleton's first wife was the daughter of Sir Richard Saltonstall, lord mayor in 1597. Sir William Craven, lord mayor in 1610, was a country boy from Appletreewick in Yorkshire. He hitched a lift to London from a carrier, who deposited him in Watling Street saying 'there may be a job for a likely lad like you'. He first entered service with a woollen draper and then gradually worked his way up in the Merchant Taylors' Company. He had his own shop in partnership with two others in Watling Street and became a wholesale cloth dealer. His success can be measured by his charities. In 1602 he founded a grammar school at Burnsall in Yorkshire and repaired and beautified the church. He left annual sums for seven Merchant Taylors and four Clothworkers and for the provision of coals and support of widows. He left money for lectures at St Antholin, as we have seen, and £50 for the library at St John's College, founded by his fellow Merchant Taylor, Sir Thomas Whyte.

Some seventeenth-century lord mayors did have an easier start in life, like Sir Henry Rowe in 1607, whose father had been lord mayor in 1568, and whose cousin William Rowe was lord mayor in 1592. Sebastian Harvey (1618) was the son of James Harvye (1581). John Gore (1624) was a Londoner whose father and grandfather were aldermen. His brother,

William, was sheriff with him and another brother, Richard, was Member of Parliament for London. John Gore married a daughter of Thomas Cambell, lord mayor in 1609. Christopher Clitherow (1635) married another of Cambell's daughters, and his father had been three times Master of his Company, the Ironmongers. Christopher became Master twice and was a leading merchant. For a while the East India Company had offices in his house in Leadenhall Street. Thomas Cambell made his way slowly through the Ironmongers' Company and founded a charity school at Barking. His son James, also an Ironmonger, was extremely successful. He was Governor of the French Company, one of the Merchants of the Staple, and on the committee of the East India Company. He had a lavish mayoral pageant, but otherwise he probably spent little on himself as he was a deeply religious Puritan whose household was 'near, austere and hard'. He left £50,000 for poor relief and prisoners, money to be lent to young freemen of his Company, £2,000 to Bridewell Hospital to establish a work scheme, and £1,000 for the repair of St Paul's. As well as all this, he left money to the Ironmongers for the redemption of poor captives from Turkish slavery.

W. K. Jordan, in his work on the charities of London, describes the early seventeenth century as the highest point of charitable donations by London citizens. We have already noted several examples among the better-known lord mayors. But many others were successful wealthy men, the thoughtfulness of whose endowments is often quite touching.

Sir Thomas Bennett (1603) left money for prisoners, as very many did, for without these donations many prisoners without friends would have starved. He also left money for the clothing of 'poor and naked men women and children wandering in London that have no dwelling', for the poor and aged in Wallingford, his home town, and for the poor of the Mercers, his own Company. Sir Thomas Hayes (1614) left £100 as stock for the City of Westminster to start work schemes, £175 to the poor of London and Weybridge, as well as money for hospitals, prisoners, and to his own company, the Drapers. Considering that he married five times and had twenty children to provide for, that is not ungenerous. Another Draper, Sir John Jolles (1615) came from Stratford Bow in Essex. He left money for almspeople at Stratford and founded a school there for thirty-five poor boys to be taught 'secrets of grammar and the Latin tongue'. He also left money to be lent to young freemen of the Company at 3 per cent. Edward Barkham (1621), another Draper, was a benefactor of Bethlem Hospital. He came from Norfolk and left money for the poor in five Norfolk villages. His monument is in Southacre Church. Ralph Freeman (1633), a Clothworker, came from Northampton and left £1,000 with an ingenious scheme for its proper use. It was to be lent to trustworthy merchants at 3 per cent. They were to set the poor to work and the income generated was to provide clothing for almspeople and a free grammar school. He died in office in March 1634 and was succeeded by Thomas Moulson, another Clothworker from Cheshire. He left money for the usual charities but also a lectureship at Hargrave, Cheshire. He married Ann Radcliffe and after his death in 1638 she increased his inheritance. She was the first major donor to Harvard in America and Radcliffe College is named after her. Christopher Clitherow left annuities to the poor of St Andrew Undershaft and Beckington, Essex, and for scholarships from Christ's Hospital to St John's College, Oxford. Nicholas Rainton left £2,000 to the Haberdashers for the poor, money for bread for two Lincolnshire villages, and for apprenticing three poor children from Enfield and three from London.

These lord mayors were in office in the period of non-parliamentary government known as the eleven years' tyranny. Charles I, who succeeded his father in 1625, soon found himself at odds with Parliament, who demanded redress of their grievances before they would consider voting taxes to pay for his wars with France and Spain. In 1629 he dissolved Parliament, determined to run the country without it. It was a quiet time politically, but, deprived of any parliamentary source of income, Charles I had to rely on various financial expedients and extra-parliamentary taxes, which antagonized even the City merchants who would normally have supported him. He irritated the aldermen, by bypassing their authority to grant new incorporations of Livery Companies. In 1635 the City's management of the Irish Society was condemned in the Court of Star Chamber. A fine was imposed, the charter revoked and the Irish estates taken over by the Crown. The unpopular tax of Ship Money was levied on the City as elsewhere, overriding the City's claim that it should be exempt. The church policy of Archbishop Laud, enforcing Anglicanism, was bitterly resented by the Puritans. In spite of all this, most of the aldermen remained Royalist. They were closely linked with the Crown as office-holders, farmers of customs, holders of monopoly patents. They had lent large sums to the King and had helped to carry out royal policies. Many had family connections with the landed gentry. So even though some had Puritan sympathies and supported lectures and Puritan colleges, they also contributed to Laud's fund for rebuilding St Paul's.

So far they had held firm control in the City. But the mass of ordinary citizens, the members of the Court of Common Council and Common Hall, as well as a minority of the aldermen, were increasingly antagonistic to the Government. The crisis of the 1640s when Charles, in desperate need of funds, was forced to call Parliament, enabled this anti-royalist party in the City to get control of the mayoral chair, as we shall see later.

Sir Morris Abbot, Draper, was elected in 1638 and it was during his mayoralty that the King and Laud launched their ill-fated attempt to force the English Prayer Book on the Scots, which was to lead to a Scottish invasion of England, recall of Parliament and ultimately the Civil War. Abbot was bound to be a Royalist. His brother was the Archbishop of Canterbury before Laud and another brother was Bishop of Salisbury. The King had knighted him on his Accession in 1625. Abbot was an eminent merchant who had accumulated great wealth by persistent application of his considerable abilities. He had visited the East Indies and been governor of the East India Company from 1623 to 1638. He was a member of the Levant Company, traded with Persia and had promoted schemes to find a North-West Passage. In 1628 he had resisted an unpopular duty on the importation of currants imposed by the King, but he had co-operated over the collection of Ship Money and during his mayoralty, when City men refused to pay the tax, he hired a ship himself. However, when Charles turned to the Lord Mayor and Aldermen in 1639 and ordered them to raise £30,000 to help against the Scots, Abbot led their refusal, not so much on political grounds as because without a Parliament to vote taxes there was inadequate security for a loan.

Sir Henry Garraway, a fellow Draper, followed him to the mayoral chair in October 1639. He too was a staunch Royalist, son of Sir William Garraway, Chief Farmer of the Customs, to which post Henry Garraway succeeded. He was a trader with world-wide commercial interests. In April 1640 Parliament was called for the first time since 1629. In Common Hall the Liverymen elected four Puritan members, leaving out the Recorder, Sir Thomas Gardiner, who would normally have been elected as a matter of course. This Parliament refused to comply with the King's demand for funds to fight the Scots, insisting on redress of grievances first. It was dismissed after three weeks of wrangling, and is thus known as the Short Parliament. Charles now attempted to raise a forced loan in the City, and Garraway was ordered to provide a list of the richest men, without consulting the Court of Common Council. Garraway ordered the

Aldermen to compile lists, and seven of them refused to co-operate. The King's Chief Minister, the Earl of Strafford, suggested that examples be made of the Aldermen. Four were imprisoned: Thomas Soames, who said before the court of the King's Bench that 'he was an honest man before he was an Alderman and desired to be an honest man still'; Nicholas Rainton, lord mayor in 1632 and a leading Puritan; Thomas Atkyn, who was to be lord mayor in 1644 and to remain a supporter of the Parliamentary cause throughout the Interregnum; and John Gayer, who would be a Royalist lord mayor in 1646. There was a public outcry and the prisoners were soon released.

By now the City was thoroughly aroused. Mobs of apprentices with their traditional cry of 'prentices and clubs' rampaged off to Lambeth Palace to seize Archbishop Laud but found him gone. Garraway suppressed the riot and doubled the watch in the City. On 28 September in Common Hall the Liverymen refused to nominate the next Alderman in succession for the mayoralty, the Royalist Sir William Acton. There was total amazement. Secretary Windebank wrote to the King: 'These 300 years no one Alderman hath been put out of his order, but in case of poverty, infirmity of age or sickness'. This was not quite accurate, as we have seen, but it was practically unheard of for the order of seniority to be put aside, and Sir William had already furnished his house in readiness. The election was postponed for a week. Sir Henry Garraway (knighted in May) consulted with the Privy Council and saw to it that the Companies gave tickets to chosen members for entry to Guildhall. As a result the next Alderman after Acton, Edmund Wright, was elected as a compromise candidate.

The mayoral election was swiftly followed in Common Hall by the election of members for a new Parliament and the Liverymen again refused to return the Recorder and chose four Puritans, including a recently elected Alderman, Isaac Penington. This was to be known as the Long Parliament because of an Act ensuring that it could only be dissolved by the consent of the members – the suggestion of the four City members. (It was eventually reduced to a rump which was thrown out by Cromwell in 1653. It was recalled after his death, dissolved again, and finally in 1660 all remaining members of the original Long Parliament met and voted for their own dissolution.) In Parliament the members got on with the work of dismantling Charles I's structure of government. The citizens of London presented the Root and Branch Petition for total reform of the church, a petition for the removal of bishops from the House of Lords and a petition

The tomb of Sir John Champneys (Skinner, 1534) in Bexley Church.

The Bowes Cup presented to the Goldsmiths Company by Sir Martin Bowes (1545).

Sir Rowland Hill (Mercer, 1549).

The Fishmongers Pageant for Sir John Leman (1616) (*a*) The Leopard; (*b*) The Fishing Busse.

The Great Fire of London, 1666.

The Lord Mayor's river procession approaching Westminster. Sir Henry Tulse (Grocer, 1683).

Sir John Houblon (Grocer, 1695). First Governor of the Bank of England.

for the arrest of the hated Earl of Strafford. Londoners' detestation of Strafford, whom they blamed for the King's policies, was intense, and when he was executed in May 1641 there was wild rejoicing in the streets. In June there was a dispute in Common Hall when the Liverymen refused to accept the Lord Mayor's customary nomination of one of the Sheriffs. The matter was referred to the House of Lords, who said that Common Hall had the right to elect both Sheriffs. In the event they chose the Lord Mayor's nominee, but the Aldermen considered the decision prejudicial to the City government and inclined more to the King's side. At the Lord Mayor's election that September there was fierce opposition in Common Hall to Richard Gurney, Clothworker and Royalist, who was next in succession. 'Each party put themselves in battle array and the Puritans were overcome with hisses.' Gurney was duly elected. He came from Croydon and had been apprenticed to a silk mercer who left him his shop and £6,000. He had also made a good marriage and had a successful business career, so he was a wealthy man and later left large sums to charity through the Clothworkers' Company and to St Bartholomew's Hospital.

The King had spent the summer in Scotland trying to win back his northern kingdom, and on his return that November the City prepared a tremendous welcome for him. The Liverymen lined the streets in their gowns, the conduits ran with wine and the Recorder presented a loyal address. Charles was greatly encouraged, for he saw 'that all those former tumults and disorders have only arisen from the meaner sort of people, and that the affections of the better and main part of the City have ever been loyal to my person and government'. He knighted the Lord Mayor, and later at Hampton Court the Sheriffs and five of the Aldermen. He promised to restore the Irish estates, maintain the true Protestant religion and uphold the City's liberties. However his optimism about his support in the City was ill-founded because at the Common Council elections in December 'the meaner sort of people' were voted in and as Clarendon wrote 'all the grave and substantial citizens were left out'. Furthermore, keen to wield their influence, the new members took up their seats before the traditional Plow Monday and so were in the Court of Common Council when the King, having failed to arrest the five leaders of the opposition in the House of Commons, rode into the City whither they had escaped by boat, to demand they be handed over. There was pandemonium in the Hall, angry cries of 'Privileges of Parliament' drowning the few shouts of 'God save your Majesty'. A discomfited Charles retreated to dine with the

Lord Mayor and Sheriffs. He had lost control of the City and so had they. The King left London on 10 January to return only for his trial and execution in Westminster seven years later.

Meanwhile the Common Council elected a Committee of Safety which prepared the City against possible attack. The gates were shut and chains drawn across the streets while women boiled cauldrons of water to pour on attackers. The Committee were answerable to Parliament, which said the Lord Mayor must call the Common Council when the Committee ordered this. In fact the Committee usurped the mayoral powers. As a contemporary tract put it, 'My Lord Mayor having no more sway than Perkins the Tailor, Riley the Bodicemaker, or Nicholson the Chandler.' Parliament moved to control the Army by issuing a militia ordinance. Gurney refused to obey this and instead read out the Royal Commissions of Array. He was deposed by Parliament and Isaac Penington was elected mayor in Common Hall on 16 August. At first Gurney tried to withhold the mayoral insignia and refused to hand them over. 'He pretended that they were at his house in London locked up and he could not come at them.' However, they were seized and Gurney was sent to the Tower, where he stayed 'almost till death' in 1647. Sir Morris Abbot died in 1642 and Sir Edmund Wright in 1643. Sir Henry Garraway was imprisoned by the Puritans after leading an attack on Parliament in Guildhall in 1643 and was incarcerated in various prisons, including Dover Castle, until his death in 1646.

Isaac Penington, Fishmonger, was a newcomer to the City government, having served as sheriff in 1638 and been elected to the ward of Bridge Without in 1639. He was certainly not due to be mayor in the usual succession, but he was the leader of the City Puritans and had presented the Root and Branch Petition to Parliament in 1640. He was a wealthy man but he impoverished himself working for the Parliamentary cause, to which he was devoted. He was given a special dispensation to continue sitting in Parliament during his mayoralty, although he did not make use of it. He was re-elected lord mayor for the year 1642–3 and resumed his seat in Parliament after that. He was appointed Lieutenant of the Tower, and so personally conducted Archbishop Laud to the scaffold in 1645. After that Parliament passed the Self-Denying Ordinance under which no member of parliament should hold a military command, so Penington relinquished the post. (The only exception to this Ordinance was Oliver Cromwell.) Penington was responsible for the demolition of Cheapside Cross and his influence in bringing about the downfall of the Church of England was recognized in a poster on the door of St Paul's which read:

> This house is to be let
> It is both wide and fair
> If you would know the price of it
> Pray ask of Mr. Mair.

Penington was present at the King's trial but did not sign the death warrant. (It was very difficult to find people who would.) He served on the Council of State under Cromwell. At the Restoration he was convicted as a regicide, but was one of those who were not executed. He remained a prisoner in the Tower where he died in 1661.

The next two mayors were Parliamentarians. Sir John Wollaston was a keen Puritan and a Colonel of the Trained Bands. Thomas Atkyn served on the Militia Committee and was Colonel of the Red Regiment of the Trained Bands. As Treasurer for War he supplied clothes and provisions to the Army. He was nominated to sit at the King's trial, refused, weathered all the political storms of the Interregnum and was discharged from his aldermanry at the Restoration.

By the end of 1645 the King had been defeated in the field and his enemies were utterly divided as to how to deal with him. In the City a Royalist reaction set in. Thomas Adams, elected in 1645, was a sturdy Cavalier who at one point in his mayoralty was suspected of hiding the King in his house after Charles had temporarily escaped from his captors. Adams was followed by Sir John Gayer. During his mayoralty he was imprisoned in the Tower by Parliament for 'abetting' a tumult raised by London apprentices, this time against Parliament. Gayer died in 1649 and was buried in St Katherine Creechurch. He gave to his home town of Plymouth land for an orphan boys' asylum, and helped found the Hospital for the Poor's Portion there. He made several other large bequests to charity, but his best known legacy is the Lion Sermon, which is still preached every 16 October in St Katherine's. This recalls one of Gayer's adventures as a merchant travelling in the Levant when he was in great danger of being killed by a lion. He prayed to be saved, his prayers were answered and he promised to institute an annual sermon in memory of this. He was followed by a Puritan, John Warner, but the next lord mayor was another strong Royalist, Abraham Reynardson, who also came from Plymouth. He was the son of a Turkey merchant and a prominent member of the Levant Company and the East India Company. His mayoralty spanned the dramatic times of Charles I's trial and execution. Reynardson adamantly refused to co-operate with any of the moves which led to the King's execution. He would not publish the Act abolishing the monarchy and was imprisoned in the Tower and fined £2,000. He survived until the Restoration when he was offered the mayoralty again but he was too ill to accept and died the following year.

The mayoralty was not abolished during the Interregnum, although it continued with a mere shadow of its former glory. It was very difficult to find anyone to serve. Ever since 1640 scores of men elected to the aldermanry had paid their fines and withdrawn. By 1650 the City finances were in a sorry state and the allowances of the mayor, sheriffs and aldermen were drastically cut back. Thomas Andrewes, a Leatherseller and the first lord mayor not from one the twelve great Companies (the next was Robert Willimot in 1742) was made mayor when Reynardson was arrested, and an attempt was made to keep up appearances in June 1649 when the Common Council entertained the Rump Parliament and the Council of State in Grocers' Hall. Andrewes delivered the Civic Sword to the Speaker, and Fairfax and Cromwell received gifts of gold. In return, Parliament presented Richmond Park to the City. (It was returned to the King at the Restoration.) Thomas Foot, Grocer, followed Andrewes, who was again lord mayor in 1650, this time in the more respectable guise of a Fishmonger. John Kendricke and John Fowke were fanatical anti-Royalists. Thomas Vyner, lord mayor in 1653, was a successful financier whose nephew was lord mayor in Charles II's reign. Christopher Pack, who followed him, was a zealous Parliamentarian who was knighted during his mayoralty by Cromwell, now the Lord Protector. Two years later he presented to Cromwell the 'Humble Petition and Advice' asking him to become King. Mayors Thomas Vyner, John Dethick, Robert Tichborne, Richard Chiverton and John Ireton were all knighted by Cromwell, who although he refused the title of King certainly chose to act like one. He died on 3 September 1658 and the same allowance of mourning cloth for the lord mayor and all the City officers was made as for a sovereign.

The attempt by Cromwell's son, Richard, to follow his father was a failure and the forces looking to a restoration of the monarchy gathered strength. General Monck marched down from Scotland with his army, occupied London, and after much negotiation in which several City aldermen were involved the Long Parliament was recalled, dissolved itself and a new Parliament was called. Charles II was invited to return and claim his throne. One of the deputation was Thomas Adams, lord mayor in 1645, who was then knighted. Thomas Alleyn, Grocer, elected in 1659, was lord mayor at the Restoration of 1660, and it therefore fell to him to proclaim Charles II as King and to meet him in the traditional way with all the Aldermen in scarlet robes at St George's Fields, offer him the Civic Sword, and lead his triumphal procession, 20,000 strong, through the rejoicing City. The diarist John Evelyn described the scene,

the ways strewed with flowers, the bells ringing, the streets hung with tapestry, the fountains running with wine; the Mayor, Aldermen and all the Companies in their liveries, chains of gold and banners; Lords and nobles clad in cloth of silver, gold and velvet; the windows and balconies all set with ladies; trumpets music and myriads of people flocking.

There has been much discussion about exactly what was restored in 1660 but there is no doubt that the traditional City government was fully restored. The mayoralty, although attenuated, had continued uninterrupted throughout the absence of the King, and the City now happily accepted the restored monarchy. Some of the mayors of the Interregnum were tried as regicides. Penington, Ireton and Tichborne pleaded 'ignorance of what they did' and were imprisoned. Some had already died, others were discharged from their aldermanries. Cromwell's knighthoods were revoked. But Charles re-knighted Vyner, Dethick and Chiverton. He also knighted the Lord Mayor, Thomas Alleyn, Abraham Reynardson, Thomas Adams and the Aldermen who would be the next six lord mayors, Richard Browne, John Frederick, John Robinson, Anthony Bateman, John Lawrence and Thomas Bludworth.

During the reign of Charles II the City was ravaged by plague and destroyed by fire. By 1672 the King was so short of money that he was reduced to the expedient of closing the Exchequer, thus ruining many City financiers. Charles's marriage to Catherine of Braganza was childless so he had no legitimate heir. This meant that the King's brother, James, a convinced Catholic, was his heir, and a party formed whose aim was to exclude him from the throne. Coffee houses had sprung up all over the City and in these gathered the groups of men who formed the first political parties. The Court party, later nicknamed Tories, supported the King, while the Country party (Whigs) led by Anthony Ashley Cooper, Lord Shaftesbury, campaigned for an Exclusion Bill. In all of this London's lord mayors were inevitably embroiled. The political nature of London's rulers became vitally important to the King and when his attempts to control the situation in the City failed he attacked their liberties. James II succeeded his brother in 1685 and all the fears that he would return the country to Catholicism proved justified. Within three years he completely lost the support of the people and ignominiously fled. The Protestant William of Orange, with his wife, James's Protestant daughter Mary, was invited to take the throne.

Sir Richard Browne, Merchant Taylor, was the first Restoration lord mayor. He had been an active Parliamentary general in the Civil War but changed to the King's side in 1648 in disgust at the way the Puritans were handling matters. He was imprisoned for five years but was released and restored to his aldermanry on Cromwell's death. Sir John Frederick, Grocer, who followed him, was a Londoner whose father, a surgeon, had fled from the religious persecution in the Netherlands in the late sixteenth century. John began his city life as a Barber-Surgeon, transferring to the Grocers in time for his mayoralty. He had extensive commercial contacts in the Mediterranean and the New World and financed several diplomatic missions. He was Member of Parliament for the City from 1663 to 1679. His home was in Frederick Place, Old Jewry, which is still named after him.

Sir John Robinson, Clothworker, (1662) was the son of Archdeacon Robinson of Nottingham and was married to a daughter of Sir George Whitmore, lord mayor in 1631. He took no part in the Civil War but was an influential member of the Corporation during the Interregnum. He was Member of Parliament for Rye from 1661 to 1679. Samuel Pepys dined with him quite often but was very dismissive of him. On 20 October 1663 he enjoyed 'a very great noble dinner', but added 'This Mayor is good for nothing else.' On 29 November 1665 Pepys was visiting Robinson in the Tower of which he was Lieutenant. There was music, always a pleasure to Pepys, and he reported that Robinson was 'in a mighty vein of singing; and he hath a very good ear and a strong voice but no manner of skill'. Sir John was said to have accepted the mayoralty at the express request of the King who was already taking a close interest in the City government. At the Common Council elections the previous December Charles had written to the Court of Aldermen requesting a peaceful election and 'a choice of such persons as are in every way well affected to the established government both in church and state.' Perhaps he was thinking about the election twenty years earlier which had turned the City against his father.

The City was very fortunate in the lord mayor elected in 1664, Sir John Lawrence, who was also Master of the Haberdashers that year. He was the son of a London merchant who was still alive when he was lord mayor, for Pepys relates: 'to my Lord Mayors to dinner where much company though little room ... a good though yet no extraordinary table ... his father a very ordinary old man, but it seems a very rich man'. John Evelyn described the banquet after his Lord Mayor's Show which was attended by the King, and the French Ambassador.

> My Lord Mayor came twice up to us, first drinking in the golden goblet His Majesty's health, then the French King's as a compliment to the Ambassador; we returned My Lord Mayor's health, the trumpets and drums sounding. The cheer was not to be imagined for plenty and rarity with an infinite number of persons in that ample hall. The feast was said to have cost £1000.

It was a fine beginning to a mayoral year. But early in 1665 plague began to stalk through the City streets, soon reaching epidemic proportions. Sir John stayed in the City throughout and ordered the Aldermen to do the same. He worked unceasingly to deal with disposal of the dead, protection of the living, problems of order and of supply of necessities.

He was followed by Sir Thomas Bludworth, who described his year as mayor as 'the severest year any man had'. It would be hard to dispute that. Not only did he have to face the Great Fire of London, but the plague was still killing thousands every week when he became mayor in October 1665, and continued through most of the year. Bludworth came from Derbyshire and was apprenticed at the age of fifteen to a Vintner. He made his way up and became a successful Turkey merchant, a member of the Levant and Africa companies. He was elected Alderman for Dowgate in 1658 but was discharged when he refused to serve as sheriff. He helped provide letters of credit for the needs of the exiled Court and was an active Royalist. In 1662 he became the Alderman for Portsoken and served as sheriff. He was Member of Parliament for Southwark from 1660 to 1679. When the Fire broke out on the night of 3 September 1666, he made the initial mistake of underestimating the danger, dismissing the blaze with: 'Pish, a woman might piss it out.' Then he panicked once it had got out of hand, and failed to create an effective fire gap by destroying buildings in the path of the fire. Pepys has pinned him down forever:

> At last met my Lord Mayor in Canning Streete, like a man spent, with a handkercher about his neck. To the King's message, he cried like a fainting woman, 'Lord, what can I do? I am spent. People will not

obey me. I have been pull(ing) down houses. But the fire overtakes us faster then we can do it'.

It must be said that Pepys already had a low opinion of Bludworth who he had earlier dismissed as 'a silly man, I think'. Royal authority was needed to pull down the houses of aldermen and influential merchants, and gunpowder was necessary to do the job quickly and effectively. Bludworth's own house in Gracechurch Street was destroyed, but the mayoral insignia were rescued and he was able to build himself a replacement in Maiden Lane.

Sir William Bolton succeeded to a ruined city. Pepys was at the swearing in at the Exchequer. 'Lord to see how meanly they now look, who upon this day used to be all little lords, is a sad sight.' Worse still, Bolton was accused of withholding money which had been contributed for the relief of victims of the Fire and was convicted of having embezzled large sums. He was removed from his aldermanry and died in obscurity. He was not the only alderman to be criticized for his behaviour in these two years. Robinson was accused of receiving contributions for plague relief and not distributing them. It was reported of Browne that he gave a group of about twenty men who struggled to rescue a chest containing £10,000 from the flames £4 between them. Samuel Starling, lord mayor in 1669, gave thirty men who saved his house from the Fire two shillings and sixpence between them.

History is much kinder to Sir William Turner, Merchant Taylor, lord mayor in 1668. He was a bachelor who devoted his energies to the City and his considerable fortune to good works. He came from Yorkshire, where he founded Sir William Turner's Hospital at Kirkleatham. He claimed from the King a traditional gift to bachelor lord mayors of £400 which he gave for the rebuilding of Guildhall. He gave Londoners enormous encouragement and help in rebuilding, so much so that there was a move to re-elect him for a second year but he declined. City tastes in building were not necessarily highly regarded. Sir John Summerson in *Georgian London* commented on Sir William's own house in Cheapside, quickly erected, as 'a brave example to the rebuilders ... robustly ornamental, but hardly elegant'. (Summerson also criticized another lord mayor's house, Swakeleys in Middlesex, which was built by Edmund Wright and later owned by Sir Robert Vyner. It was 'wholly traditional, modern only in its boastful display of "Holbein" gables and even those were by 1638 not particularly modern'.)

Turner was concerned in an affront to mayoral dignity when on 3 March 1669 he and his entourage attended the Feast of the Lent Reader of the Inner Temple. The Temple claimed immunity from civic jurisdiction as an ecclesiastical liberty since medieval times, so the Lord Mayor was requested not to insist on bringing the Civic Sword. Sir William replied 'My service to your Reader. Tell him I will come and dine with him. I will bear up my Sword and see who dares take it down.' The students of the Temple did dare and the Lord Mayor and his attendants were forced to retreat ignominiously. He complained to the King who promised to settle the case at law, but this was never done. The City got its revenge in 1678 when there was a fire in the Temple. The Lord Mayor, Sir James Edwards, offered assistance if he could be admitted to the liberties of the lawyers. They refused and the City fire engines turned back.

In 1672 Charles II was planning to wage war on Holland, which was not popular with Parliament who refused to vote the necessary funds. As a temporary financial expedient he stopped payments from the Exchequer for a year. The Goldsmiths, who were the bankers, deposited their reserves in the Exchequer and in return received interest. Deprived of access to their funds for a year, many were ruined. Sir Robert Vyner, the King's goldsmith, lost £416,000 and was in financial difficulties thereafter. Nevertheless he was able to accept his election as lord mayor in 1674 and sustain the appropriate state. He began as an apprentice to his uncle, Thomas Vyner (1653), became very successful, and it was in his workshops that the new royal regalia were made to replace those melted down during the Interregnum. In spite of his losses Sir Robert was a devoted Royalist. He presented to the King a statue showing Charles on horseback trampling Cromwell. In fact it was a statue of the Polish hero, John Sobieski trampling a Turk, which the Polish ambassador had commissioned but never paid for. Vyner had Charles's head substituted for Sobieski's but 'Cromwell' still looked very Turkish. The statue stood in the Stocks Market until the site was cleared for the Mansion House. It was offered for sale but there was little interest. Eventually it was claimed by a descendant and now stands in the grounds of Newby Hall, Ripon. Vyner's enthusiasm for the King was most memorably manifested at his inaugural banquet, when he got drunk and 'overfond' of the King. The story was told in the *Spectator* many years later. The King got up to leave but Sir Robert seized his arm and insisted, 'Sir you shall stay and finish t'other bottle'. Charles gave in, saying good-humouredly, 'He that is drunk is as great as a King'. Vyner was rewarded for his loyalty by spending his latter days in Windsor Castle. He died in 1688, only fifty-seven years old but broken-hearted at the death of his only son, aged twenty-two.

In 1667 Pepys was surprised, and a little miffed, to discover that Thomas Davies who had been at St Paul's School with him had been elected sheriff, 'the little fellow, the bookseller, my schoolfellow and now Sheriff, which is a strange turn methinks'. Indeed Thomas Davies was an unlikely person to attain civic rank. He was a good bookseller and an excellent linguist, specializing in foreign books. He quietly pursued the business of stationer in St Paul's Churchyard apparently with no great ambitions. His attitude changed in 1662 when he and his brother inherited a fortune from their great-uncle Hugh Audley. Davies decided to enter civic life and during 1667 was elected Alderman for Farringdon Without, and sheriff, and was knighted at the laying of the foundation stone of the new Royal Exchange. The following year he became Master of the Stationers' Company. He transferred to the Drapers' Company for his mayoralty and was lord mayor in 1676. The Stationers' Company still own two fine silver cups which he presented to them. Thomas Davies's brother left his share of the fortune to his daughter Mary, who at the age of twelve married Sir Thomas Grosvenor. Part of her dowry was land to the east and south of Hyde Park, then open fields, but later to be developed as the Grosvenor Estate – the richest property in London.

The most impressive lord mayor in Charles II's reign was the Draper, Sir Robert Clayton. He came from Northamptonshire and was apprenticed to his uncle, a scrivener. He was fortunate to be left a large sum of money by his uncle and went into partnership with a fellow apprentice, John Morris, who later left him all his estates, including the great house at Marden Park, Surrey, which they bought in 1670. Clayton and Morris were well established by 1660 and did well in helping to sort out the tangle of land-ownership problems which the Restoration brought. (Their clients included the Duke of Buckingham and Judge Jeffreys.) They developed the new and highly efficient system of deposit banking. They were criticized by envious contemporaries for exploitation because they lent money on the security of deeds, and the owners sometimes failed to get them back. John Dryden included Clayton in 'Absalom and Achitophel', a satirical poem which spared very few of the notable figures of that time.

> Ishban of conscience suited to his trade
> As good a saint as usurer ever made.

On top of his business success Clayton acquired through his wife, Martha

Trott, a huge plantation in Bermuda. John Evelyn described him as: 'This prince of citizens, there never having been any who for the great stateliness of his palace, prodigious feasting and magnificence, exceeded him. He was a discreet magistrate and though envied, I think without cause'. Clayton used his wealth in many ways. After the fire he rebuilt the front of Christ's Hospital at a cost of £10,000 in gratitude for his recovery from a serious illness. He founded and endowed the Mathematical School there. He gave money for the rebuilding of St Thomas's Hospital. He was at various times director of the Bank of England, governor of the Irish Society, president of St Thomas's, on the governing body of Christ's Hospital, President of the Honourable Artillery Company and Commissioner of Customs. In 1673 he decided to join the Country Party, and became a leading Whig and sat as Member of Parliament for London, representing the City during his mayoralty, all through the Exclusion crisis and several times thereafter. He was instrumental in presenting the address offering the throne to William of Orange. When later he failed to get elected for the City as a Whig he sat for his pocket borough of Bletchingley in Surrey. He died in 1707 aged seventy-eight and is buried in Bletchingley church with a splendid monument, if pompous, showing him in his mayoral robes.

By 1680 Charles II was thoroughly disillusioned with the City which was now totally in Whig hands. Sir Patience Ward's election to the mayoralty that autumn was deeply embarrassing to the Court. Sir Patience was an ardent Protestant and Whig MP for Pontefract. (His strange Christian name he attributed to his father's desire for a daughter, after six sons. His father swore that if the next child was a boy he would call him 'Patience'. It was and he did.) Not only was the Lord Mayor a Whig, the Sheriffs were too. In 1681 the King tried to bring his adversary, Lord Shaftesbury, to trial for treason. The Sheriffs empanelled a Whig jury which threw the case out. The sheriffs' election that June produced two more Whigs, Pilkington and Shute, but in September Sir John Moore, a Tory, was elected lord mayor. He was a Dissenter at heart but had decided to support the King. He was the younger son of the most important lead merchant in London. The King was so keen to have him lord mayor that he declared if anyone else was chosen 'he will refuse him positively if by law he can do it'. A poll was demanded for the first time in living memory, but Moore was duly nominated by the Liverymen and elected by the Aldermen. The invitation to his banquet was taken to the King by the Recorder and the Sheriffs to which Charles replied 'Mr. Recorder, an invitation by my Lord Mayor and Sheriffs is very acceptable to me and to show that it is so notwithstanding that it is brought by messengers that are so unwelcome to me as these two Sheriffs, yet I accept.' When the time came for the next election of sheriffs Sir John was persuaded to revive the old custom of drinking to his nominee. He drank to a Tory, Dudley North, and issued the customary mayoral precept to the Livery Companies to attend at Common Hall, confirm his choice, and elect the other sheriff. This led to an uproar in Common Hall. The Lord Mayor was jostled and his hat knocked off. The Liverymen refused to nominate North and put forward their own two candidates. The row went on for weeks, with several adjournments, until at length the Tories won and their Sheriffs were sworn in on 28 September in a Guildhall guarded by the Trained Bands for fear of a riot.

Meanwhile the King decided to get control in the City by a court action. The Crown instituted proceedings of quo warranto, accusing the City of breaches of its charters. The case took over a year and in 1683 was decided in the Crown's favour. The City's privileges were removed by law and for the next eight years the Lord Mayor and the Sheriffs were royal nominees. The Livery Companies also had to surrender their charters and so did towns all over the country.

Thomas Pilkington, the Whig sheriff, was brought to trial for libel against James, Duke of York, having accused him of burning the City in 1666, and was fined and imprisoned. Patience Ward appeared on behalf of Pilkington and was indicted for perjury. He escaped to Holland and remained there until 1688 when he came over with William of Orange. He sat as MP for the City in 1689–90 and died in 1696. His estate was greatly impaired by losses and charges of nearly £40,000, but what remained he left to his nephew, John Ward, who was lord mayor in 1718.

William Prichard (1682) was the last lord mayor to be elected before the removal of the City's liberties. He was a Tory and his election could hardly be described as 'free'. At the show of hands the Recorder put him third, and when a poll was demanded that proved unsatisfactory until the Court of Aldermen had disqualified enough of the Whigs (on the grounds that as Dissenters they could not take the proper oath) to give him the majority. Charles was 'so well pleased with their choice of so honest and loyal a man' that he ordered that the Lord Mayor should be presented to him personally rather than, as was usual, to the judges.

Throughout the rest of Charles' reign and James' short reign the City remained quiet, and although the lord mayors were now royal nominees the usual traditions continued. Perhaps this took the edge off the Londoners' anger at the loss of their ancient rights. Macaulay, in his *History of England* commented sarcastically that

> the external splendour of the municipal government was not diminished, nay was rather increased by this change. For under the administration of some Puritans who had lately borne rule, the ancient fame of the City for good cheer had declined; but under the new magistrates, who belonged to a more festive party, and at whose boards guests of rank and fashion from beyond Temple Bar were often seen, the Guildhall and the halls of the great companies were enlivened by many sumptuous banquets.

Sir Robert Geffery (1685) was the first Ironmonger lord mayor for fifty years and his Company gave him a splendid pageant with a triumphal procession by water to Westminster, watched by the new King James II. Geffery came from a poor family in Landrake, Cornwall. He came to London and made his fortune as a merchant, particularly in the import of tobacco. He had no children and when he died at the age of ninety-one in 1704 he left money for an almshouse in East London and for a school in Landrake. The buildings of the almshouse are still there, now well known as the Geffrye Museum. Other benefactions of lord mayors of this time included those of Sir John Moore who not only paid for the rebuilding of the Grocers' Hall and for a writing school for Christ's Hospital, but also founded a grammar school at Appleby in Leicestershire, in a building designed by Sir Christopher Wren. Sir William Prichard was a major benefactor to St Bartholomew's Hospital. He also left money for an almshouse and a school at Great Linford in Buckinghamshire.

Sir John Peake (1686) son of Sir William Peake (1677) had a fine procession which is portrayed on a fan from the period. Sir John Shorter (1687) ended his mayoralty prematurely when attending the opening of Bartholomew Fair on 24 August 1688. He was drinking the traditional tankard of ale with the Keeper of Newgate when the lid of his tankard flapped down so loudly that his horse shied and threw him. He died the next day and Sir John Eyles was appointed to take over. That October James, in a last ditch attempt to save his throne, restored the City's liberties, so the mayoral election was properly held and Sir John Chapman was chosen. He went to Westminster by water as usual and was duly sworn in. But James's efforts were in vain, his throne was tottering and he anxiously watched the weather vane on the Banqueting House for the

'Protestant' wind which would bring William of Orange to supplant him. William finally landed at Torbay on 5 November. After weeks of alarms, flights, casting of the Great Seal into the Thames, hopes raised and lowered, James finally left London for good on 18 December, and on that day William took up residence in St James's Palace. He called an assembly of all who had ever sat in Parliament under Charles II. The Corporation of London was in the unique position of being the only body in the country unaffected by the lack of a legal government, so the Lord Mayor, Aldermen and fifty representatives from the Common Council sat with the Members of Parliament as a separate estate of the realm. This gathering agreed to call a Convention Parliament. The Glorious Revolution had taken place.

Sir John Chapman did not live long to enjoy it. When James first tried to escape, the notorious Judge Jeffreys also attempted to get away disguised as a sailor. He was recognized and captured at Wapping and dragged before the Lord Mayor who was overwhelmed by the responsibility. Macaulay called him 'a simple man who had passed his whole life in obscurity and was bewildered by finding himself an important actor in a mighty revolution'. He was so upset 'that he fell into fits and was carried to his bed whence he never rose'. He died in March 1689.

The new lord mayor was Thomas Pilkington whom we last saw on his way to prison for libelling James, when the latter was Duke of York. On succeeding to the throne James pardoned Pilkington and released him. He was elected in March 1689 to succeed Chapman, re-elected at the usual time that autumn and elected again in May 1690 under an Act of Parliament reversing the quo warranto judgment and officially restoring the City's liberties. His mayoralty continued through to October 1691.

8

BANKERS AND POLITICIANS

The Act of May 1690 under which Sir Thomas Pilkington was re-elected lord mayor reversed the quo warranto verdict which had removed the City's right to elect its own rulers. The Act declared the verdict 'illegal and arbitrary'. It stated: 'The City of London now is and from time immemorial hath been an ancient city and the citizens and freemen thereof from the time aforesaid have been a body corporate.' Never again would the City's charters be forfeited. During much of the eighteenth century City men were to form the main focus of opposition to the Government of the day, but no attempt was made by the Government to overthrow the Corporation.

By the early eighteenth century London's own phenomenal success and expansion were a greater potential threat to the City's government than interference by the Crown, although the problems would not become acute until the mid nineteenth century. Until the seventeenth century the ancient City comprised London, with the exception of the royal and parliamentary headquarters at Westminster and the Inns of the lawyers which lay along the banks of the Thames between the City and Westminster. The suburbs were few and straggling. The majority of the inhabitants lived in one of the City's twenty-six wards and were ruled by the City government. But the constantly expanding population began to overflow into the suburbs and already before the Fire of 1666 a considerable proportion of Londoners lived outside the City boundaries. After the Fire there was no stopping London's expansion. Many of the handsome new houses in the City's reconstructed streets remained empty for years. The rich took up residence in the new fashionable squares of the West End. The poor moved out to Clerkenwell, Stepney, Spitalfields, Bermondsey and Wapping, away from high City rents and livery company controls.

By the year 1700 the population of the City was about 130,000, whereas that of the whole of London was about 500,000. The City had always been a great commercial and financial centre as well as the place where Londoners lived and worked. Now the commercial institutions grew and multiplied, and the banks, insurance companies, trading companies and exchanges began to take over from the residents. Many great merchants chose neither to live in the City nor to take up the Freedom. Nevertheless there were still many eminent men who elected to play a part in the City government. There were some who saw it as an arena where national causes could be pursued.

At the beginning of this period those who rose to be lord mayor tended to be directors of the Bank of England, of the East India Company and the South Sea Company. Many of them served as president of one of the great London hospitals and were members of the Honourable Artillery Company and colonels of the Trained Bands. Several of them were related to other lord mayors. Sons followed their fathers in the Child, Hoare, Heathcote, Parsons, Garrard and other families. John Ward (1718) followed his father Patience Ward (1680), and Thomas Rawlinson (1705) was followed by his cousin Thomas Rawlinson (1753). There were many family links, but it was by no means a closed oligarchy. Several immigrant families who had come to England in the late seventeenth century produced lord mayors, for example, Houblon, Bateman, Delmé and Janssen.

When William of Orange accepted the throne of England he was in the midst of wars against Louis XIV of France, and his chief concern was the prosecution of those wars, which required funds. The founding of the Bank of England in 1694 provided the finance without which the later campaigns of the Duke of Marlborough could never have succeeded. Several lord mayors played a crucial part in setting up the Bank. Sir William Ashurst (1693) headed the founding commission and six of the founding directors became lord mayor at later dates. Sir John Houblon was the first Governor of the Bank during his mayoralty in 1695. He came from a well-established Huguenot family, and had been very successful in business with his father, trading with Spain. Several members of his family were involved in the Bank, especially his brother James, who was also an MP. Sir John sat as MP for the City, was a director of the new East India

Company (a reformed version of the old company) and a Lord of the Admiralty. The earliest subscriptions to the Bank were received in the Mercers' Hall, but the first proper headquarters was the Hall of Sir John's own Company, the Grocers. In the 1720s, after his death, the first building of the Bank was on the site of his house.

In 1696 the Bank ran into serious trouble over recoinage. Much of the existing silver had been clipped and had to be called in. There was a delay over issuing the new coinage and there was a run on the Bank. The directors were determined to fulfil their obligations to the Government, so in 1696 no dividends were paid to shareholders, and the price of the Bank's stock fell. Throughout this trying time Houblon controlled the affairs of the Bank with exemplary skill, and was presented with a silver tankard 'in token of his great ability, industry and strict uprightness at a time of extreme difficulty'. The other original directors who became lord mayor were Sir Edward Clarke (1696), Sir Thomas Abney (1700), Sir William Gore (1701), Sir Gilbert Heathcote (1710) and Sir James Bateman (1716).

Not all the wealthy lord mayors involved in finance were supporters of the Bank of England. Some regarded it as an unwelcome rival. Sir Francis Child, lord mayor in 1698, was a successful goldsmith banker who was described as 'the father of the profession'. Goldsmiths had acted as bankers over the centuries, but Francis Child was the first to turn entirely to banking. His career was a classic of an industrious young man working his way up, and as such he was the model for William Hogarth's *The Industrious Apprentice*, a series of prints illustrating the rise of a worthy young man to become lord mayor. Child began as an apprentice to a City goldsmith, William Hall. He married Elizabeth Wheeler, from a goldsmith family whose sign was the Marigold. Soon after the marriage her father died and her mother married another goldsmith, Robert Blanchard, who took Francis into partnership. They are noted in the 1677 London directory as keeping 'running cashes'. In due course Child inherited the whole business and turned it over entirely to banking. Among his clients were two of Charles II's mistresses, Nell Gwynn and Barbara Villiers. He was jeweller to the King and lent large sums to the Government. He was a Member of Parliament for the City and for Devizes, and he was one of the original Commissioners for Greenwich Hospital, and President and benefactor of Christ's Hospital. Late in life he bought a great house, Osterley in Middlesex, once the property of Sir Thomas Gresham. Of his twelve sons, four survived, and one of them, Francis, was lord mayor in

1731. Three sons succeeded to Osterley, where his grandson, also Francis, brought in Robert Adam to transform it into one of the finest classical houses of the eighteenth century. Child's Bank at Temple Bar always used to accommodate the lord mayor and the aldermen when they waited to receive the monarch for a ceremonial entry to the City. The bank was rebuilt in the nineteenth century and is now a branch of the Royal Bank of Scotland. The sign of the Marigold can still be seen on the front.

Sir Richard Hoare, lord mayor in 1712, was another goldsmith banker who did not support the Bank of England. He was in business with his cousin, James Hoare, at the sign of the Golden Bottle in Cheapside. One of his customers was Samuel Pepys. He was Member of Parliament for the City, president of Christ's Hospital and the London Workhouse, and on the committee set up to build fifty new churches in London, under the Act of 1711 which aimed to bring Christianity to thousands of Londoners in the newly developing areas. His second son, Henry, purchased Stourhead and settled there in 1720 and Henry's second son, Richard, was lord mayor in 1745.

Some lord mayors of this period were caught up in the religious controversies, which were still a matter of deep public concern, and closely linked with politics. On the whole, High Churchmen and Catholics were Tories, and Dissenters were Whigs. Sir Humphrey Edwin, who was a Dissenter, was lord mayor in 1697, the year before Sir Francis Child. He came from an ancient family in Hereford, where his father had twice been mayor. He married the daughter of a wealthy merchant in London and did well in business. He joined the Barber-Surgeons and later transferred to the Skinners. He was made Alderman of Tower Ward in 1687, during the suspension of the City's liberties by James II who, in order to relax the laws on religion which penalized Catholics, looked for support to the Dissenters, because they were also penalized. In 1688 Edwin was sheriff and so attended William III on his entry to London. His Lord Mayor's procession was a very quiet affair, possibly on religious grounds, but he held a grand reception for the King on his return after the Treaty of Ryswick, which temporarily ended the fighting on the Continent. It was possible for Dissenters to hold corporate office at this time provided they occasionally attended Church of England services. But Sir Humphrey provoked a storm of protest from the church party when, one Sunday, he blatantly attended afternoon service at a Dissenter meeting house, having done duty at church that morning. His attendants were shocked and all deserted him, except the Swordbearer, who was locked in a pew protesting loudly. The episode aroused satirical comment from Swift and Defoe, and the Lord Mayor promised not to do it again. But it was believed that his performance led to the Occasional Conformity Act of 1711, which penalized Dissenters who took this harmless way of getting round the Corporation Act (which made membership of the Church of England a prerequisite for holding corporate office).

Attitudes on religion affected City politics, and there were several disputed mayoral elections while the Whigs were in power, in which Tories were deliberately kept out of office. Sir Thomas Abney, lord mayor in 1700, was the youngest son of a Derbyshire family, who made his own way in London and early in life joined the Non-conformist church in Silver Street. He was one of the original directors of the Bank of England and was president and benefactor of St Thomas's Hospital, to which he gave £200 in honour of his mayoralty. He was elected ahead of his turn to keep out the Tory, Charles Duncombe. Abney was a keen Whig and sat as Member of Parliament for the City. He rallied support to William III when the King's health was failing, and later backed the Hanoverian succession. He was a patron of Sir Isaac Watts, the hymn writer, who lived with him in his house at Abney Park. (Later the grounds became a cemetery for Dissenters which was opened in 1840 by the Lord Mayor.) Sir Charles Duncombe was again kept out of office the following year by Sir William Gore, another of the original directors of the Bank. Eventually he became lord mayor in 1708. Duncombe was another goldsmith banker opposed to the founding of the Bank of England. He came from Buckinghamshire and started life in the City as an apprentice in Cannon Street. He lodged in Southwark and every day walked over London Bridge and past St Magnus Church to work. He was late several times and was dismissed. He resolved that if he did well in life he would donate a large clock to St Magnus, and this he did in 1709, having done very well indeed. It is still there, now overshadowed by Adelaide House, but it would have been clearly visible to everyone walking over old London Bridge. Duncombe was one of the few goldsmiths who withdrew their money from the Exchequer before the stoppage in 1672, having had warning of what was about to happen. It is possible that his election was disputed in 1700 not only because he was a Tory, but because of a case against him for 'false endorsing of exchequer bills' in 1698, which put him in the Tower. A Bill of Pains and Penalty, promoted by the Whigs, was before Parliament by which two-thirds of his property would be forfeit. It passed the Commons but was turned down by the Lords, thanks to the Tories and the Duke of Bolton whose money he had saved with his own in 1672. He survived this crisis to become the richest commoner in England. When he retired from banking he bought Helmsley Castle in Yorkshire. (The Castle is a ruin but Duncombe Park is still there.) At his country house at Teddington the ceilings were by Verrio and there were carvings by Grinling Gibbons. He died in 1711, leaving no will, so his sister inherited his fortune which passed to her daughter who married the Duke of Argyll.

Sir Samuel Garrard, the next lord mayor, was a Tory and keen High Churchman. He was the great-grandson of Sir John Garrarde (1601) and of Sir Edward Barkham (1621), through whom he was distantly related to Sir Robert Walpole. The celebrated High-Churchman, Dr Sacheverell, preached an inflammatory sermon before him and the Corporation on the text, 'Perils among false brethren', in which he violently attacked the Dissenters. Sir Samuel congratulated him, saying he hoped it would be printed, as was customary with City sermons. The Whig majority on the Court of Aldermen objected, so Sacheverell printed and circulated it himself. The House of Commons decided it was libellous to the Queen and the Protestant succession and Sacheverell was brought to trial in Westminster Hall. The trial attracted wide public notice and outside the Hall there were fights among the mob. He was found guilty but his sentence was so light that the outcome was regarded as a victory for the Tories. Sacheverell was not to preach for three years and his existing sermons were to be burnt at the Exchange by the Common Hangman. This event was supervised by the Sheriffs. Garrard, who at the trial had denied encouraging Sacheverell, stayed away.

By now Queen Anne was tiring of the Whigs, who had been in power for some time, and her fondness for the Duchess of Marlborough was giving way to her friendship with Abigail Masham, who was an ally of the Tory, Sir Robert Harley. The public were weary of the war, which the Whigs supported, and the Tories began to gain ascendancy in Court circles and in Parliament. The next lord mayor, however, was a staunch Whig, Sir Gilbert Heathcote. His election was described by a German visitor, Conrad Von Uffenbach (*Travels*, 1710), who was not greatly impressed either by Guildhall, which he found 'neither large nor elegant', or by the actual election.

There was such a throng of people that we could hardly fight our way in; it was ridiculous to watch various persons standing at the door and not only calling out to those entering, but also handing them different printed papers recommending the competitors. We too had several given to us.

Heathcote was elected by the Whig majority in the Court of Aldermen, but was very unpopular with the City Tories. This appears to be the reason why he did not have a water procession to Westminster, but rode there while the Livery Companies went by barge. There is a story that he fell off his horse, and because of that thereafter the lord mayors went by coach. It is not substantiated. But ever since then the lord mayors have in fact made the land journey by coach. Heathcote was a self-made man from Chesterfield, who began as an apprentice to a wine merchant and joined the Vintners' Company, of which he became Master in 1700. He ran a successful business with Jamaica and the East Indies. He was a founder member of the Bank of England of which he was director during his mayoralty, president of St Thomas's Hospital, president of the Honourable Artillery Company, a Fellow of the Royal Society and a Commissioner for the American colony of Georgia, which he helped to found. He sat as Member of Parliament for Helston, Lymington and St Germans as well as the City. He was one of the wealthiest commoners of his time, with a fortune of £700,000. He gave £500 to St Thomas's and £500 to the poor of Chesterfield, but otherwise he had a reputation for stinginess. Alexander Pope (a Tory and a Catholic) condemned him with the lines:

> The grave Sir Gilbert holds it for a rule,
> That every man in want is knave or fool.

His nephew became lord mayor in 1742.

By the end of Queen Anne's reign the war in Europe had been ended by the Peace of Utrecht and the succession to the throne was assured to the Protestant, George of Hanover. Now the Whigs were the party in power and continued so until the Accession of George III in 1760. The Tories were in opposition and some of them supported the Jacobite risings of 1715 and 1745 in favour of the exiled Stuarts, pretenders to the throne.

When George I arrived in London to secure his inheritance he was received at Southwark with the usual splendour. The City fountains ran with wine and the Lord Mayor, Sir Samuel Stanier, the son of an Italian, led the procession, clad in a new crimson velvet gown. Sir William Humfreys, the next lord mayor, had the honour of entertaining the King and the Royal Family at his feast, after they had watched his procession from a special box in Cheapside. The banquet was splendid, but it was a disaster for the Lady Mayoress, who laid great store on receiving the salutation of a kiss from the Princess of Wales (the first royal lady on this occasion). This was an old custom which had been dropped by Queen Anne, but Lady Humfreys expected it would be revived. When the Princess failed to kiss her, the furious Lady Mayoress ordered one page to pick up her train, threw her bouquet to another and stalked out.

Relations between the City and the Court became strained under the Georges. At first the City was divided politically, with the Tory Common Council opposing, and the predominantly Whig Court of Aldermen supporting the Government. This Whig majority was gradually eroded as Government policies conflicted with City interests. During the early years of George I's reign every lord mayor was knighted, usually when he became sheriff if he had not already received a knighthood on some royal occasion. But the rise of Sir Robert Walpole to power altered the City's attitude to the Government. By 1730 the Tories were getting the upper hand in the City and three lord mayors in succession, Humphrey Parsons, Francis Child and John Barber were not knighted, although Child was knighted towards the end of his mayoralty (when he went with a City deputation to congratulate George II on his safe return from Hanover). Richard Hoare, in the diary he kept of his year as sheriff, described how he deliberately avoided being knighted when presenting an address to the Crown, but he succumbed during his mayoralty. The ebullient Humphrey Parsons declared that he avoided coming near the King for fear he might be knighted for 'he was sure his wife would never bed him afterwards'. In the second half of the eighteenth century only a sprinkling of lord mayors were knighted.

The division between the City and the Court was marked by indifference to honours on the part of the Londoners themselves and by the scorn which was heaped on the 'cits' by the fashionable world of the West End. However the aristocracy were often happy to marry their children into wealthy City families, many of whom were not averse to such a social rise, as was portrayed by William Hogarth in *Marriage à la Mode*.

The City opposed the Government on specific issues, but on the whole they were loyal to the Crown, and civic independence changed to civic obsequiousness on the many journeys made by lord mayor, aldermen, sheriffs and other City dignitaries to Westminster to present loyal addresses of congratulation on safe returns from Hanover, marriages and births of royal children and grandchildren. Civic independence was expressed in petitions to Parliament protesting against Government bills. By the 1740s it was clear there was a strong body of support for the Jacobites.

One constant feature of political life under the Hanoverians was the poor relationship between each King and the Prince of Wales, which meant that the opposition among the Whigs gathered around the heir to the throne. Sir James Bateman, lord mayor in 1716, was a Fishmonger whose grandfather had come to England to escape religious persecution in the Netherlands. Bateman was one of the greatest financiers of his day, a founder director of the Bank of which he was governor from 1705 to 1707. He was MP for Ilchester and then East Looe. He was essentially involved with the Government, but when the Prince of Wales went into opposition he went with him, as did Sir John Ward. Sir John Fryer began his career as a strong supporter of the Hanoverians, and for his loyalty was made a baronet in 1714. He had been a Dissenter in his youth and liked to tell how he used to play truant from church and once or twice frequented a public house on the Sabbath day. As lord mayor in 1720 he was a firm supporter of the Whig Government. But when Walpole became First Minister he, like most City men, went into opposition, even though remaining Whig in principle. Sir John wrote of Walpole, 'he is detested in the City for he never did anything for the trading part of it'.

There are two threads to follow in City politics in this period. One is the political division on national lines between the Whig majority in the Court of Aldermen and the predominantly Tory Common Council and Common Hall. The other is the dispute between the Court of Aldermen and the Common Council over the aldermen's claim to a veto on Common Council acts.

In 1725 Walpole's Election Act restricted voting in Common Hall to Liverymen and limited the freeman franchise for the Common Council to £10 householders. Furthermore the Act confirmed the aldermen's veto on Common Council acts. It received enthusiastic support from most of the aldermen, although Francis Child and John Barnard (lord mayor in 1737) vigorously opposed it as a move by the Government to interfere in the City's control of its own affairs. It certainly indicated how seriously the Government took City politics. Lord Townshend wrote to the King of the 'City of London, whose influence and example is of so great consequence to the whole nation'. The Government took care to have someone to watch over 'the ministry interest' in the City, and in 1727 that was the Lord Mayor, Sir John Eyles. When he proclaimed George II King, the Common Council produced, as was customary, a 'Loyal Address' of congratulation. This one, however, reflected strong Tory views, criticizing the Government's foreign and financial policy. Sir John set it aside and substituted a properly dutiful address, put together by the Aldermen and a few loyal Common Councilmen. That October the new King and Queen attended a splendid banquet given by the next lord mayor, Sir Edward Becher, with a consort of musicians playing music 'composed by Mr. Handel'.

During the next few years the City became virtually united against Walpole over his policy of conciliation towards Spain and especially over the hated Excise Bill. This bill was intended to restrict smuggling and to raise more money from import duties, thus enabling Walpole to reduce the Land Tax, which was very unpopular with his chief supporters, the Whig landowners. Instead of duty on tobacco and wine being levied on importation, the goods were to be kept in bonded warehouses, untaxed, and only to be sold in shops licensed for the purpose. This aroused a storm of protest among merchants and traders, who saw it as interference with their liberties and damaging to trade. Soon the popular press were attacking it as a threat to freedom with cries of 'No Slavery – No Excise – No Wooden Shoes' (a reference to the French). Even Sir John Eyles turned against the Government and several other leading City men who were to be lord mayor were in the forefront of the attack.

Humphrey Parsons was lord mayor in 1730. He had inherited from his father, lord mayor in 1703, his country house of Reigate Priory and a successful brewery in Aldgate. Their porter was famous, celebrated in Goldsmith's lines from *Description of an Author's Bedchamber*:

> Where Calvert's butt and Parsons black champagne
> Regale the drabs and bloods of Drury Lane.

He controlled the export of beer to France, where he had an exemption from customs duty as a special favour from Louis XV. Parsons was a flamboyant character and a keen huntsman. At a royal hunting party at Versailles his English courser outstripped the rest and was in at the death. This breached Court etiquette, but the King was so impressed that he asked the price of the horse and was promptly presented with it by Parsons, who received in return the King's portrait set in diamonds. Parsons was extremely popular, a strong Tory and ardent opponent of the Excise Bill. He was MP for Harwich from 1722 to 1727 and for London from 1727 to 1741.

Francis Child, who followed him as lord mayor, was a Tory MP for

London and Middlesex who also firmly opposed the Government. He had served on the Common Council committee which drew up the dubious Loyal Address of 1727. When he was lord mayor he received a friendly message from the Stuart Pretender and at the end of his year was thanked particularly warmly by the Common Council – an indication of their approval of his politics.

In 1732 John Barber was elected lord mayor. His career is unusual and of interest for the light it throws on how a comparatively humble man might rise to join the great financiers who formed the bulk of the City oligarchy. He was the son of a barber-surgeon who lived in Gray's Inn Lane; was apprenticed to a printer and became a member of the Stationers' Company. He set up his own printing house and became a very successful printer. His first £100 came from printing *The Diet of Poland* by Daniel Defoe, and he was soon well known to famous Tories like Bolingbroke, Pope and Swift. When the Tories rose to power in the last years of Queen Anne's reign he became the Queen's printer. The arrival of George I and the ascendancy of the Whigs was a set-back. But his business kept going and Barber was one of those who managed to do very well out of South Sea stocks. In 1722 he gave up active printing work and became an alderman. At this point he had to go to Italy for his health and was given leave of absence, being away for about three years. In 1729 he was sheriff, in which office he was very fortunate. The sheriffs were entitled to the property of men convicted in their jurisdiction, and one Colonel Charters, who was hanged for raping a maid in his house, was worth £7,000, which Barber and his brother sheriff shared between them. While he was sheriff, Barber noticed that, even when prisoners in Newgate were acquitted at their trial, they still had to pay the gaolers' fees. If they were unable to pay they had to return to prison. When he became lord mayor he stopped this practice.

He translated to the Goldsmiths' Company and became lord mayor in 1733 when the Excise Bill was before the House of Commons. He managed to procure an advance copy of the bill and organized a City petition against it. The City's determined opposition was also expressed by two of its MPs, Sir John Barnard and Micajah Perry, whose speeches in the House were accompanied by noisy protests from the mob outside. Walpole referred to these as a gang of 'sturdy beggars' and was sharply reproved by Barnard. Although Walpole got a small majority for his bill in the Commons he had to bow to the onslaught of the opposition and withdraw it. Bonfires greeted its failure in the City and the following year the mob tried to make it an annual celebration. The next lord mayor, Sir William Billers, was a Whig, a director of the East India Company and the South Sea Company and a Fellow of the Royal Society. He ordered a special watch and the arrest of persons trying to light bonfires. In the riots that followed his windows were broken, he himself was pelted with dirt and stones as he patrolled the streets, and the crowds tried to smash his coach.

The City Tories also joined in an attempt to repeal the Septennial Act which had been passed in 1716, just after the first Jacobite rising, to give Parliament a secure seven-year term. At the time Walpole easily defeated this, but it was an important issue of parliamentary reform to be taken up again later. Walpole's Gin Act of 1736 also aroused hostility in the City. However, the City's main quarrel with the Government was over dealings with Spain. British merchants were indignant at the Spanish insistence on searching British vessels in the West Indies. Stories of ill treatment of British sailors began to circulate, culminating in that of Captain Jenkins, who appeared in Parliament to exhibit his severed ear, wrapped in cotton wool. Walpole endeavoured to maintain the peace which he considered was essential, and persuaded Parliament to agree to a Spanish Convention. But agitation against this eventually drove England into war with Spain (the War of Jenkins' Ear). As the City bells tolled in triumph Walpole wryly commented, 'They now ring their bells, but soon they will be wringing their hands.'

Sir John Barnard became lord mayor in 1737. He was the outstanding lord mayor in the first half of the eighteenth century and led the popular forces in the City for over twenty years. He was born in Reading, the son of Quaker parents, but joined the Church of England before he was twenty. He began work at fifteen in his father's counting house, then came to London, joined the Glovers' Company, translating to the Grocers' when he became lord mayor. He had great financial ability and made marine insurance his main business. In 1737 Walpole was said to have offered him the Chancellorship of the Exchequer, but 'Sir John absolutely refused it, saying it was a laborious and envied place by which he could honestly get but £4,000 a year, and so much he gets by his trade without trouble'. He and Walpole clashed later that year when Walpole turned down his scheme for reducing interest on the national debt from 4 per cent to 3 per cent.

Micajah Perry, who followed Barnard in 1738, had been his close ally over opposition to the Excise Bill and the Spanish Convention, and also had supported his proposals on the national debt. Perry's grandfather was the greatest tobacco merchant in England. Micajah inherited the business and handled the affairs of Virginia planters in London. He was frequently consulted by the Board of Trade, and his evidence to a Commons committee investigating customs frauds in Scotland led to the Act putting customs administration in England and Scotland under one Commission. Two things distinguish Perry as lord mayor. One is that he laid the foundation stone of the Mansion House, and the other that he kept a diary of his year as mayor, which gives us a picture of the lord mayor's life and duties at that time. The ceremonies of election and handover of office were much as they are now. The procession was, of course, by barge to Westminster, returning to Blackfriars, whence he proceeded to Guildhall, 'my own Company and the Artillery Company marched all the way before me'. He dined in state in Guildhall, 'having put off the Scarlet Robe and put on the Entertaining Gown'. On 23 December he 'went a begging with the Sheriffs through the several markets for the several prisons'. This was an ancient custom which was revived in the 1720s.

His time, like that of all lord mayors in the eighteenth century was greatly taken up with the various City courts of Aldermen, Husting and Common Council, as well as sessions at the Old Bailey and Guildhall. He was a member of parliament during his mayoralty and during one week in March 1739 there was no Court of Aldermen, 'by my desire, I was so engaged in Parliament'. There were river journeys up to Putney and down to Greenwich to hold Courts of Conservancy. There were many church services and dinners with judges, but far fewer social occasions than nowadays.

On 25 October 1739 he 'Went to the Stocks Market preceded by the City Musick and my Officers with the Sunday Sword and Mace and laid the chief corner stone of the Mansion House.' Much of the money for the Mansion House had been raised by fines imposed on those who refused office, particularly the office of sheriff. It was said that it was built for those who wanted to be lord mayor out of the pockets of those who did not. It had been customary, as has been seen, for the lord mayor to 'name a sheriff' in a toast at a City dinner. Sometimes this was a genuine expression of preference, but more often it was a way of imposing a penalty. Sir John Barnard had named several Non-conformists knowing they would not serve, and Perry hardly seemed to get through a dinner in the spring and summer of 1739 without 'naming a Sheriff'.

Now the Tories were so strong in the City that the Whigs began to lose their majority on the Court of Aldermen. At the next election for lord mayor in 1739, George Champion should have been chosen according to seniority, but he had voted for the unpopular Spanish Convention and so was rejected and Sir John Salter was chosen in his stead. Common Hall then proceeded to present a paper to the City MPs, Parsons, Barnard, Perry and Willimot, thanking them for their conduct in Parliament in opposing the Spanish Convention and the Excise Bill. It urged them to press harder for the removal of placemen from the Commons (a long standing grievance) and for the repeal of the clause in the 1725 Act giving the aldermen the veto. It pointed out that some of the aldermen had wanted to use their veto over the petition against the Convention, thus attempting 'to deprive the citizens of the most valuable of their rights, that of addressing themselves to the legislature, or to the throne'. Such 'instruction' of their MPs was to be used frequently by the Liverymen in the eighteenth century. When Salter retired the following year there was another disputed election. The two candidates nominated by the Livery were Sir Robert Godschall and George Heathcote. Godschall was a Portugal merchant, very much against the Convention and the Excise Bill. He was the son-in-law of Sir William Lewen (1717) and brother-in-law of Sir John Barnard. Heathcote was the nephew of Sir Gilbert Heathcote (1710) and a wealthy West Indies merchant. He was at this date a Whig, although he later became a Tory. Godschall was the senior, but the majority of Aldermen voted for Heathcote, who had only just finished his shrieval year and declined. The Whigs were determined not to have Godschall and the situation was saved only when Humphrey Parsons, who was senior to Godschall and very popular, agreed to stand for a second term, 'let the expense be what it would'.

The Sheriffs in charge of this disputed election were Henry Marshall and Richard Hoare, grandson of the lord mayor in 1712. He kept a journal of the year in which he described how he was elected sheriff, 'to my great surprise by a majority of hands', at midsummer. He and Marshall went with the then Lord Mayor, Sir John Salter, to be presented to the Barons of the Exchequer on 30 September, where they witnessed a ceremony of cutting twigs and counting horseshoes and nails which City people today know as the Quit Rents Ceremony. (This is said to be the oldest surviving ceremony next to the Coronation. It now takes place every October in the Lord Chief Justice's Court in the Royal Courts of Justice. The City Solicitor renders a Quit (i.e., token) Rent for two properties outside the City boundaries. One is a piece of land in Shropshire known as 'The Moors' and the rent for this is a blunt knife and a sharp knife. The City

Solicitor bends a hazel rod over the blunt knife and breaks it over the blade of the sharp knife. For the other property, 'The Forge' in the parish of St Clement Dane, the rent is six horseshoes and sixty-one nails, which the City Solicitor painstakingly counts out.) On 28 October, after Parsons was sworn in, the senior Aldermen and the Sheriffs dined with the old Lord Mayor, the junior Aldermen with the new one. Salter failed to give the customary farewell supper to the Aldermen and their ladies, which gave some offence, especially to the ladies.

The Lord Mayor's procession was very grand with six horses to draw the coach, but several Aldermen did not attend owing to ill-feeling over the election. Parsons went to Westminster by coach, the Sheriffs by barge. Parsons did better because when the Sheriffs got into their barge for the return they discovered they were stranded by the tide and had to wait two hours before the barge would move.

A great deal of Hoare's time as sheriff was spent in court. (He was very interested in the famous case of William Duell, who was hanged, taken down as dead and removed to the Barber-Surgeons' Hall for dissection, where to everyone's astonishment he recovered. Hoare's theory about his extraordinary survival was that he had a high fever at the time so that his blood was circulating with particular force.) As Sheriffs of Middlesex he and Marshall went in May to hold the County Court at Brentford and preside over the parliamentary elections. They were handsomely enter-tained and returned home about five o'clock 'attended by as many of our officers and bailiffs as were able to sit their horses'.

During his time as sheriff, Hoare was elected Alderman of Farringdon Without in place of Francis Child who had died. Hoare was in Bath at the time and knew nothing about it until he returned. One great worry was the risk of serious financial loss. The sheriffs were liable for the debts of prisoners, so they were alarmed when some debtors owing £17,000 attempted to escape. They were prevented by being chained to the floor and doubly ironed. Hoare clearly was uncomfortable about this harsh treatment, but said he felt justified in 'a more severe sort of imprisonment for our better security'. His journal ended with an expression of relief, 'and after being regaled with sack and walnuts, I returned to my own home in my private capacity, to my great consolation and comfort'.

Humphrey Parsons' second mayoralty proved too much for his con-stitution and he died on Palm Sunday 1741. A new lord mayor had to be found and Common Hall was again in a dilemma, because the Whig Aldermen still rejected Godschall. Barnard was approached, but refused to take on a second term; Heathcote still declined and Robert Willimot, next in seniority and a possibly acceptable candidate, still had not served as sheriff. That left Daniel Lambert, a merchant from Banstead in Surrey, who had worked his way up in City politics, was MP for London and was acceptable to the Livery. He was chosen and served until October when Godschall was at last elected. Robert Willimot served his shrievalty that year and was elected lord mayor in 1742. He was a Cooper and approached the Clothworkers' Company with a view to translation for his mayoralty. He met with little encouragement so he 'consulted eminent counsel' and discovered that there was no legal reason why he should belong to one of the top twelve Companies. Therefore he became lord mayor as a Cooper and so broke a long practice. A few still chose to translate, but from this date more and more lord mayors came from the minor Companies.

By now Walpole had resigned, and government influence on City politics weakened. City opposition to Walpole had made London the champion of independent political opinion. The citizens now issued instructions to their MPs, urging them to demand the active prosecution of a sea war, a Place Bill (to remove MPs who held government sinecures), repeal of the Septennial Act and repeal of the Aldermanic veto. These instructions were in themselves a way of avoiding the veto, since the petitions and addresses could be vetoed. The usual Common Council addresses to the throne continued to be presented but it was noticeable that the summer address of 1742 snubbed George II by totally ignoring his victory at Dettingen in which he personally led the British Army – the last King of England to do so.

However, a much more serious form of opposition was growing in the City, where the more extreme Tories were now Jacobites, looking with interest at the moves which the Young Pretender was beginning to make towards recovering what he regarded as his throne. He was informed that there was a groundswell of Jacobite sympathy in the City and that several of the London aldermen were prepared to rise for him. There is a portrait in Goldsmiths' Hall known as *Benn's Club* which shows six subsequent lord mayors – Benn, Marshall, Blachford, Ironside, Alsop and Rawlinson – drinking to the Pretender. It was commissioned for the Hall by John Blachford in thanks for the use of the Hall and Company plate during his mayoralty (1750). George Heathcote, who became lord mayor only for the last few months of 1742 after the death of Godschall, had been a Whig but had swung to Toryism and was certainly a Jacobite. It is uncertain how extensive support for the Jacobites was in the City. Rumours were rife but it remains doubtful how many supporters would have emerged if the Pretender had not abandoned his advance on London.

In reaction to these fears, loyalist associations were formed in the City. Sir John Barnard rallied popular support and prepared a Loyal Address. Heathcote wanted grievances tackled first, but he was overruled. During the panic run on the Bank when the Pretender advanced to Derby, Barnard persuaded other City merchants to join him in promising to take Bank notes rather than coinage. The lord mayor in 1745 was Sir Richard Hoare, who, having avoided his knighthood as sheriff, received it on 31 October upon the presentation of a Loyal Address to the King. He was a Tory, but also a loyalist, and was responsible for the defence of the City, ordering the Trained Bands to take up quarters at the Royal Exchange, and the City Marshals to supervise the night watch.

After the failure of Bonnie Prince Charlie's invasion, Jacobitism was finished. George Heathcote resigned his aldermanry and retired to Bath, disillusioned. At Westminster Henry Pelham, now First Minister, was determined to win over the City's support. In 1746 that part of Walpole's 1725 Election Act which gave the aldermen a veto in Common Council was repealed. In 1747 Pelham followed Sir John Barnard's recommendation to raise a government loan by open subscription. Barnard was at the height of his popularity in the City and in 1748 his statue, by Scheemakers, was erected in the Royal Exchange. The following year Pelham introduced a scheme which Barnard had long advocated for reducing the interest on the national debt from 4 per cent to 3 per cent.

One item in Richard Hoare's diary refers to insanitary conditions in Newgate Gaol, which led to outbreaks of gaol fever so infectious that the magistrates caught it by sitting in court. Hoare described special cleansing of the gaol and the provision of fresh clothes for the prisoners. The danger was very real. Sir Samuel Pennant, lord mayor in 1749, died in May 1750 of gaol distemper and Sir Daniel Lambert died the same year. Thomas Winterbottom, lord mayor in 1751, died in June 1752.

In the midst of all this the Mansion House was nearing completion. Designed by the Clerk of the City's Works, George Dance, it had taken over fifteen years since Micajah Perry laid the 'chief corner stone', but now the builders promised it would be ready by Michaelmas. The Lord Mayor Elect was Crisp Gascoyne, Brewer. He was sworn in at Westminster on 9 November, for this was the year of the change to the Gregorian calendar which removed eleven days from the calendar that year in order to bring England into line with most of Europe. He was sworn in 'with the usual solemnities, making a fine appearance with a superb coach and six horses decorated with ribbons and gilt furniture'. The Lord Mayor's Banquet was held in Guildhall, where the Lady Mayoress was Crisp Gascoyne's daughter, Mrs Fanshawe, his wife having died some years before. After the ball which followed the banquet they returned to the Mansion House where Gascoyne spent his year of office as lord mayors have done ever since (except when it has had to be closed for repairs). The house was not quite finished, but the Easter Banquet was held in the Egyptian Hall in 1753.

Stephen Janssen, Stationer, was lord mayor in 1754. His father was a Flemish Protestant who came over in the late seventeenth century. He was one of the directors of the South Sea Company and after the 'Bubble' burst his estate was confiscated, but he was allowed to retain £50,000 to pass on to his heirs. Janssen, a printer by profession, opened an enamelling business in Battersea, using a new technique of transfer printing. The novelty of the idea had a great impact, and although Janssen was declared bankrupt in 1756 and could not continue the business, copper plates of the designs were used elsewhere, so the name 'Battersea' continued to be used for English enamels. Janssen's bankruptcy was the consequence of his heavy expenses as lord mayor. He struggled to repay his debts and cut back his household. After his wife's death he lived in lodgings on eighteen shillings a week. It was a hard struggle, but he succeeded and in 1765 was made Chamberlain of London, the first former lord mayor to attain this lucrative post, which was to be held by eight more former lord mayors.

A few years after they at last obtained their own house the lord mayors acquired their own coach. Although lord mayors had ridden in coaches since 1710 there had been no specific civic coach. Now a coach was specially constructed by Joseph Berry to a design of Sir Robert Taylor. The total cost was £860 towards which the Lord Mayor contributed £100 and the Aldermen £60 each. It was gilded and decorated with panels attributed to the painter Cipriani. The first lord mayor to ride in it was Sir Charles Asgill in 1757, who had risen from a humble clerk to be partner in a bank. As the *Gentleman's Magazine* reported: 'He was a strong instance of what may be affected, even by moderate abilities when united with strict integrity, industry and irreproachable character.'

By the mid-1750s Sir John Barnard's position as leader of the City was beginning to be challenged by William Beckford, and a new era in City politics was dawning. As lord mayor, Barnard had worked hard to ameli-

Statue in Guildhall of William Beckford
(Ironmonger, 1762, 1769).

William Hogarth's caricature of John Wilkes
(Joiner, 1774).

Banquet given by the Corporation of London for the Prince Regent, at Guildhall, 18 June 1814. A painting by George Clint.

Benn's Club. Painting in Goldsmith's Hall showing six subsequent lord mayors drinking a toast to the Pretender.

Brook Watson (Musician, 1796) whose leg was bitten off by a shark in America when he was a boy.

Sword rest of John Boydell (Stationer, 1790) in St Margaret Lothbury.

MOMENTS of PLEASURE.

London Publ. by G. Humphrey 27 St James's St. 1820.

Cartoon of Matthew Wood (Fishmonger, 1815–16) satirizing his support of Queen Caroline.

CONJUNCTION of TALENT

The GREAT DICTATOR and his Mighty Councillor, the DONKEY MARE

Cartoon of Sir John Key (Stationer, 1830–1) criticizing his warning to the Duke of Wellington not to attend the Lord Mayor's banquet because of City hostility over the Reform Bill.

THIS BRASS WAS PLACED HERE BY
THE CORPORATION OF THE CITY OF LONDON
IN MEMORY OF THE RIGHT HONOURABLE
GEORGE ✦ SWAN ✦ NOTTAGE
LORD MAYOR, WHO DIED DURING HIS MAYORALTY
IN THE FORTY EIGHTH YEAR
OF THE REIGN OF QUEEN VICTORIA,
ON THE 11TH DAY OF APRIL 1885, AGED 62 YEARS
AND WHO LIES BURIED BENEATH THIS SPOT.

The tomb of George Nottage (Spectacle Maker, 1884) who died in office and was buried in St Paul's Cathedral.

On the threshhold of the City by S. J. Solomon, Sir George Faudel-Phillips (Spectacle Maker, 1896).

orate the condition of poor debtors, to raise the standard of London policing and to suppress begging. He was a keen churchman and encouraged better Sunday observance. After his mayoralty he wrote a little booklet for his apprentices. It was called 'a present for an Apprentice; a sure guide to gain both esteem and an estate'. It is given to all freemen of the City of London as *Rules for the Conduct of Life*. In 1758 he resigned his aldermanry and retired from public life. He died in 1764, aged nearly eighty, and was buried in Mortlake Church.

9

RADICAL REFORMERS

From 1756 William Pitt, the 'Great Commoner' as he came to be known, was the focus of City loyalties. At last the reformers had a national figure whom they could wholeheartedly support. Pitt appealed to City men through his vigorous foreign policy and his unwavering support of trade. As he said, 'when trade is at stake you must defend it or perish.' On a higher plane he attracted those who worked for political reform and were opposed to reactionary Government policies. He lifted politics above petty squabbles to concentrate on major issues. City opponents of Government policies in the early part of the eighteenth century had concerned themselves with attacking measures which directly affected particular interests, like the Excise Bill and the Aldermanic veto. Now they turned their attention to more general matters: parliamentary reform, freedom of the press, the treatment of the American colonists.

It was public indignation at Government conduct of the war against France which brought Pitt to power in 1756. When in April 1757 he was dismissed for opposing the King's policy of pursuing a continental rather than a sea war, there was a public outcry, especially in London, where he was promptly presented with the Freedom of the City. Indeed honours came in from all over the country until his wife commented, 'it rained gold boxes'. By June Pitt was back in office, and during the next two years the war was prosecuted with tremendous vigour and success, culminating in Clive's victories in India and Wolfe's capture of Quebec in 1759. In that year the Lord Mayor, Sir Thomas Chitty, laid the foundation

stone for a new bridge across the Thames. It was named after William
Pitt but subsequently became known as Blackfriars Bridge.

Pitt remained in office until 1761. Meanwhile George II had died and
been succeeded by his grandson. George III was twenty-two when he
became King, and unlike his predecessors, whose sympathies remained
with Hanover, he gloried in the name 'Briton'. This might have endeared
him to Pitt and to the City. But he was immature and excessively dependent
on his close friend and Chief Minister, the Earl of Bute. In 1761 Pitt
resigned when the Government refused to declare war on Spain. In
acknowledgement of his recent great service to the nation he was offered
and accepted a peerage for his wife and a pension of £3,000 for himself.
For this he was criticized by his popular following, but he was encouraged
to attend Sir Samuel Fludyer's Lord Mayor's Banquet, and received a
tumultuous reception in the City. The enthusiasm for Pitt was far greater
than that for the King and Queen, while the Earl of Bute was hooted by
the crowd and pelted with mud. In 1763 the Treaty of Paris brought the
war to an end. Pitt was utterly disgusted at the terms, declaring 'we retain
nothing, although we have conquered everything', and his attitude found
support in London, particularly from two men who were to lead the City
in opposition to the Government through one of the liveliest periods in
its political history – William Beckford and John Wilkes.

With the Accession of George III the complexion of English politics
changed. Now the Tories came to power in support of the Crown and
the Whigs went into opposition. In the City the opposition movement
was concerned with parliamentary reform, demanding shorter Parliaments
and a fairer suffrage with an end to rotten boroughs. Its leaders looked
not only to the City but to a wider area of London, to Westminster,
Southwark and Middlesex, and beyond. The majority of aldermen were
now Tories, monied men loyal to the Government interest. But several
Radicals as well as Beckford and Wilkes became lord mayor: Brass Crosby,
James Townsend, Frederick Bull and John Sawbridge. The outstanding
Tory lord mayors of the period were Sir Thomas Harley and Sir Thomas
Hallifax.

It was William Beckford who had persuaded Pitt to attend the Lord
Mayor's Banquet in 1761 and had masterminded the mob's enthusiastic
reception of him. Beckford came from a family long established in
Gloucestershire. In the seventeenth century his great-grandfather had
gone out to Jamaica and set himself up as a sugar planter. William was
born in Jamaica in 1709. At the age of fourteen he was sent to England

to be educated at Westminster School, where a close friend was the boy who was to become a great judge, Lord Mansfield. Beckford showed uncommon ability at school, and was fortunate in inheriting the family's lucrative West Indian business on the death of his elder brother. Although he became the leader of the popular movement in the City, in some ways he had more in common with the landed classes. He owned an estate in Wiltshire with a fine house, Fonthill, which his son, famous as the author of *Vathek*, rebuilt in the then fashionable Gothic style. As a West Indian planter, Beckford was also a slave-owner, and so this advocate of liberty was open to jibes such as that which appeared in the *Public Advertiser* in 1769:

> For B(eck)f(ord) he was chosen Mayor
> A wight of high renown,
> To see a slave he could not bear
> Unless it were his own.

Beckford entered politics in 1747 as Member of Parliament for Shaftesbury, for which he sat until 1754. His rise in the City hierarchy was swift. In 1752 he became an Ironmonger by redemption and was elected Alderman for Billingsgate. The next year he was Master of the Ironmongers. In 1754 he stood in the parliamentary elections for Petersfield and for the City and succeeded in both constituencies. He chose London and declined Petersfield, sending the town £400 to pave its streets. Beckford's political progress was not only swift, but deliberate. Many lord mayors, as we have seen, were members of parliament. But Beckford was the first who entered City politics in order to further his national aims. In 1755 he was elected sheriff and in 1762 he duly became lord mayor. Beckford used his position to help promote Pitt's policies in Parliament and to fan the fires of discontent in the City. During his mayoral year the peace negotiations which so disgusted Pitt were going on, and in 1763 Beckford refused to call Common Hall to make the customary vote of thanks to the Crown. None of this prevented him from having a year of unprecedented splendour, with banquets so sumptuous that gourmets talked of them long afterwards.

Already a rival leader of the popular movement in the City had appeared – John Wilkes, London's most controversial and colourful lord mayor. The aims of the two men were close, but they were not friends. Beckford did not like Wilkes and often found him an embarrassment. But the devotion Wilkes attracted from the mob meant that Beckford could not dissociate himself from his cause. John Wilkes was born in Clerkenwell in 1727, second son of a thriving malt distiller. He too was very able at school and went on to the University of Leyden. He married, at his father's suggestion, a wealthy woman much older than himself. They had one daughter, to whom Wilkes was devoted, but the marriage soon broke up, leaving Wilkes a rich man. However his tastes were expensive and his habits profligate. Furthermore he was determined to get into Parliament and spent a great deal of money unsuccessfully contesting Berwick-upon-Tweed. He finally secured Aylesbury, for which he sat from 1757–1764. He looked to Pitt to provide him with a lucrative post so that he could recoup his finances, and hoped for either the Embassy at Constantinople or the Governorship of Quebec. When neither of these came his way he blamed the detested Bute rather than Pitt. He turned instead to journalism, and began to use his own publications to criticize the Government. In 1763, in issue no. 45 of *The North Briton*, he published an anonymous attack on Government foreign policy which criticized the King. This caused a furore, and Wilkes was arrested under a general warrant, his house was ransacked and his papers were seized. This was a breach of parliamentary privilege, and Wilkes was released a few days later, spoiling for a fight with the Government.

By now Wilkes's cause had aroused intense popular concern, and the slogan 'Wilkes and Liberty' was displayed everywhere. In November 1763 Parliament ordered issue no. 45 to be burnt by the Common Hangman. Thomas Harley was one of the sheriffs who had to attempt this task in front of a city mob who pelted the sheriffs with 'hard pieces of wood and dirt', rescued the offending periodical from the flames and smashed the windows of Harley's coach. Instead the mob burnt a boot and a petticoat (for the Earl of Bute and the unpopular Princess Dowager). Wilkes was called out to fight a duel by Samuel Martin, a member of parliament, and was seriously wounded. Soon after this he went to Paris, spent the next four years on the Continent in voluntary exile, and was declared an outlaw by Parliament. He returned to England early in 1768 and stood as a parliamentary candidate for the City. He came bottom of the poll, but immediately stood for Middlesex instead and was elected with a huge majority. There was tremendous exultation among his followers, who rampaged through the City, smashing the windows of all houses not illuminated in Wilkes's honour. One such house was the Mansion House, where Sir Thomas Harley, Goldsmith, was now lord mayor. Harley was a distinguished and honourable man, only thirty-seven at this time, a leading merchant and banker and Member of Parliament for the City. During a severe frost and trade depression that winter he had fish brought into Billingsgate to be sold cheaply to the poor. But the mob hated him for his Tory politics.

Having won his electoral victory, Wilkes surrendered to the King's Bench prison as an outlaw. There he remained for two years. The mob tried to prevent his imprisonment and gathered in large numbers in St George's Fields outside the prison. Troops were called in to disperse them and some people were killed in what was described as a 'massacre'. In the City, Harley made a firm attempt to control the riots, reminding freemen of their pledge to keep their apprentices from going on to the streets in times of disorder. He was thanked by the House of Commons for his efforts and made a Privy Councillor.

Wilkes did not languish in prison, but received a constant stream of visitors and well-wishers. His friends formed the Society of the Supporters of the Bill of Rights, which put forward a radical programme of reform and raised £17,000 for Wilkes, who was by now totally penniless. Meanwhile the House of Commons rejected the choice of the Middlesex electors and ordered a new election. The voters stubbornly persisted in re-electing Wilkes three more times. Finally Parliament declared Wilkes's opponent, Colonel Luttrell, elected MP for Middlesex, although he had only polled a fraction of the votes. This was seen by reforming elements as a dangerous infringement of the rights of electors. Petitions came in from all over the country, protesting at this high-handed action, and ranging more widely, criticizing the King's ministers, denouncing taxation of the American colonists and complaining of attacks on the freedom of the press.

With Wilkes in prison, Beckford, who had lost his prominence, came to the fore again as the leader of Wilkes's followers and promoter of his reforming causes. In 1769 he was nominated by the Livery for a second mayoralty, and was elected by a reluctant Court of Aldermen, who had anticipated he would refuse. His second term of office was as splendid as the first, even though the majority of aldermen did not attend the Lord Mayor's Banquet. It was during this term of office that William Beckford won his lasting fame and a statue in Guildhall (the only lord mayor there). He went with the Aldermen and representatives of the Common Council to St James's Palace to present strongly worded remonstrances to the King about the treatment of Wilkes at the Middlesex elections. The King's replies were very curt, and on the second occasion Beckford, instead of accepting the royal reply and retiring, as was usual, stood his ground and protested. The words he is supposed to have spoken are engraved at the base of his statue:

> Permit me, Sire, farther to observe that whosoever has already dared, or shall hereafter endeavour, ... to alienate your Majesty's affections from your loyal subjects in general, and from the City of London in particular ... is an enemy to your Majesty's person and family, a violator of the public peace, and a betrayer of our happy Constitution, as it was established at the Glorious Revolution.

There has been some discussion over whether he actually said the words, or whether they were written later by Horne Tooke, but it is not important. Although they may not seem very forceful to a modern observer, at that time to make any riposte was unprecedented. Beckford had shocked the Court and thrilled the nation. The Tory Aldermen signed a protest dissociating themselves from the remonstrance, and three of the Livery Companies, the Goldsmiths', Grocers' and Weavers', questioned the lord mayor's power to summon Common Hall for political purposes. Pitt said of him 'the spirit of Old England spoke on that never to be forgotten day'. It was Beckford's swan song, for he died a few weeks later, on 21 June 1770.

Meanwhile Wilkes had been making his way in the City. On 10 March 1768, shortly before his success at the Middlesex election, he was admitted to the Freedom of the Joiners' Company by redemption. Two years later they elected him Master. In 1769, shortly before his discharge from prison, he was elected Alderman of Farringdon Without. In 1771 he served as sheriff and so was now in line for the mayoralty.

On Beckford's death Barlow Trecothick was elected lord mayor for the rest of the year. He was one of the City MPs elected in 1768 when Wilkes came bottom of the poll. Trecothick was lampooned in 'The City Races', a popular skit on the election, as 'Lord Rockingham's wall-eyed horse Mercator'. He had attached himself to Lord Rockingham's party for its pro-American line. By now there was considerable opposition in the City to Government policy towards the colonists, and Trecothick was an American. There is some question about where he was born, since his baptism was registered at Stepney, but possibly he was born on the sea voyage. He certainly grew up in America, returning to England in his early twenties. In London he acted as colonial agent for New Hampshire and retained a close interest in American affairs. It is perhaps an indication of the strong pro-American feeling in the City that in 1773 both the

Sheriffs were Americans: Stephen Sayer, framework knitter, and William Lee, haberdasher. Sayer joined the army before Quebec, got a commission and came to England. He married the daughter of a judge and became a partner in a banking house. He was briefly arrested on a trumped-up charge of trying to seize the Tower for American rebels, but soon freed. Lee was a Virginian, whose brother presented a petition from the first Congress in Philadelphia to George III.

Trecothick was not re-elected the following September when Brass Crosby was chosen lord mayor. Crosby was born in Stockton-on-Tees, worked for a Sunderland solicitor, then came to London and worked as an attorney in Little Minories, Seething Lane. He made the money he needed to take up civic office through three wealthy marriages. In 1760 he purchased the office of City Remembrancer and sold it the following year. He was elected to the Common Council, became sheriff in 1764 and Alderman for Bread Street in 1765. He sat as Member of Parliament for Honiton from 1768 to 1774. When he was elected lord mayor he declared he would protect the privileges and liberties of the City at the risk of his life. His first protest was against the issue of press warrants when he ordered the City constables to chase off the press gangs, which seized men for enforced service in the Navy. (Immunity from the press gangs was one of the privileges of citizenship.) Then the matter of printing of House of Commons debates arose. This was against existing Commons regulations and Members complained that reports of debates were appearing in the press. The offending printers were ordered to appear before the Bar of the House and when two failed to turn up the House sent a messenger into the City to arrest one of them. The messenger duly made the arrest and brought the prisoner before the City Magistrates sitting at Mansion House, who happened to be the Lord Mayor, Alderman John Wilkes and Alderman Richard Oliver. They released the printer and arrested the messenger. An infuriated House of Commons summoned Crosby and Oliver before them and committed them to the Tower. Wilkes, who was not then an MP, they decided to leave alone: no lord mayor had been imprisoned in the Tower since the Civil War. The event aroused very little notice in the country but the City mob were thoroughly aroused. They burnt effigies of members of the establishment, including the unfortunate Thomas Harley, and when Crosby and Oliver were released six weeks later the people accompanied them back to the Mansion House in a triumphal procession with 'loud and universal huzzahs'.

In 1772 Wilkes contested the mayoralty. He came head of the Livery poll but was rejected by the Aldermen, who chose James Townsend instead. Wilkes's supporters made a great commotion on Lord Mayor's Day, shouting 'D—n My Lord Mayor for a scoundrel, he has got Wilkes's right and we will have him out.' Townsend had been one of the Supporters of the Bill of Rights, but turned against Wilkes when he used some of the funds raised for personal expenditure. The following year again Wilkes headed the Livery poll, but the Aldermen were divided and Townsend gave his casting vote for Frederick Bull, another Radical and a supporter of Wilkes. George III had watched these elections anxiously, hoping against hope that 'that devil Wilkes' would not succeed. But in 1774 the courtiers at last lost control of the Court of Aldermen and Wilkes was elected lord mayor and that same month was re-elected Member of Parliament for Middlesex. In the City delighted crowds unhitched the horses from his coach and drew him to the Mansion House in triumph.

Wilkes's mayoralty was conducted with great splendour, sparing no expense, and his beloved daughter was a dignified and charming Lady Mayoress. George III's fears proved groundless. In 1775 Wilkes presented a remonstrance with such tact that the King declared he had never known such a well-bred lord mayor. The expense of the year nearly undid Wilkes. He calculated that the receipts from the office amounted to £4,889 0s. 6½d. while his expenses were £8,226. 13s. od. He decided to try for the post of Chamberlain and stood for election in 1776, but was defeated by the Court candidate, Benjamin Hopkins. Flouting tradition he attempted three times to oust Hopkins and failed, but on the latter's death in 1779 he won the post which he held for the rest of his life. As Chamberlain he granted the Freedom of the City to many famous men, including General Cornwallis, Admiral Howe and Lord Nelson.

Wilkes had become respectable. He used to say that he never was a Wilkite and to refer to himself in his later years as 'an extinct volcano'. But when he was active he was a powerful force in politics. Despite his dubious reputation he was clearly a man of great charm, with the power to attract not only the mob, but civilized men like Dr Johnson, who abhorred his politics, and the historian Edward Gibbon, who wrote of him, 'I scarcely ever met with a better companion; he has inexhaustible spirits, infinite wit and humour and a great deal of knowledge.' Not all the achievements of the radical movement in eighteenth-century London were attributable to him, but his leadership and experience were crucial. After Wilkes's wrongful arrest general warrants could not be used to prosecute libel. He got his expulsion from the House of Commons expunged from the records. Never again could Parliament keep out a Member who had been properly elected by his constituents. Nor, thanks to Wilkes and Brass Crosby, could the Commons prevent their debates from being published. The Supporters of the Bill of Rights pursued a programme of Parliamentary reform which was a forerunner of later achievements, even universal suffrage. Wilkes himself proposed that the franchise should include 'the meanest mechanic, the poorest peasant and day labourer'. His name will not be forgotten in America where he was regarded as the champion of liberty; his activities received more favourable press comment there than those of any other British politician.

John Sawbridge followed Wilkes in the Mansion House. He came from Kent and was in business with his father as a hop merchant and distiller. He was a JP for Kent and Colonel of the East Kent Militia. He inherited a country estate, but was a radical and a founder member of the Supporters of the Bill of Rights. He sat as Member of Parliament for Hythe from 1768 to 1774 and then for many years for the City. He was first nominated for the mayoralty in 1771, but on that occasion William Nash, a confirmed courtier, was chosen. As lord mayor, Sawbridge vigorously opposed press gang warrants, and petitioned on behalf of the American colonists. The King issued a proclamation suppressing rebellion and sedition, to be read officially by the Lord Mayor. Sawbridge duly read the proclamation at the Royal Exchange, but deliberately left behind the Sword and Mace, which ought to have been there. He was a popular man, clever, but coarse and well known as the best whist player in St James's. His great reforming cause was a bill for shorter Parliaments, with which he persisted year after year.

Sawbridge was the last of the Wilkites to serve as lord mayor. Several courtiers followed him. The next lord mayor was Sir Thomas Hallifax, Goldsmith, the son of a Barnsley clockmaker, who went to London, started as a clerk in Martin's Bank and became a partner in the firm of Vere, Glyn and Hallifax. As sheriff in 1768 he was one of the returning officers during the Middlesex elections when Wilkes was repeatedly returned. At that time Hallifax maintained the right to free elections, but shortly afterwards he joined the Court party and was one of those who opposed Wilkes's election as lord mayor. He invited to his Lord Mayor's Banquet leading members of the ministry who had not been asked for seven years. Nevertheless, he too opposed the activities of the press gangs in the City. He was followed by Sir James Esdaile who supported the Government over the American war. The King strongly approved of his election, and on his presentation to the judges the Lord Chancellor said he was glad to see 'a return of that dignity, peace and tranquillity which has been lost and disturbed for many years past'.

Following the disagreement over Beckford's protest to the King, a joint committee of the Common Council and the Livery met and decided that the Lord Mayor did have the right to compel attendance, and that refusal could be punishable by disenfranchisement. In 1773 they decided to make an example and proceeded against Alderman Samuel Plumbe, Goldsmith, who had signed the protest. He was duly disenfranchised, but the decision was reversed in 1775, since when it is established that the Lord Mayor cannot compel the attendance of Liverymen at Common Hall. Plumbe was re-enfranchised and became lord mayor in 1778.

In 1779 Brackley Kennett, Vintner, was elected lord mayor. According to the *City Biography*, a scurrilous commentary on city notables published in 1800, he was a waiter in a tavern in Pall Mall. He had been Alderman of Cornhill since 1767 and had served as sheriff in 1765. He was one of the Tory Aldermen who dissented from the City remonstrance in 1770. He came to the mayoralty at a most unfortunate time and so was destined to play an inglorious part in the worst riots London has ever known, and the worst fires since 1666 – another occasion when sadly the lord mayor was found wanting.

The Gordon Riots of June 1780 began with a large, but orderly, protest against the recent Catholic Relief Act, led by Lord George Gordon. Anti-Catholic feeling was widespread in the City and the London mob joined the protest and got totally out of hand. They burnt Catholic chapels and tore down the houses of known Catholics. They sacked Newgate prison and burned Lord Mansfield's house in Bloomsbury. They broke into a huge distillery in Holborn, got drunk on the gin and set the place alight. London was in chaos for a week and thousands of troops had to be brought in to restore order. By the end of it all over 300 people had been killed and 450 prisoners were taken, of whom 25 were hanged. Over fifty buildings were damaged or destroyed. Brackley Kennett failed to get the situation under control early on. Part of the trouble was that his sympathies, like those of so many City men were against the Catholics. He was reported as having refused to read the Riot Act, saying that the people were only destroying the houses of those they disliked. Anyway, as he said, 'I must be cautious lest I bring the mob to my own house'. According to a contemporary court report, John Cole, a witness to the outbreak, said:

If I had dropped from the clouds and had known nothing of the present business, or the laws of this country, I should have thought that the rioters were executing the sentence of the law by razing the house of some state criminal, and that the Lord Mayor and soldiery were attending to protect them in their business.

It is worth recording that Wilkes played a distinguished part in bringing the rioters under control, and led the London Military Association in defending the Bank of England.

Kennett was taken to task by the Privy Council at the time, and the next year he was brought to trial before the Court of King's Bench on a charge of having 'wilfully, obstinately and contemptuously neglected to do his duty during the riots in June last'. His defence was that he had shown too great fear and exercised too great humanity, in not wishing to injure innocent bystanders. It was stated at the trial that:

If on a riot a magistrate neither reads the proclamation from the Riot Act nor gives any order to fire on them, nor makes any use of a military force under his command, this is 'prima facie' evidence of a criminal neglect of duty in him; and it is no answer to the charge for him to say that he was afraid unless his fear arose from such danger as would affect a firm man; and if, rather than apprehend the rioters his sole care was for himself, this is also neglect.

He was found guilty, but died before sentence was passed on him.

The Gordon Riots brought to an end the alliance between radical City leaders and the London mob. The attacks on the Royal Exchange and the Bank of England were too close to home. As George Rudé wrote in *Hanoverian London*, 'they began to shut their ears against the voices of popular clamour ... in so doing they snapped the threads that had so long linked the activities of the streets with the debates and resolutions of the Guildhall'.

London's lord mayors continued to be actively involved in politics and nearly half of them were at some time members of parliament. But they were not so controversial nor so closely linked with the mob. There were fewer wealthy bankers. Indeed it is noticeable that the majority came from the minor Companies, and several were men of humble origin. A few had strong literary and artistic interests. Often they were ridiculed by cartoonists and satirical writers and yet officially the lord mayor was still treated with elaborate respect and ceremonial. The City rulers of the late eighteenth century had to cope with difficult times. The French Revolution of 1789 stimulated radical movements and led to wars which brought hardships, food shortages and financial crises. Politics again took on a new form, as William Pitt, son of the 'Great Commoner', rose to take over the leadership of the nation. Aged twenty-four, he became the youngest-ever Prime Minister in 1784. Those who supported him were Tories, and in the City included the majority in the Court of Aldermen and in the Common Council. In opposition was Pitt's great rival, Charles James Fox, the leader of the Whigs, and a close friend of George, Prince of Wales, who in true Hanoverian tradition was antagonistic to his father and looked forward to supplanting him. Pitt first came to power after the failure of Fox's attempt to reform the East India Company. Fox's India Bill would have transferred the Company's affairs and its extensive and valuable patronage to a government commission. This was inimical to the interests of City merchants, and George III took the City's part. The bill passed the Commons, but the King saw to it that the Lords threw it out – and Fox fell from power. He had hopes of recouping his fortunes when in 1788 George III had his first attack of madness. It looked as though the Prince of Wales would take over, and the Foxite Whigs were in power for a few months. However, the King recovered in 1789, and a great thanksgiving service was held in St Paul's. William Gill, the lord mayor, received the King at Temple Bar and surrendered the Pearl Sword. The King returned it, saying, 'My Lord, the Sword cannot be in better hands.' The Lord Mayor rode on a white palfrey in front of the King to the Cathedral. For the rest of his reign George III enjoyed public sympathy and external dangers drew the nation together.

In the City the majority were Tory and supported the Government, but Whig sentiments dominated in Common Hall, whose attempts to present radical resolutions to the Crown and to have Whig aldermen elected lord mayor were frequently frustrated by the Court of Aldermen. Sir Watkin Lewes, who succeeded Brackley Kennett as lord mayor, was the son of a Pembrokeshire clergyman. As a Welshman he was frequently shown in caricatures wearing a leek. He had assisted Wilkes in defending the Bank from the rioters, and was a fellow liveryman of the Joiners' Company, but he complained that Wilkes frequently made a butt of him. 'How can you say so?' exclaimed Wilkes, 'when you know I never was fond of an empty butt.' (Another target for Wilkes was John Burnell who became lord mayor in 1787, aged eighty-four, the oldest lord mayor ever. He began life as a working stonemason. At a City banquet he was very awkward about cutting open a pie. 'You had better take a trowel to it', shouted Wilkes.) Sir Watkin made a wealthy marriage, but spent much of his fortune on unsuccessful attempts to get elected for Worcester. He subsequently sat for the City from 1781 to 1796, first as a Whig, later as a supporter of Pitt. The diarist William Hickey attended his Lord Mayor's Banquet and gave an account of it, which praises the standard of the Lord Mayor's hospitality but is scathing about the behaviour of the guests. Hickey complained of the crowded conditions.

> The heat from the crowd assembled and immense number of lights was disagreeable to all, to many quite oppressive and distressing. The Lord Mayor's table, at which I was, and nearly opposite his Lordship, was less so than other parts of the hall, from being considerably elevated above the rest. The wines were excellent, and the dinner the same, served, too, with as much regularity and decorum as if we had been in a private house; but far different was the scene in the body of the hall, where, in five minutes after the guests took their stations at the tables, the dishes were entirely cleared of their contents, twenty hands seizing the same joint of bird, and literally tearing it to pieces. A more determined scramble could not be; the roaring and noise was deafening and hideous, which increased as the liquor operated, bottles and glasses flying across from side to side without intermission. Such a bear garden altogether I never beheld.

In his later years Lewes got into severe financial difficulties and spent much time in the Fleet prison. On Wilkes's death he tried and failed to win the position of Chamberlain. It was offered to Sir Thomas Harley, who was also in difficulty because his bank had lost heavily in the financial crisis which followed the threatened invasion of 1797, but he declined the offer because he had promised to support Richard Clark. Clark, a Joiner, was lord mayor in 1784. He was a successful attorney who had strong literary interests. He was a friend of Dr Johnson, with whom he used to attend suppers at the Mitre tavern, and a Fellow of the Society of Antiquaries. He held the post of Chamberlain for thirty-three years.

The next lord mayor was Thomas Wright, Stationer, a publisher, partner and brother-in-law to his fellow Stationer, William Gill, lord mayor in 1788. The outstanding Stationer lord mayor in this period was John Boydell, who became a famous print-seller and publisher. Boydell was born in Shropshire in 1719, son of a land surveyor who expected his son to succeed him in business. But at twenty-one John walked to London and enrolled as a student at the St Martin's Lane Academy. He became apprenticed to W. H. Toms, an engraver, began selling small engravings of landscapes and amassed some capital. He was a competent artist, but recognizing his own talent was not outstanding, he decided to concentrate on publishing and printing the works of other artists. The business flourished and he began to sell his prints on the Continent, where they were very successful. For the first time English engravers and painters became known abroad. By the time he was lord mayor in 1790 the balance of foreign trade in prints had turned from import to export. In that year he published a collection of his engravings, commenting that it was 'the only book that had the honour of making a Lord Mayor of London'. In 1789 Boydell had begun a new venture. He built a gallery in Pall Mall, designed by George Dance the younger, and commissioned leading artists to paint scenes from Shakespeare, which were then printed. By 1802 it contained 162 works and 3 sculptures, including Thomas Bankes's *Apotheosis of Shakespeare*. Unfortunately the gallery was not a commercial success and Boydell's foreign trade was ruined by the wars. He had to apply to Parliament for permission to dispose of his property by lottery to clear his debts. (The gallery passed into the hands of an artists' group called the British Institution and was eventually demolished in 1868.) Boydell died in his house in Cheapside in December 1804, before the lottery was drawn. He had continued to live there, rising every morning at 5 a.m. and washing at the pump in Ironmonger Lane before beginning his work. His life may not have ended with commercial success but he was a public-spirited man who did much to encourage artists and raise England's prestige in the artistic world.

The artist Thomas Malton was full of praise for William Pickett, who was lord mayor the year before Boydell, because of his plans to widen the Strand and demolish Temple Bar to give traffic an easier passage. He got no support so Temple Bar remained until 1870, when it was removed to Theobalds Park, north of London. Pickett was a Goldsmith, whose firm, Pickett and Theed, took on Philip Rendell as a partner. Today Rendell, Bridge and Rendell, the successor of that firm, is one of London's major goldsmiths. The Goldsmiths' Company have a sad story about Pickett's daughter. When he was an alderman in 1772, she was dressing to accompany him to a civic feast, when her ballgown caught fire and she was killed.

The 1780s had been a comparatively quiet period in the City, but the mayors of the 1790s had to cope with many problems. Sir James Sanderson,

Draper, lord mayor in 1792, was thanked by the Common Council for the way in which he had controlled outbreaks of revolutionary enthusiasm and suppressed seditious meetings. He was later recommended for his baronetcy by Pitt, who wrote to the King, 'this will probably produce a very good effect in the City'. Paul Le Mesurier, Goldsmith, who followed him, was an outstanding lord mayor, and one of the youngest, being only thirty-eight when elected. He was born in Guernsey, son of the hereditary Governor of Alderney. He went into partnership with his wife's uncle and they made large sums as prize agents in the American war. He sat as Member of Parliament for Southwark from 1784 to 1796, and spoke mostly on East India affairs. For his opposition to Fox's India Bill he was made a director of the East India Company. During his year as sheriff he was noted for his humane treatment of prisoners in Newgate, where there was dreadful overcrowding because America was no longer available for the transportation of convicts. As lord mayor he skilfully handled mobs in the City who were angry about army recruitment. He was highly respected as a shrewd, courageous and public-spirited man, sober and enlightened in an age of affectation and excess.

Le Mesurier had been a Tory. The next lord mayor, Thomas Skinner, Haberdasher, was a staunch Whig, but he put party politics aside during his mayoralty. The ministry feared there would be riots, and wanted to bring in troops, but Skinner promised to keep the peace without resorting to force and succeeded. He was an eminent auctioneer, pilloried by Peter Pindar (a contemporary writer of satirical poems) as:

> Emperor of auctioneers
> Who, with a hammer and a conscience clear
> Pompously gets ten thousand pounds a year.

Few mayors escaped the satirists' notice, but Sir William Curtis attracted more ridicule than most. He was the son of Joseph Curtis of Wapping, a baker of ship's biscuits. He was an excellent example of a man of humble origins who made good in the City. The story is told of a prisoner brought before him, who pleaded 'Don't be hard on me. I remember how we used to stand side by side with our porters knots in Mincing Lane.' 'Yes', responded Curtis crisply, 'and if I'd been a fool like you I'd be standing there still.' William became a successful banker and was a friend of George IV, whom he accompanied to Scotland. He sat as a member of parliament almost continuously from 1790 to 1826 and held many official posts. He was likeable and convivial, but very fat, and an unconscious buffoon, so he was often caricatured as the City Gourmandiser, or in Highland dress as 'Wandering Willie'. He is popularly credited with being the originator of the phrase 'the three Rs', and is supposed to have fined himself five shillings as an example to the City for failing to keep the pavement outside the Mansion House clean.

Brook Watson, Musician, came from a poor Yorkshire family, was orphaned and sent to America to join a relative in business. When he was fourteen he was attacked by a shark at Havana and lost a leg. He recovered, went to Canada and was in business in Halifax, Nova Scotia. In 1759, having served under Wolfe, he returned to England and continued in trade, mostly with America. From 1786 to 1793 he acted as Colonial Agent for New Brunswick. He was a director of the Bank of England and MP for London 1784 to 1793. He then resigned his seat in order to take up the post of Commissary General to the Duke of York's Army in Flanders. He served with the Army until it returned to England in 1795. His mayoralty in 1796–7 spanned the worst year of the war with France. Ireland was in revolt, invasion was threatened, there was a serious mutiny in the Navy and terrible shortages of food. In Common Hall, Whig critics of the Government attempted to pass a resolution 'to investigate the real cause of the awful and alarming state of public affairs'. Brook Watson, a Tory, ruled this out of order and had the Mace taken up. At a subsequent Common Hall he was censured and a resolution was passed condemning the ministry for having plunged the country into an unnecessary and unjust war.

John William Anderson, who followed him, was fortunate in taking over at a time when the tide of war turned. However, he cut a comic figure at the royal service of thanksgiving for naval victories in December, when he had to lead the procession on horseback with two grooms holding him on. As a member of parliament he prided himself on his regular attendance, but had been absent from a debate at which he had intended to speak, so the current joke was that he had been busy taking riding lessons. Sir Richard Glyn, the next lord mayor, was a Tory, the eldest son of the lord mayor of 1759, and the most notable banker of his day. Then in 1799 Harvey Christian Combe was elected. He was a leading Whig, who had been chosen by the Livery as their preferred nominee for the last six years, but every time he had been passed over. Even now the Tory Aldermen tried to avoid electing him by choosing Thomas Skinner, a Whig and a respected lord mayor in 1794, but he refused to serve a second term. Combe, the son of an attorney in Andover, was apprenticed to his uncle, a corn factor. He married his cousin and went into the brewery business with his brother-in-law and became very wealthy. He was MP for London from 1796 to 1817. During his mayoralty there were bread riots in the City which he had to control with the aid of massed troops. Nonetheless he remained popular with the people, who at the next Lord Mayor's Banquet gave Combe, as late lord mayor, the accolade of removing the horses from his carriage and drawing him in it from Blackfriars to Guildhall. He continued as one of the most important Radicals in Parliament until his death in 1818.

Sir William Staines, lord mayor in 1800, also had his carriage drawn by the crowd as a sign of popularity. He was born in Southwark and was apprenticed to a Mason but ran away to sea. He soon regretted this, for he was taken as a prisoner of war for several months. He returned repentant and set to work. When he was working as a bricklayer in Uxbridge a parson's wife told him she had dreamt of him wearing a golden chain. Perhaps this spurred him on to become a successful paviour. He made a fortune honourably and by 1786 was wealthy enough to build and endow nine almshouses. His Lord Mayor's Day was outstanding because Lord Nelson, recently home from his victory on the Nile, attended the banquet and received a Sword of Honour from the Corporation. On this great occasion it was reported that 5,000 were present.

Sir John Perring, who was lord mayor in 1803, also had a connection with the Nelson family. He befriended Lady Hamilton and Nelson's daughter, Horatia, after the Admiral's death. Lady Hamilton was in desperate straits by then and was most grateful for his help. She wrote:

> I have been staying in Alderman and Lady Perrings last week Horatia had a great dinner given to her on her birthday the Lord Mayor drank her health and she was put on the table after dinner and she made a speech which made them all cry their is more Hospitality in the City than any where.

Another Alderman, Joshua Jonathan Smith, lord mayor in 1810, helped her to leave for France, where she ended her days.

Sir James Shaw became lord mayor in 1805, just after the battle of Trafalgar. News of the victory and of Nelson's death reached London on 5 November, a few days before his Lord Mayor's Day. The great Admiral's portrait was hung above the Lord Mayor's seat in Guildhall and his bust, garlanded with oak and laurel stood on the Sheriff's table. At the Lord Mayor's Banquet Pitt was the guest of honour and, in proposing the toast, the Lord Mayor thanked him for saving Europe. To this Pitt made his famous reply, 'I return you many thanks for the honour you have done me; but Europe is not to be saved by any single man. England has saved herself by her exertions and will, I trust, save Europe by her example.' Two months later Pitt himself was dead. Nelson's impressive funeral at St Paul's, took place in January 1806. The Lord Mayor, on horseback, with the Aldermen in scarlet gowns, met the procession at Temple Bar. The King was too ill to attend and the Prince of Wales attempted to take his place in front of the Lord Mayor, but Sir James insisted on his right to precedence over all save the King.

Shaw was the son of a Kilmarnock farmer. He went to America when he was seventeen and spent three years with a Scottish shipping firm in New York. He returned to London as a junior member of the firm and did well. He was a Tory MP and with his interest in shipping supported the London Port Improvement Bill. This was to set up new docks down river to relieve the congestion in the Thames, and was opposed by many City men who feared loss of business if the docks were removed from their control. In 1831 Shaw became Chamberlain after the death of Richard Clark, aged ninety-one. As Chamberlain he inadvertently invested £40,000 held by him as Banker to the Corporation in spurious Exchequer bills, which then flooded the market. Shaw was prepared to sacrifice his fortune to make good the loss, but a government commission exonerated him and he was repaid the full amount. He was zealous in aiding his fellow Scots and in particular made provision for Robert Burns's widow and arranged commissions for her sons. A statue to him was set up at Kilmarnock Cross in 1848.

City attitudes to the war veered from enthusiasm at the beginning to repeated demands for peace after the first two years. When peace was signed at Amiens in 1801 there was jubilation, but on the resumption of hostilities with France there was more support for the Government, and volunteer regiments were raised to face the threat of invasion. However, by 1808 the City was utterly dissatisfied with the conduct of the war and there were demands for parliamentary reform. In 1811 George III went into a hopeless decline and his son was at last made Prince Regent. City men looked to the dawn of a new era but were soon disillusioned when the Regent refused to receive a livery petition for parliamentary reform on the throne.

Finally the war turned in the Allies' favour, and in 1814 there was a great thanksgiving service in St Paul's for the fall of Napoleon; the Duke of Wellington was presented with the Freedom of the City. During the last few years most of the lord mayors had been men of no particular distinction. Samuel Birch, elected in 1814, was an interesting exception. He was the son of a London pastrycook who went into his father's business and became known as 'Mr Pattypan'. He inaugurated the famous turtle soup, which was first served at a Lord Mayor's Banquet in 1761, as a regular feature of the meal, and continued to be served until recent years. He was a man of strong literary and musical tastes, a poet and playwright, whose works were produced at Drury Lane. In 1836 he disposed of his father's business to Ring and Brymer, the well-known City caterers. He was also active politically and sat as MP for London 1817–43 as a Tory. He worked hard to raise volunteer regiments in the City, and was successful when there was real fear of a French invasion. He was Colonel Commandant of the first regiment of Loyal London Volunteers.

The post war period was a time of depression with food shortages, unemployment and general discontent. The City was crowded with vagrants, discharged soldiers and foreign seamen. Demands for parliamentary reform grew, but in this movement the City was no longer the leader. London was now too big and diverse for the City to be the focus of a reform movement and the initiative passed to Westminster and to the provinces. But there was a strong opposition party in Common Hall and several of the aldermen who became lord mayor were supporters of reform. They were: Harvey Christian Combe (1799), Thomas Smith (1809), Joshua Jonathan Smith (1810), Matthew Wood (1815 and 1816), John Thomas Thorp (1820) and Robert Waithman (1823).

Matthew Wood was the son of a sergemaker in Tiverton, Devon. He was brought up as a Dissenter and was sent for a time to Blundell's Free Grammar School, but left at an early age to assist his father. At fourteen he was apprenticed to his cousin, a chemist in Exeter. He began travelling for a druggist, came to London to work for a firm in Bishopsgate, and set up his own business. He was elected to the Common Council for Cripplegate in 1802, and in 1807 was elected alderman for that ward. He was an able man, admirably suited to serving as lord mayor in a tense and difficult time. As lord mayor he was very popular for the way he promoted resistance to repressive government measures and for his campaign against the London underworld. Improvements in the City planned in his time were the new London Bridge, a new debtors' prison and a new post office. His popularity was such that he was re-elected in 1816, although the

Government was so hostile that all the Ministers absented themselves from his second Lord Mayor's Banquet (as they had from his first). The Prince Regent referred to him as 'that beast Wood'. A splendid new barge, which had been completed that September and was named the *Maria Wood* after his daughter, carried him to Westminster.

In December 1816 Matthew Wood had to deal with one of the most serious public outbursts against Government repression: the Spa Fields Riots. A huge public meeting got out of hand and the crowd marched from Clerkenwell towards the City, breaking into a gunmaker's shop on the way. Matthew Wood, with a few supporters, went to meet them as they advanced down Aldersgate Street. He described how 'a man with a tricoloured cockade in his hat came up to me with a desire to explain. I had him in the centre, when two fellows levelled their Musketts at me. I said, "Fire away you rascals". One of them fired.' Fortunately he missed and, nothing daunted, Wood, followed by Sir James Shaw, 'whose zeal, activity, coolness and undaunted courage gave valuable assistance', pursued them to the East End where they dispersed. On his return to the Mansion House he was touched to find Sir William Curtis, lord mayor in 1795, 'who in his zeal for public service had lost sight of all his personal ailments and had come, ill as he was, to offer me his best services'. 'Repertory of the Court of Aldermen' (Sharpe, *London and the Kingdom*).

Wood had done his duty as chief magistrate, but he sympathized with the demands of the rioters for reform. A City petition in 1817 declared that all they desired was 'to see the House of Commons in conformity with pure constitutional principles, a fair and honest organ of the public voice, exercising a controlling power over the servants of the Crown and not an instrument in their hands to oppress the people'. Further Government repression gave added impetus to the movement for reform. In 1817 habeas corpus was suspended. In 1819 the massacre known as 'Peterloo' when the troops charged a peaceful crowd in Manchester, was followed by the repressive Six Acts which restricted public meetings and curbed the freedom of the press.

It is against this background that we should look at the affair of Queen Caroline. Caroline of Brunswick was married to George, Prince of Wales, in 1795. The marriage was a disaster, for George, who was anyway illegally married to Mrs Fitzherbert, rejected Caroline early on. She retreated to Europe, where stories of her eccentric behaviour multiplied. In England, and especially in the City, popular feeling was sympathetic to her as an ill-treated wife. Common Hall was strongly on her side and even in the Court of Aldermen she had friends in Matthew Wood and Robert Waithman. In 1820 George III died and the Regent at last succeeded to the throne as George IV. He decided to start divorce proceedings against Caroline, but she was determined to take her place as Queen. Matthew Wood went to France to meet her, advised her to come to England at once and escorted her back for a triumphal entry to London. The enthusiasm of the Londoners is difficult to explain simply as compassion for a wronged woman. Caroline provided a focus for the radicals' resentment of Government policies. A Bill of Pains and Penalties condemning her behaviour was brought against her in Parliament. The enquiry went on for weeks until the bill was dropped for lack of support. Public rejoicing was overwhelming. London was illuminated for three nights, the mob as usual smashing the windows of all houses not lit up. The Duke of Wellington's coach was stopped by an angry crowd which demanded that he drink the Queen's health. 'Well, gentlemen, if you will have it so, the Queen', replied the Duke coolly, 'and may your wives be like her.' Caroline went to St Paul's to give thanks for the failure of the bill and was ceremonially met at Temple Bar by the Lord Mayor, John Thomas Thorp, with the Sheriffs and several Aldermen, including Matthew Wood. The following summer she made a pathetic attempt to get into Westminster Abbey for the Coronation but found all doors barred against her. After this her health declined and she died a few weeks later. Her funeral journey from her house in Hammersmith to Harwich for her burial in Brunswick was deliberately directed away from the City. The Londoners refused to accept this and simply blocked all the alternative roads so that the military were forced to bring the cortège through the City streets. In Knightsbridge there was a fracas when the mob pelted the soldiers with sticks and mud. The soldiers opened fire and two people were shot. Then the procession passed in an orderly way through the City with the Lord Mayor, John Thomas Thorp, at its head. Two weeks later Robert Waithman, then sheriff, was involved in supervising the funeral of the two men who had been shot. There was trouble and he narrowly avoided injury when a bullet passed through his carriage.

George IV was the last monarch to hold a coronation banquet in Westminster Hall, so Thorp was the last lord mayor to serve as butler and receive the traditional cup and ewer for his services. Robert Waithman became lord mayor in 1823. He was born in Wrexham in 1764 and orphaned at four months. His uncle, a Bath linen draper, adopted him, and by the time he was thirty he had established himself in business and moved to London, where he amassed a considerable fortune. Fired by enthusiasm for the French Revolution, he threw himself into politics, beginning with the Common Council in 1794. In 1818 he was elected Member of Parliament for the City, and was one of the most ardent reformers.

The restrictive laws against the Catholics were the first to succumb to the reformers and in 1828 George IV most unwillingly gave his assent to the repeal of the old Test and Corporation Acts. The offensive anti-Catholic inscription on the Monument, which had been placed there in 1681 by Sir Patience Ward, and read 'But Popish frenzy which wrought such horrors is not yet quenched' was removed in 1830. Parliamentary reform had to wait for a new king. In 1830 George IV died and his brother William IV succeeded to the throne. The Livery prepared an address of congratulation, disclaiming 'the fulsome strains of unmeaning flattery' and pointing out that the people were not fairly represented, but the King refused to receive the address on the throne, so it was never presented.

The Lord Mayor in 1830 and throughout the passage of the Reform Bill was Sir John Key. He had joined his father's wholesale stationery business, and duly became a Liveryman of the Stationers' Company, of which he was Master in 1830. He was then thirty-six years old. He faced a dangerous situation with his Lord Mayor's Banquet because Wellington, who was now Prime Minister, was opposed to parliamentary reform and therefore very unpopular in the City. He and the King and Queen had as usual been invited to the banquet, but it was clear that there would be riots. Key took the decision to write and advise them not to come and his advice was taken. Common Council criticized him for 'this indiscreet and unauthorised action' but he was probably right. As it was there was a minor affray at Temple Bar where the mob threw stones across the City boundary at the recently formed Metropolitan Police.

Lord Grey became Prime Minister and introduced a Reform Bill into the House of Commons in 1831. It passed the Commons in September but was promptly rejected by the Lords. There were riots and demonstrations all over the country. Common Council presented an address to the King, warning of commotions. The King received them graciously and urged them to do all they could to prevent violence. In this tense atmosphere the election of the lord mayor took place. Key was nominated for a second term by Common Hall, but turned down twice by the Court of Aldermen, who attempted to persuade first John Thomas Thorp and then William Thompson, both ex-lord mayors, before reluctantly electing

Key. The Livery warmly thanked him for his zeal over parliamentary reform and for upholding the election rights of Common Hall against the 'secret tribunal' of the Court of Aldermen. He was made a baronet at the opening of Rennie's London Bridge in 1831 and was Chamberlain from 1853 to 1858.

The struggle to pass the Reform Bill continued. In May 1832 the House of Lords again rejected the Bill and Lord Grey urged the King to create enough new peers to outvote the diehards. When the King refused to do this Grey resigned and there was widespread public dismay. The newspapers came out in mourning with black borders. For nine days there was no effective government and there was genuine danger of revolt. Then the King gave way, Grey returned, the threat of an influx of Whig peers forced the Lords to give in and the Reform Act became law. Not all the democratic measures for which the City radicals and other reformers had fought were included. There was no secret ballot, no annual Parliaments, no universal suffrage. But the rotten boroughs were abolished, parliamentary representation was more fairly distributed throughout the country and every man owning property worth £10 per annum got the vote. In the City these voters were added to the Liverymen, who had until then elected the City's Members of Parliament. The Freedom of the City was presented to Lord Grey, to Lord Althorp, then Leader of the House of Commons (he succeeded to the Earldom in 1834), and to the great Birmingham reformer, Thomas Attwood, who said of the City, 'It has ever stood in the van of the people in their fight for liberty.'

10

RETRENCHMENT AND
REVIVAL

Although the City had played a leading role in the movement for parliamentary reform, it took a very different view when the reformers turned their attention to the government of London itself. By the mid nineteenth century the problems of running the vast and ever-spreading metropolis, the Great Wen, as William Cobbett called it, had become acute. Already in the seventeenth century the City of London burst over its borders and new areas of concentrated population had grown up which were not administered by the Lord Mayor and the Corporation. At that time the population of London as a whole was about 250,000 and that of the City about 150,000. Charles I's Government put forward a plan for the incorporation of the suburbs in London but it received no support from the City leaders, who preferred to concentrate on an area, defined by established ward boundaries, which they could control. The outbreak of the Civil War prevented further discussion of the project and it was not taken up again. By the beginning of the eighteenth century the population of the City numbered about 200,000 while that of all London was about 600,000. When the first official Census was taken in 1801 the City's population was 127,621, and that of all London over 860,000. The 1811 Census revealed that nine-tenths of Londoners lived outside the ancient City. This vast population was administered by a motley collection of parish vestries. There was no overall policy for sewerage, burial grounds, housing or police.

In the face of these enormous problems the City presented a picture of reactionary complacency. The Corporation of London would not concern itself with the administration of Greater London, although it had a monopoly of markets within seven miles, it collected coal duties over a radius of twelve miles (some of the coal posts marking this area can be seen in outlying suburbs to this day) and it governed the River Thames for eighty miles from Staines to the Medway, including, of course, the Port of London. The members of the City Livery Companies, who took part in the election of the lord mayor, himself a liveryman, and who elected the sheriffs and the City members of parliament, controlled the accumulated wealth of centuries and presented a picture of a body of men 'replete with privilege'. To many would-be reformers it was intolerable that the City refused to take any responsibility generally beyond its historic borders, and the City government came under successive attacks during the nineteenth and twentieth centuries.

It would be satisfying to be able to portray London's lord mayors as playing a major role in these matters, either as heroic defenders of the City's liberties against all comers, or alternatively as high-minded reformers. The usual assumption about nineteenth-century lord mayors is that they were a dull and mediocre lot, inclined to be old and fat. In fact no generalization about them stands up to close inspection of the men involved. Some were indeed diehard reactionaries; others supported reforming measures. They did tend to be less colourful than those of the eighteenth century, and from the beginning of Victoria's reign party politics gradually ceased, at least in any obvious way, to influence the choice of lord mayor. Only a few of them now were among the ranks of the leading bankers and company directors. But the office of lord mayor was sturdily maintained by a succession of men who, as we shall see, had strong individual interests and many merits. In time they began to find a new role in a changing society.

Meanwhile, they were often the butt of satire and adverse comment. In 1843 an imaginary conversation on the subject of the lord mayors was published in the *Westminster Review*, which sums up the main points of criticism.

Who is the Lord Mayor? I read in your journals that he lately gave a dinner at which nearly all the Cabinet Ministers were present, with the Governor of the Bank of England, and the Chairman of the East India Company; is it that he is a man so remarkable for talent or superior intelligence that your great men are proud of his society?

Why – not exactly.

Is it from respect to the interests of commerce? The Lord Mayor is perhaps the first of your London merchants?

There are greater.

Is it then because of his position; and certainly it is a noble one – the representative of London – the metropolis of the world; a population of two millions –

Of whom not more than one fifteenth portion are under his control.

But did I not read somewhere that there were more than a hundred parishes in the City?

All of them not so large as the one parish of Marylebone, the vestry of which has more power over the church, the poor, and the ordinary business of local government than all the officers of the London Corporation! The respect of which you speak is paid only to a dream of the past, and to custom, the chains of which bind even a strong mind, till they are broken by a stronger.

And this chief of a subordinate department who invites our ambassador to dine; whose accession to office, as I have heard, is honoured by a state procession; whose expenses for any one year must exceed the revenues of a German prince – this Lord Mayor –

Is only the Alderman in rotation, the worthy representative of perhaps eighty resident freemen in the Ward of Bridge.

We have seen that in the eighteenth century the lord mayor could actually be the governor of the Bank of England or the chairman of the East India Company. Many were among the City's greatest merchants. Now it was a different matter. The great leaders of commerce and finance were far too busy to become involved in civic government. In any case the work of the lord mayor would not have interested them. Most of his time at this period was spent on what Sidney and Beatrice Webb, in their analysis of local government, described as 'the dull decorum of the Aldermanic bench' and 'the daily grind of the Justice Room'. The lord mayor had to spend hours of every day trying cases in the Mansion House Justice Room and dealing with a stream of applicants. Small wonder that the job did not appeal to men of distinction. The reformer Francis Place wrote in 1833 'they always catch a fool to make a Lord Mayor of; there is, however, very little difficulty in this fool catching, as no-one who approximated to a wise man would take the office'. But this was less than fair to many mid nineteenth century lord mayors.

The Lord Mayor for the year 1832–3 was Sir Peter Laurie, a good example of an honourable and hard-working chief magistrate. He was a Scottish farmer's son, who came to London as a lad and worked his way up in business. In due course he made money as a contractor for the Indian Army and was able to retire from business in 1827, having taken his nephews into partnership. In 1829 he became chairman of the Union Bank and remained so until his death in 1862. He was a member of the Saddlers' Company, served as sheriff in 1823 and became the Alderman for Aldersgate in 1826. He was fifty-four when he was elected lord mayor, in which office his chief work was indeed as a magistrate. He had a reputation for exceptional shrewdness and fairness. He was unfairly satirized by Dickens as Alderman Cute in *The Chimes* with his plan for cutting down the number of suicides from Blackfriars Bridge by punishing them for the attempt. A more typical picture of his fairness and common sense comes from the case of a costermonger's son who was accused of ill-treating a donkey. Giving evidence, the costermonger said the donkey was 'as good a hass as ever goes on two legs'. 'He goes on four legs, father,' said the boy, 'hasses never goes on two legs.' 'Don't contradict your father, boy,' reprimanded Sir Peter Laurie. 'He's perfectly right in talking of two-legged asses. There are more of that sort than the other.'

Henry Winchester, elected mayor in 1834, was an example of the worst type of lord mayor of this period. A diehard reactionary, he had held out against Sir John Key and the Reform Bill to the end, and refused to listen to the views of liberals in Common Hall and the Court of Common Council. The Court of Aldermen was sharply divided over his election, and the doubts of those who opposed him were fully justified when he refused to call Common Hall and Common Council when requested and would not allow political meetings and discussions in Guildhall. At the end of his mayoralty the customary vote of thanks by the Common Council gained a negative response, and shortly afterwards they passed a vote of censure upon him.

The next lord mayor, William Taylor Copeland, was a much more stimulating man. He came from Stoke-on-Trent and at thirty-eight was one of the youngest lord mayors. He was the son of Josiah Spode's partner and a very successful salesman, who persuaded the Goldsmiths' Company, of which he was a member, to buy Spode china for the Hall. He became head of the firm, which he ran very efficiently. He was instrumental in regenerating the potteries industry and in making Spode china famous all over the world. He sat as Member of Parliament for Coleraine, and then for Stoke-on-Trent for many years, and was later involved in defending the City against reforming proposals in the 1850s.

Thomas Kelly, lord mayor in 1836, began life as a shepherd boy. He was the son of a Kent farmer and came to London when he was fourteen to work in a brewery. Later he worked for a bookseller in Paternoster Row and eventually became a successful publisher himself, doing particularly well out of printing bibles. He was lord mayor when Queen Victoria acceded to the throne. On the death of William IV on 20 June 1837, Kelly received a personal letter from Lord John Russell, requesting him to give instructions for tolling the great bell of St Paul's. He went with the Aldermen to Kensington Palace to meet the eighteen-year-old Queen and then proceeded with the Heralds to proclaim her Accession at St James's Palace; opposite Northumberland House; at the corner of Chancery Lane; in Cheapside; and at the Royal Exchange. Another significant event in his mayoralty was the opening of London's first railway, the London to Greenwich line, in December 1836. Improved transport, at first with omnibuses and then with railways, was one of the most influential factors in London's growth, making it possible for people to travel in to work in the capital from an ever-widening radius.

From the beginning of Queen Victoria's reign relations between the City and the Crown were harmonious, and it was through this relationship that the lord mayor's role as host for royalty and national and international figures developed. This had been an important function of the mayoralty from very early days, as we have seen, but from the mid nineteenth century onwards, the entertainment of visiting royalty and heads of state provided the highlight of most mayoral years. Critics of the mayoralty might scoff, but with centuries of tradition behind him, the lord mayor, even if of humble origin, was able to carry out this important duty with dignity and not a little pageantry.

Possibly because the City no longer played a major role in national politics these gradually ceased to have a significant influence on the choice of aldermen or lord mayors. This is not to say that individual lord mayors took no interest in politics. Several of them served as members of parliament throughout the nineteenth century and well into the twentieth century, although the proportion was nowhere near as high as it had been in the eighteenth century and it became very rare for a man to be an MP during his year of office. As members of parliament, lord mayors belonged to political parties, but they did not allow this to influence their actions as lord mayor. The Corporation had begun to be non-party-political.

Another important aspect of the mayoralty noticeable from the mid nineteenth century onwards was the use of the influence of the lord mayor to raise large sums of money for charitable use. Earlier lord mayors had bequeathed much of their personal fortunes to charity. Eighteenth-century lord mayors had gone round the streets collecting for the poor. In the nineteenth and twentieth centuries they set up funds to help, for instance, the victims of disasters in Britain and all over the world.

To return to the vexed question of reform, well before the Reform Act of 1832 the Corporation had been forced to agree to the setting up of docks outside the City. It was not until the Thames became hopelessly clogged with ships that they agreed to co-operate in the building of new docks down river, the West India, East India, and London and Surrey Docks. Another question was that of policing London. Robert Peel founded the Metropolitan Police in 1829, but the City, with which Peel said he was 'afraid to meddle', refused to have their policing arrangements amalgamated with the new London force. Ten years later they set up the City Police on similar lines to the 'Met' and kept them independent, as they are to this day. The office of City Marshal, hitherto in charge of law and order in the City, became purely ceremonial. The Municipal Reform Act of 1835, which reconstituted local government on more democratic lines, left the Corporation of London untouched, this task being simply put off. In fact the Corporation of London compared well with most other city governments, with a relatively democratic franchise and an efficient administration. It was even held up as a model for the new councils. A small change by the City itself was the reduction of the Freedom fine (i.e., the charge for purchasing the Freedom). The City was exempted from the Public Health Act, but fear of cholera led the Corporation to appoint a Medical Officer of Health and put through its own, very necessary, programme of health reform.

It was not until 1852 that the first Royal Commission was set up to investigate the City government and make proposals for change. Its findings did not reveal any great scandal. Indeed the City's officers were found to be very competent, notably Sir John Key, lord mayor during the passage of the Reform Act and now Chamberlain (i.e., Treasurer). But not one of the Aldermen lived in the City and only twenty-five of the Common Councilmen did. The men of highest rank in finance and commerce were not involved in the Corporation and the Common Council was 'a parliament of shopkeepers'. With a few exceptions, the great Livery Companies had lost interest in the City government and most lord mayors now came from the smaller companies. By now the Lord Mayor's Show retained little of its former splendour, although it continued every year, with a few men in armour to remind people of the City's historic traditions. Critics were inclined to be dismissive. Charles Pearson, a reforming Common Councilman, later to be the City Solicitor, wrote in 1834 (W. Carpenter, *The Corporation of London*):

> The time has arrived when the civic exhibitions, with the Mayor as chief performer can no longer be tolerated. I have, in disguise, mixed with the attendant crowd on a Lord Mayor's Day, and I declare that the whole parade is the subject of the most contemptuous sneering, even amongst children; and the apprentices, instead of being moved, as in the days of Whittington, with the spirit of competition and glory, at seeing the gilt coach, laugh aloud as it trundles along.

In 1854 an article entitled 'The Decline and Fall of the City of London' in *Fraser's Magazine* stated: 'It cannot survive the year; the last Lord Mayor's Show has been given; the stage coach has been bespoke by Madame Tussauds – Gog and Magog doing duty as humble firewood will frown no more over turtle and champagne.'

But they were wrong. The difficulty of finding an alternative to the City government led to the failure of a series of parliamentary bills containing radical proposals: either to abolish the Corporation; to alter the system of electing its officers; to extend its boundaries; or to leave its boundaries and set up separate municipal districts in the outlying areas. A major problem was the reformers' own fear of creating a huge new authority. Within the City itself there was a strong faction determined to resist any tampering with ancient rights and privileges, even though there were many City men, particularly in the Common Council, and even among the aldermen, who were in favour of reform of some kind. However they examined all proposals critically and were scornful of the reformers' failure to come up with ideas which won general support. Sir James Duke, lord mayor in 1848, had written: 'My experience has shown me that the office of Lord Mayor is one of great responsibility, of great labour and of very great anxiety'. As a City Member of Parliament he fought the 1856 bill for the reform of London, together with William Taylor Copeland, lord mayor in 1835, and William Cubitt, lord mayor in 1860. The Corporation sought to modify, rather than destroy the bill, but the Government, caught between City opposition and the demands of the more extreme reformers, dithered and the bill collapsed. 'Nothing could be more lamentable', said Duke, 'than to see a feeble government abandoning a good measure in order to please a section of its supporters.' Other City leaders involved in its defence at this time were William Lawrence, lord mayor in 1863, and his brother James Lawrence, lord mayor in 1868, who was dubbed the City Demosthenes for his ardent attack in Common Hall on the Government measure. David Williams Wire, lord mayor in 1858 and an eminent solicitor, claimed that the City would have done more to promote reform of its constitution if Parliament had left it alone. Part of the trouble in 1856 was that the Government was distracted by the Crimean War and subsequent changes of ministers meant that the question of reforming the City was shelved for the time being.

However, something in London as a whole had to be done about the urgent problems of public hygiene. The Metropolis Local Management Act set up thirty-eight local units which, together with the City, were to send delegates to a Metropolitan Board of Works which was given the job of supervising improvements. The chairman was Sir Benjamin Hall (after whom Big Ben is named). An immediate priority was the condition of the River Thames which was so full of sewage that the stink penetrated the handsome new Houses of Parliament. In the hot June of 1858 the closed windows had to be covered with curtains soaked in chloride of lime. One of the first acts of the Metropolitan Board of Works was to construct a main sewer to carry the sewage away downstream. By then the City no longer controlled the Thames, because in 1857 the Thames Conservancy had been set up. This had a board of twelve Conservators which included the Lord Mayor, two Aldermen and four members of the Common Council, as well as the Deputy Master of Trinity House, three nominated by the Government and one by Trinity House Corporation. From this time on the Lord Mayor's Show ceased to include a water procession.

An examination of the lord mayors in the mid nineteenth century shows them to be men whose careers illustrate new developments in the character of the office. Thomas Farncomb, Tallow Chandler, 1849, came from Sussex and was a merchant and shipowner, who became a successful wharfinger. He was one of the earliest promoters of the London and Westminster Bank. He held a lavish banquet in the Mansion House for mayors from all over the United Kingdom, at which Prince Albert announced plans for the Great Exhibition of 1851. As a native of Sussex, Farncomb made a state visit to Rye. This illustrates not only the interests outside the City of the lord mayors, but also the new freedom of the lord mayor to travel during his year of office. Sir Francis Child, for example,

The Coronation luncheon for Queen Elizabeth II in Guildhall by Terence Cuneo, 1953 (Lord Mayor, Sir Rupert De La Bère).

The Silver Jubilee luncheon for Queen
Elizabeth II in Guildhall, 1977 (Lord
Mayor, Sir Robin Gillett).

Queen Elizabeth the Queen Mother's
eightieth birthday service, 1980. On the
steps of St Paul's Cathedral with
Sir Peter Gadsden (1979).

Sir Christopher Leaver (1981) with the
Prime Minister of Singapore, Lee Kwan
Yew, in the Mansion House.

Dame Mary Donaldson (1983) in the
Mansion House.

Sir Alan Traill (1984) with President Julius Nyerere of Tanzania.

The Prime Minister, Margaret Thatcher, speaking at Sir Allan Davis's Lord Mayor's banquet, 1985.

The Silent Ceremony, 1986.

A fanfare after the election of Sir Greville Spratt (1987) *right*, with Sir David Rowe-Ham (1986).

The Lord Mayor's coach in the Show with pikemen and musketeers from the Honourable Artillery Company.

in 1731 had had to write to the Secretary of State to ask leave of absence from the King 'to go sometimes for a day or two to my house in Middlesex' (Osterley).

Thomas Challis, Butcher, 1852, was born in Fore Street, became a hide merchant, and was known as a painstaking magistrate who, 'throughout his term of office', as his *Times* obituary put it, 'took a leading part in encouraging the formation of schools of art and other educational matters'. There was no Lord Mayor's Show in his year because of the death of the Duke of Wellington that September and his stupendous funeral in St Paul's in November. But the Show for Thomas Sidney in 1853, inspired by the Great Exhibition, had allegorical representations of Justice, the Nations, and Prosperity. It was a change which met with much public criticism, and a *Punch* cartoon illustrated the 'Lament of the Man in Brass' (the traditional men in armour), but it was the beginning of a new attitude to the display, which now proclaimed national themes rather than the values of an individual livery company.

Francis Moon, Stationer, 1854, was one of London's outstanding publishing lord mayors. The youngest son of a gold and silver smith, he was placed as a boy with a Mr Tugwell, book and print seller. Moon took over the business on Mr Tugwell's death and became a large-scale printseller. When the successors of John Boydell (lord mayor 1790) became bankrupt he purchased most of their stock. He was a man of fine taste and judgement who received the patronage of the English and many European courts and was invited to St Cloud by King Louis Philippe of France. One of his most celebrated publications was David Roberts's *Sketches in the Holy Land*, which are still sold throughout the Middle East. On his Lord Mayor's Day Guildhall was decorated with a huge painting by David Roberts, representing the French and English as allies. In April 1855 Moon entertained the Emperor Napoleon III and his Empress and was created baronet. He later visited Paris where he was fêted by the aristocracy.

The election of David Salomons, the first Jewish lord mayor, the following year was a milestone on the way to religious toleration, and showed the City, even in this period, as far from reactionary in all matters. Salomons was the second son of a merchant and underwriter of London and was brought up to the commercial life. In 1832 at the age of thirty-five he was one of the founders of the London and Westminster Bank. He distinguished himself by his charitable contributions and benevolent efforts in the City, and was clearly eminently suited for the municipal office which he sought. The difficulty was whether a man could be bound by an oath not taken on the Christian Bible. In 1830 a Common Council Act extended the Freedom to all natural-born subjects not professing Christianity but otherwise qualified, allowing them to take the freemen's oath in accordance with their own religious beliefs. Salomons was elected sheriff, the first Jew to hold the office, in 1835. At the close of that year he was presented with a massive silver ornament by fellow Jews as 'an acknowledgement of his exertions in the cause of religious liberty'. He became the Alderman of Cordwainer Ward in 1847 and lord mayor in 1855. He had been trying for years to get into Parliament and was returned for Greenwich in 1851, but could not take his seat because of the parliamentary oath. A fellow Jew, Lionel Rothschild, had been returned for the City since 1847, but had been likewise unable to take his seat. Thanks to his family's influence the parliamentary oath was finally altered in 1858 and Rothschild duly entered Parliament. Salomons was elected Liberal MP for Greenwich in 1859 and held the seat until this death in 1873. At the end of his mayoralty he received a unique address of congratulation from merchants and bankers of the City. Both he and Rothschild endowed scholarships at the City of London School. Salomons left £1,000 to the Guildhall Library.

Thomas Finnis was lord mayor in the year of the Indian Mutiny. His brother, a famous colonel in the Indian Army, was killed at the outbreak of the Mutiny, and in memory of his brother Finnis inaugurated and promoted the Indian Mutiny Relief Fund, the first of the great Lord Mayor's relief funds. William Cubitt, Fishmonger, and younger brother of the famous builder, Thomas Cubitt, became lord mayor in 1860. He began work with his brother at their Gray's Inn Road works, and continued to run those works when Thomas turned to large-scale house-building. William Cubitt retired from building work in 1851, aged sixty, and concentrated on his civic duties. He was MP for Andover from 1847 on, and in that same year served as sheriff. In 1851 he was elected Alderman for Langbourn. He was actively involved in the defence of the City against Government bills in the 1850s. During his mayoralty he extended splendid hospitality to foreign commissioners and others connected with the International Exhibition of 1861. He was so successful that he was re-elected the next year and so was the last lord mayor to serve two years running. He took a leading part in originating the public subscription for a memorial to Prince Albert, who died in December 1861. Over a quarter of a million pounds was sent to the Mansion House for charitable funds, especially to provide relief for the victims of a dreadful explosion in the Hartley Colliery, and for distress among the Lancashire cotton-workers (caused by the American Civil War). He died at Andover in 1863. Funeral sermons were preached in many Lancashire towns at the request of the workers, who appreciated how much he had helped them.

Warren Stormes Hale, Tallow Chandler, lord mayor in 1864 at the age of seventy-three, was an orphan from a Hertfordshire family, who began in the City as an apprentice to his brother, a Wax Chandler in Cannon Street. Hale became a member of the Common Council in 1826, Alderman of Coleman Street in 1856 and sheriff in 1858. Back in 1833 he was instrumental in getting the Corporation to use the medieval John Carpenter foundation of a school for poor boys as the basis for setting up a large public day school, the City of London School. It opened in 1837 in Milk Street, moved to the Victoria Embankment in 1883, and has recently moved to new premises nearby. He also promoted the foundation of the Freemen's Orphans' School in 1854, and founded the Warren Stormes Hale Scholarship.

Benjamin Phillips, Spectacle Maker, was the first Jew to become a member of the Common Council in 1847. He became sheriff in 1859 and lord mayor in 1865. He was a fancy goods warehouse-owner, and married the sister of his business partner, Faudel. Their son, George Faudel-Phillips, was lord mayor in 1896. Phillips was a fine linguist and orator, who was proud of being an ordinary citizen who had made his own way. Montague Williams in *Leaves of a Life* described how Sir Benjamin (he was knighted in 1866) took him to Commercial Road and pointed out a little bead shop where he and his wife began the business which was now the great house of Faudel, Phillips and Company.

During his mayoralty Phillips entertained the King and Queen of the Belgians at the Mansion House, and set up a fund for the relief of cholera in London. In 1866 he held a great meeting in Guildhall in favour of the Second Reform Bill, another occasion on which the City supported parliamentary reform. There were said to be 5,000–6,000 people present. In the 1867 Reform Act the City's government was reformed, in that the freedom qualification for the franchise in the wards was abolished, and £10 ratepayers and those on the parliamentary register could vote for Common Councilmen and Aldermen.

Thomas Gabriel, Goldsmith, 1866, was the fourth son of a Brixton timber merchant and began his business life in his father's firm. His mayoralty was eventful in a variety of ways. The City had now begun to undertake certain important building improvements, and during his year the chief stone of the new Holborn Viaduct was laid and the cornerstone of the new Smithfield dead meat market. (The old live cattle market, a serious health hazard, had been moved to Islington in 1855.) The first Day Census was held in the City on 13 December, revealing that it had a night population of 113,387 and a day count of 283,520 thus showing that more than twice as many people travelled in to work as lived there. Gabriel held a magnificent reception for Sultan Abdul Aziz of Turkey and Ismail Pasha, Viceroy of Egypt, for which he was created baronet. He went on a return visit to Turkey and also headed the corporation visit to Paris for their Great Exhibition.

In contrast, the mayoralty of William Ferneley Allen, who followed him, was a rather dour affair. When Allen was lord mayor elect the Lord Chancellor warned him: 'This is an age in which nothing can be expected to stand on the foundations of mere custom and antiquity.' Taking heed, Allen dispensed with the Lord Mayor's coach in his procession. This caused much public dissatisfaction and his Show was satirised in poems and cartoons. He said he preferred his private carriage to being jolted in the state coach. In 1858 he had published a defence of the City entitled *The Corporation of London, Its Rights and Privileges*. In it he asked: 'Are the citizens of London, are the people of Great Britain, prepared to resign without a struggle the last of the glorious rights and privileges bequeathed to them by their Saxon ancestors?'

The lives of all these men illustrate different aspects of the mayoralty – personal endeavour and achievement, lavish hospitality, raising of funds for victims of disasters, concern with education, liberal philosophy. They demonstrate that the mayoralty was by no means a 'mere magistracy'. By the 1870s the City was attracting men of a higher calibre and beginning to look for more ways of making a positive contribution to the well-being of the people. The Livery Companies too were becoming more active and attracting new members from among businessmen. Some of this interest had a political motive as men saw the City as a bulwark against radicalism. As national politics became more clearly defined in the late nineteenth century the Conservatives aimed to preserve the City, the Liberals to reform it.

In 1871 the Corporation made its first approach to the Government about the possibility of buying Epping Forest as a place of recreation for the people of London. In 1872 a meeting was held in the Mansion House when Sills Gibbons was lord mayor to consider how the City guilds could revert to their ancient function of directing the arts and manufactures of the country.

In October 1872 a leading Liberal philanthropist was elected lord mayor. Sydney Waterlow, Stationer, was born in Finsbury in 1822, the fourth son from a family of Walloon descent. They were printers and stationers, and Sydney began his working life as an apprentice to his uncle. With his brothers he built up a highly successful business. They did particularly well out of publishing the *Bankers' Magazine*. In 1862, at his own expense, he built a block of dwellings for working-class families. He took great care to ascertain what sort of homes workmen actually wanted and put the enterprise on a proper business footing by setting up the Improved Industrial Dwellings Company Limited. He entered civic government through the Common Council and then was elected Alderman of Langbourn. In 1866–7 he served as sheriff, visited Turkey and the Paris Exhibition with Thomas Gabriel and was knighted. In 1868 he was elected Liberal MP for Dumfriesshire and afterwards sat for Maidstone and for Gravesend. He was deeply concerned with work for St Bartholomew's Hospital, of which he was Treasurer, and in 1871 he bought Lauderdale House in Highgate and presented it to the Hospital as a convalescent home. When they ceased to use it he presented the house and grounds to the newly formed London County Council (LCC) in 1889. The grounds now form Waterlow Park, and his statue, donated by public subscription, stands at the top of the hill. During his mayoralty he set up the Hospital Sunday Fund at a meeting in the Egyptian Hall, which was based on the idea of making a collection in the metropolitan churches on one Sunday in each year. It was followed by many similar funds. An entirely different event in the Egyptian Hall was a brilliant fancy dress ball held there during his year. He also entertained the Shah of Persia. He continued an active public life long after his time as lord mayor and was chairman and treasurer of various organizations. As a member of parliament his liberal principles led him to speak in favour of reform of the Corporation, and he advocated a single large municipality, while retaining the City's control and traditions.

Andrew Lusk, who followed him, was also a Liberal, sitting as MP for Finsbury from 1865 to 1885. He was a farmer's son from Ayrshire who set up a grocery business with his brother in Greenock, moved to London when he was thirty, and dealt in groceries and the supply of ships' provisions. He became the chairman of the General Life and Fire Insurance Company, and was founder of the Imperial Bank. During his mayoralty there was a great Corporation banquet to Tsar Alexander II, a grand ball for the marriage of the Duke and Duchess of Edinburgh and a reception for Sir Garnett Wolseley on his return from the Ashanti campaign. The sum of £150,000 was raised for the relief of the Bengal famine. David Stone, the next lord mayor, received the Sultan of Zanzibar at Mansion House and attended the opening of the new Paris Opera in full state with coaches and retinue.

Although the aldermen had the reputation of being Tories, it is clear this was not true of all of them. In fact Common Hall had continued to be Liberal ever since the Reform Act, and consistently returned Liberals to Parliament. William Cotton, lord mayor in 1875 and MP for London from 1874 to 1885, was the first Conservative alderman to be elected as MP for the City since 1830. He was one of the leading defenders of the City's liberties. He became Chamberlain in 1892 and was knighted that year. William McArthur, lord mayor in 1880, on the other hand, sat as Liberal MP for Lambeth from 1868 to 1885. He was Irish, the fifth child of a Wesleyan Minister in Donegal. He began as an apprentice to a woollen draper in Londonderry and started a lucrative trade with Australia, doing business with his brother, who had emigrated. McArthur transferred the headquarters of the flourishing business to London in 1857 and duly made his way into the City hierarchy through the Spectacle Makers' Company, the starting point for a great many lord mayors in this period. He became a director of the City Bank and the Bank of Australia, and chairman of the Star Life Assurance Company. He retained a deep concern with religious enterprises and an interest in colonial matters. In the year before his mayoralty he travelled round the world visiting religious foundations throughout the Empire. There was considerable alarm in March 1881 when a bomb was discovered and defused under the Wat Tyler window in Mansion House. It was believed to have been planted by the Fenians and there is some question whether the Lord Mayor's Irish origins had anything to do with it.

William Gladstone became Prime Minister in 1868 and during his first term of office made no move to reform the Corporation. A period of Conservative rule under Benjamin Disraeli followed from 1874 until 1880 when Gladstone and the Liberals returned to power. A commission was set up to investigate the Livery Companies, and the Home Secretary, Sir William Harcourt, began to prepare plans for the total reform of London government. Ex-lord-mayors Sir Sydney Waterlow and William Cotton, and Robert Fowler who would be lord mayor in 1883, were members of the Royal Commission on the Livery Companies, which emerged unscathed, the enquiry into the use of their charitable funds showing that they were properly administered.

A succession of Conservative lord mayors followed William McArthur, but they avoided expressing political views during their year of office. When John Whittaker Ellis was host to Gladstone at his banquet in 1881 he banished any fears that he might annoy the Prime Minister in his speech. In his reply Gladstone said that there had been lord mayors for more than 500 years and he hoped they would still be there 500 years in the future. Ellis was able to demonstrate the value of the Corporation's activities when he accompanied Queen Victoria to Epping Forest in May 1882, declared the forest open as a place of recreation for the people and was created a baronet. He defended the Livery Companies at the enquiry, as did Henry Knight, who succeeded him as lord mayor. He dedicated two more open spaces, Burnham Beeches and Coulsdon Commons, as recreation grounds. He had been Captain of the City of London School and attended the opening of its new building on the Embankment. During his year Mansion House relief funds were raised for a terrible fire in Jamaica, an earthquake on the island of Ischia and gales in the Western Highlands. He was the last lord mayor to be sworn in at Westminster and attended the opening of the new Law Courts in the Strand.

In 1883 the first eminent businessman to join the Corporation for many years was elected lord mayor. Robert Fowler was an only child from a Quaker and Liberal family who grew up to be a firm Church of England Conservative. He was a brilliant mathematician and classical scholar, an MA from University College, London. He entered Parliament as Member for Penryn in 1868, for which he sat until 1874 and sat for the City from 1880 to 1891. He joined the family firm of Drewett and Fowler, one of the precursors of the National Westminster Bank. He devoted his energies to reorganizing the Conservative Party in the City but was at first unwilling to become involved in the civic government. However, he joined the Spectacle Makers' Company, was elected sheriff in 1870 and in 1878 agreed to become the Alderman of Cornhill.

His election as lord mayor was the cause of an uproar in Common Hall, where the City's supposed neutrality as far as national politics were concerned appeared temporarily to break down. The Livery believed they had nominated two Liberals, Simon Charles Hadley and George Nottage, but the Sheriffs announced that the nominees were Hadley and Fowler. The Aldermen then retired to a chorus of boos and hisses. They were out for half an hour and when they returned Fowler was on the Lord Mayor's left hand. For a while there was pandemonium as the Liverymen protested and the Recorder attempted to make himself heard to announce the result. Finally the Court settled down and Fowler proved an excellent lord mayor. He too was host at his banquet to Gladstone, whom he delighted with a quotation, in Greek, from Homer's *Iliad* in his speech. The Prime Minister paid tribute to him as 'a frank and courageous opponent in the House of Commons'.

In 1884 Sir William Harcourt attempted to bring in a bill to reform London government. This would have extended the area of Corporation control to the whole of greater London. The City would have had only 30 out of 240 elected members and its existing constitution would have been swept away. On 29 March 1884 about 2,000–3,000 Liverymen crowded into Guildhall to consider the bill. Robert Fowler presided as Lord Mayor. Political opinion among the Liverymen must have swung right round now that the ancient liberties of the City were being attacked. A few Liberals tried to put forward a motion supporting the bill but the majority shouted them down and cheered loudly as resolutions were passed condemning it. In the House of Commons sixty-one petitions were received against the bill and one in favour. The matter was dropped for that session and soon afterwards a long period of Conservative government began under Lord Salisbury.

George Nottage, another Spectacle Maker, was elected lord mayor that autumn. His family came from Nottage in Glamorgan, and he started work at the age of sixteen in his uncle's iron foundry. He became interested in photography and when he came to London founded the London Stereoscopic and Photographic Company, which was a pioneer in photographic work. In April 1885 Nottage fell ill but tried to keep going, developed pneumonia and died at the age of sixty-three. The last lord mayor to die in office, he is buried in St Paul's, where there is a magnificent brass plaque to commemorate him in the crypt. Robert Fowler was invited to take over for the rest of the year, so he was the last lord mayor to serve two turns of office. He was made a baronet in July 1885.

Sir Reginald Hanson was lord mayor during Queen Victoria's Jubilee celebrations in 1887. There was a splendid ball in Guildhall attended by the Prince and Princess of Wales and members of many European royal families. The Queen herself paid a personal visit to the Mansion House on 14 May which is commemorated in a tapestry in the Saloon. That autumn Polydore de Keyser was elected lord mayor. The son of a Belgian who came to London as a waiter, he was the first Roman Catholic to hold the office since the Reformation. In 1874 he opened De Keyser's Royal Hotel on the site of the old Bridewell Palace by Blackfriars Bridge. It had 400 rooms and was described in the 1879 Baedeker as 'conducted in a continental fashion, well situated, but somewhat expensive'. After the First World War the hotel was closed, and in 1930 Unilever House was built on the site. De Keyser joined the Common Council in 1868 and became a member of the Spectacle Makers' Company. He was elected the Alderman of Farringdon Without in 1882. As lord mayor he made a state visit to Belgium, where he received a particularly warm welcome. He was knighted in December 1888. In 1889 he accepted the presidency of the British section of the Paris Exhibition, although the Government declined to be associated with it and made no grant. De Keyser's optimism was justified. The Exhibition, whose star attraction was the brand-new Eiffel Tower, proved to be very successful. The French Government made de Keyser a Chevalier Legion d'Honneur.

James Whitehead, who followed him as lord mayor, was completely different. He was the youngest of six children from Sedbergh in Yorkshire. He attended Appleby Grammar School and was apprenticed to a draper when he was fourteen. He moved from there to Kendal, thence to Bradford, and first came to London as an agent for the Bradford company. He became a partner in a big wholesale firm and showed his business acumen in backing a rising young shopkeeper, John Barker. At the age of forty-seven he was able to retire from business, and went on a world tour. His involvement with civic life began when he took on the job of honorary secretary to the Rowland Hill Memorial Fund. A statue was erected to the founder of the Penny Post (who was distantly related to the Rowland Hill who had been lord mayor in Queen Elizabeth I's reign). With the money that remained Whitehead set up a fund for post office workers which still exists as the Rowland Hill Benevolent Fund.

In 1882 Whitehead was elected Alderman of Cheap. Queen Victoria, when she met him, commented: 'He is quite unlike a City Alderman, being thin and good-looking.' He stood for Parliament as a Liberal advocate of Irish Home Rule, but was defeated, finally becoming MP for Leicester from 1892 to 1894. His Lord Mayor's Show was deliberately quiet, as he preferred to save the money to spend on special meals in various work-houses in London. It was a very wet day (as the cover of this book reveals) and in the streets newsboys were shouting about Jack the Ripper and the ' 'orrible murder in Whitechapel'.

Nevertheless, Whitehead's Lord Mayor's Banquet was a brilliant occasion and although he was himself a teetotaller there was no shortage of drink. During his year the Mansion House was undergoing repairs, so he was housed in the Hotel Metropole (in Northumberland Avenue). He went to the opening of the Paris Exhibition with de Keyser and was so impressed that he set up a fund for seventy-five British workmen to pay a visit to study the exhibits. On 1 July 1889 he gave a lunch to the Shah of Persia to which several members of the Royal Family came. The Prime Minister, Lord Salisbury, in reply to the Lord Mayor's speech, said, 'You spoke just now of being the mouthpiece of the City. On this occasion you are much more. You are the mouthpiece of the entire nation.'

It was an eventful year in many ways. On 13 August the great Dock Strike began. Shipping was brought to a halt and the men and their families were soon starving. Public sympathy was with the dockers, who wanted the end of a pernicious piecework system and a minimum wage of 6d per hour. The Lady Mayoress organized free meals and clothing for the dockers' families and the Lord Mayor formed a conciliation committee to urge the employers to give way. By 16 September the strike was over. On 22 October Whitehead entertained 300 provincial mayors and provosts at Mansion House at a grand ball to celebrate the 700th anniversary of the mayoralty. He was given the Freedom of Appleby and made a baronet by the Queen 'for highly valuable services in an eventful Mayoralty'. He was invited to stand for another year, but declined.

Sir Henry Isaacs' Lord Mayor's Show in 1889 was historical, to commemorate the 700th anniversary of the mayoralty, and displayed a series of English worthies who were descended from lord mayors, including Queen Elizabeth I, the Duke of Marlborough, Oliver Cromwell and Robert Walpole. There was a procession of lord mayors, one representing each of the seven centuries which, as the brochure commented, 'is interesting as exemplifying the strange and peculiar changes in the colour and shape of the Mayoral robes'. Those selected were: Henry FitzAilwyn, Gregory de Rokesley, Richard Whittington, Edmund Shaa, John Gresham, William Craven and John Wilkes. The Court of Common Council resolved 'that the Court ... do commemorate the event in a suitable manner' but nothing particular was done. The Library Committee suggested that a history of the City be commissioned, showing its part in English history, a distinctive feature of which was to be a record of the lord mayors. This led to the publication of Dr R. R. Sharpe's *London and the Kingdom* in 1894.

David Evans, 1891, was the first Welsh lord mayor for nearly fifty years, and one of the youngest at the age of forty-one. Stuart Knill was the second Roman Catholic lord mayor and was heckled by the Livery at his election, and greeted by a crowd shouting 'No Popery' in the street. He really did arouse resentment when he gave a banquet at the Mansion House to an entirely Roman Catholic assembly (with the exception of the Sheriffs) and proposed the toast 'The Holy Father and the Queen'. This caused a public outcry and the Court of Aldermen passed a resolution of regret, although they asserted they did not believe he was actuated by any disloyal motive. His son John, lord mayor in 1909, was careful to avoid such provocation.

Meanwhile the question of London government was being settled. In 1889 under the County Councils Act the London County Council was set up (and many subsequent lord mayors were members of it). The City was left untouched, but the reformers assumed that the new body would in due course swallow up the City or the two would amalgamate. Sir George Faudel-Phillips, lord mayor in 1896, denounced the idea of a 'Mammoth County Council'. All plans for including the City collapsed, and in 1899 the London Government Act created twenty-eight separate boroughs which, as one disappointed reformer put it, surrounded the City like 'a sort of Praetorian Guard'.

The Lord Mayor in that year was Alfred James Newton. He founded the City Imperial Volunteers to serve in the Boer War. He persuaded Livery Companies, bankers and merchants to back the venture and was granted a donation of £25,000 from the Common Council. On 1 January 1900 the first volunteers were sworn in by the lord mayor, sheriffs and five aldermen. All received the Freedom of the City. They served for nine months and were welcomed back with a triumphal march through the City on 29 October. The force was disbanded on 31 October and the remaining money provided pensions. (The last surviving recipient died in November 1978.)

The Census of 1901 revealed that the population of the City was 26,897, whereas that of Greater London was now 4,509,166. These figures clearly demonstrate that the character of the City had changed completely over the last half-century. The lord mayor, although still the head of the City's own local government, was now of national rather than purely local importance. State entertaining, attendance at public functions, and national and international charities were his chief concern. It was essential for these purposes to maintain the dignity of the office and already in the last twenty years of the nineteenth century nearly all the lord mayors were knighted, either before their year of office, often when they were sheriff, or during the year. Many were created baronet and some were elevated to the peerage after they had served as lord mayor. Sir Marcus Samuel, lord mayor in 1902, became Lord Bearsted; Sir Horace Marshall, 1918, became Lord Marshall; Sir George Blades became Lord Ebbisham; and Sir Charles Wakefield became Lord Wakefield. Some still rose from humble origins but most came from established families. During their careers they acted as governors of hospitals and chairmen of charities. They were Masters of their Livery Companies and many of them became members and often Masters of several Companies. They acquired exotic foreign decorations. Several of them were leading Freemasons.

One consistent factor in the mayoralty for over fifty years was Sir William Soulsby, the Lord Mayor's Private Secretary. He first went to work for William Cotton, who had known him as a child, in 1875. As he wrote himself in a special edition of *The Times* published in 1927: 'I came intending to stay for a year – I have remained for 52'. He finally retired in 1931 after fifty-six years of service to lord mayors. He was an invaluable aid to the lord mayors, his experience covering the change from the age of quill pens and horse omnibuses to typewriters and tube trains. He felt that the prestige of the office of lord mayor had greatly increased during his time in the Mansion House. He also commented that there was far less heavy drinking. He wrote many of the lord mayors' speeches, as became apparent when one lord mayor, opening a new building in the City, stumbled in his speech, peered at his paper and grumbled: 'I can't always read Soulsby's writing.'

The Lord Mayor's unique position in the country was emphasized on 22 January 1901, when Frank Green received news of Queen Victoria's death by cable before the notice was posted at Osborne. Sir Joseph Dimsdale, lord mayor in 1901, became Chamberlain in 1902 and retained the office until his death in 1912. He was the last ex-lord-mayor to hold the office. He was also made a Privy Councillor, the first lord mayor to be so honoured since Thomas Harley in 1768. Sir Thomas Vesey Strong, lord mayor 1910, was made a Privy Councillor in 1911, and Sir Horace Marshall in 1919.

A few names from this period stand out. William Treloar was the second son of a family from Cornwall who had settled in Southwark. His father was a carpet manufacturer on Ludgate Hill. William entered the family business when he left school at fifteen and went through every department. He was well established in the business before he entered civic life, becoming Alderman of Farringdon Without in 1892 at the age of forty-nine. He was sheriff in 1899, the year of the City Imperial Volunteers, and was knighted in 1900. He became lord mayor in 1906 and during his mayoralty entertained the King and Queen of Norway and of Denmark as well as receiving Edward VII and Queen Alexandra at the opening of the new Central Criminal Court. He is best remembered for his work for children. He married but had no children of his own, although he and his wife adopted a nephew and niece. He liked to give huge parties for poor children every year at Guildhall. His major work was to set up a hospital for children crippled by tuberculosis, which combined treatment and education. The Lord Mayor Treloar College is still helping disabled boys and girls today. He wrote *Ludgate Hill Past and Present*, *Wilkes and the City* and *A Lord Mayor's Diary*, giving a detailed account of his year of office. This indicates a busy year, not so very different from that of a modern lord mayor, full of official engagements, meetings and speeches. He said he had read of an archbishop of Canterbury who had told a lord mayor to mind his own business. 'A Lord Mayor cannot do so. I have not attended to mine since I became Lord Mayor, and I am glad to say that the business is better for it.'

Lord mayors had often visited Paris and Brussels, but Treloar decided to go further afield and visit Berlin in June. Sir Edward Grey, the Foreign Secretary, warned him that the Germans intended to use the anniversary of the Battle of Waterloo on 18 June to make a propaganda point against the French, with whom Britain was now in alliance. He urged Treloar to alter his plans, but Treloar refused to do this. However, he managed the affair very skilfully, by avoiding an official dinner on the evening of 18 June. There was a lunch at which he had to make a speech, in which he firmly stated that France was our staunchest ally. On his return to England he was made a baronet.

At Sir Thomas Vesey Strong's banquet to the Bankers, Lloyd George made his famous speech about the threat posed by a German gunboat at Agadir, in Morocco, warning the Germans that Britain would not tolerate gunboat diplomacy conducted from Berlin. Sir Thomas Vansittart Bowater was lord mayor when war broke out in 1914. During the war, life in the City continued as usual, except that the Lord Mayor's Show became a stirring military parade and the Lord Mayor's Banquet became more frugal.

Sir Charles Johnston, lord mayor in 1914, organized the City of London National Guard. He was followed by Sir Charles Wakefield, one of the outstanding lord mayors. He came from Liverpool and was educated at the Liverpool Institute. He started work with an oil broker and set up his own firm dealing in lubricating oils. He foresaw the expansion of the motor industry and made a fortune. 'Castrol' was the trade name of his product. At the Mansion House during the war he played an invaluable part in the recruiting movement. From 8 a.m. to 8 p.m. he was there to welcome and shake the hand of each recruit. He visited the Western Front and the Grand Fleet at Scapa Flow. He was obviously an immensely likeable man, a kindly and considerate employer, very fair and honest. Soulsby, who was unwilling to single out any individual from among the lord mayors, said 'he was one of the kindest and most generous citizens who ever filled the civic chair'. He gave money to finance Sir Alan Cobham's flight to Australia and back, and for Amy Johnson. Wakefield gave scholarships for RAF cadets and was chairman of the RAF Benevolent Fund. A great enthusiast for the Empire, he supported the Imperial Cadet movement. He was very keen on motoring and sponsored speed trials. As well as all this he was the author of two books, *America Today and Tomorrow* and *On Leaving School and the Choice of a Career*. He bought and presented to the nation the Thomas à Becket Cup, the Armada Jewel, the papers of Sir Isaac Newton and Nelson's personal logbook. He gave the Matz and Kitton collection of Dickens literature to the Dickens Fellowship at Doughty House. He was a major benefactor to a host of charities. He was made an Honorary Freeman of Hythe, and in 1930 was created Baron Wakefield of Hythe. In 1935 he was presented with the Honorary Freedom of the City. The only other lord mayor to be honoured in this way was Sir George Wyatt Truscott in 1937, after fifty-five years of service to the City, having been lord mayor in 1908.

At Sir Horace Marshall's Lord Mayor's Banquet in 1918 Lloyd George announced the abdication of the Kaiser, to rousing cheers. Marshall's Lord Mayor's Show was a great military parade. On the Sunday following he attended service at St Paul's, a practice started by Wakefield, who also was the first to stop at the Cathedral on his way to the Law Courts to ask for a blessing on his mayoralty. Two days later the Lord Mayor announced the Armistice to cheering crowds from the balcony of the Mansion House. A year of celebrations followed in the City culminating in a great Peace Parade. The Freedom of the City was presented to President Wilson, who addressed his speech of thanks to 'Mr Lord Mayor'.

During the period between the two World Wars the mayoralty continued with high prestige and undisturbed by any moves to alter the City government. James Roll, lord mayor in 1920, was one who rose from his arrival in London as a 'small and friendless boy from the country' (as he said in a speech at the end of his year of office) to the mayoralty at the age of seventy-three. Actually he began at the age of fourteen with his uncle and served with Pearl Assurance for fifty years. He was made a baronet in 1921. Sir John Baddeley, who followed him, was the author of several books on the City. Sir J. E. Kynaston Studd stands out as the third twentieth-century lord mayor to be featured in the *Dictionary of National Biography* (the other two being Treloar and Wakefield). He was also the second Etonian to be lord mayor (the first being Dimsdale). He was the eldest of three well-known cricketing brothers, and captained Cambridge in 1884. He intended to train as a medical missionary, but when that idea did not prosper he was asked by Quintin Hogg to join in pioneering the Regent Street Polytechnic. He became honorary secretary in 1885, vice-president in 1901 and president on Hogg's death in 1903. He entered civic life in middle age at the instance of members of the Polytechnic, joined the Fruiterers' Company and later the Merchant Taylors'. He became Alderman of Farringdon Without, following Treloar, and sheriff in 1922. As lord mayor he entertained King Fuad II of Egypt and paid an official visit to Amsterdam. His year was also remembered for a Mansion House dinner to leading cricketers.

Sir William Neal gave up the Mansion House for his year so that it could undergo renovations and was housed at the Hotel Metropole and given a motor car. Sir Maurice Jenks, 1931, flew to open Morecambe Town Hall in an aeroplane bearing the City Arms. Sir Stephen Killik started as an office boy, became a stockbroker and travelled widely in North and South America. He was a leading authority on Argentina and published a manual on the Argentine railways and many articles on finance and the working of the Stock Exchange. He was one of the smallest lord mayors physically. (Another was Sir George Faudel-Phillips in 1896, who had enormous footmen.) Sir Percy Vincent attended Vancouver's Jubilee celebrations in April 1936 and so was the first lord mayor to make an official overseas visit to the Empire. He travelled 12,000 miles, made 500 speeches and was made freeman of five cities. Sir George Broadbridge carried the City's Crystal Sceptre before King George VI at his Coronation. He was Unionist Member of Parliament for the City, 1938–45, and was created Baron Broadbridge of Brighton in 1945.

Sir Frank Bowater, lord mayor in 1938, the brother of Sir Thomas Vansittart Bowater, lord mayor 1913, was in office when the Second

World War began. On 11 October he made an official visit to the Temple to inspect troops marshalled there. It was the first time the lord mayor had officially entered the Temple since 1669 when Sir William Turner had clashed with the students who pulled down his sword. During the war the mayoralty continued at the Mansion House, the daily routine punctuated by air raid precautions and fire-watching duties. Life was restricted, with rationing of food and petrol, and a smaller Lord Mayor's Banquet was held in the Mansion House instead of in Guildhall. George Wilkinson, lord mayor in 1940 and made a baronet in 1941, opened the Lord Mayor's National Air Raid Distress Fund, which was run by succeeding lord mayors and was one of the biggest undertakings in the history of Mansion House charities. The lord mayors visited gun positions round London and held receptions for troops at the Mansion House. The lord mayor in 1941 was Sir John Laurie, the great-nephew of Sir Peter Laurie, 1832. Sir Samuel Joseph, father of Sir Keith Joseph, followed him. Sir Frank Newson-Smith, lord mayor in 1943, had the Cadet Battalion of the Honourable Artillery Company as a Guard of Honour outside the Mansion House, instead of a Show. An article in the *Sunday Times* at the end of his year reported on the continuing national status and international fame of the mayoralty. Although a simple lunch now replaced the Lord Mayor's Banquet, the Mansion House gold plate was displayed and the Prime Minister still attended.

11

THE MODERN MAYORALTY

The City of London suffered heavily from enemy air raids. Huge areas were devastated, many Livery halls were destroyed and City churches lay in ruins. Guildhall was burnt out and its roof collapsed. A temporary roof was erected in 1941 which served until 1953 when the present roof was built. Many of the churches and Livery halls were reconstructed. The area of worst destruction, north of the City wall, became the Barbican, providing residential housing within the City as well as an arts and conference centre. Concentrated in the heart of the square mile the soaring towers of banks, insurance companies and business offices have transformed London's skyline. Now the City has a night time residential population of about 6,000 and a daily commuter influx of about 300,000. It is one of the three most important financial centres in the world, with New York and Tokyo, and generates invisible earnings of around £8 billion a year.

The lord mayor, as the chief citizen of such a City, has an exacting and important part to play. The previous chapter has described how the role of the lord mayor has evolved during the past 100 years. Just as business life has changed enormously during the past forty years, so has the lord mayor's activity during his year of office. He now has, in addition to all his usual duties, a significant diplomatic and public relations role, which occupies a great deal of his time and energy. But he does not neglect traditional activities. It is the historic background which gives the office of Lord Mayor of London its special character.

The Lord Mayor still has precedence in the City over all but the Sovereign. Outside the City he ranks with, but after, Cabinet Ministers. On the death of the Sovereign he attends the Privy Council and signs the proclamation of the successor to the throne. He has the right to be present at the Coronation, where he has an accustomed position. At the opening of Parliament he has a seat in the Peers Gallery of the House of Lords. Every quarter the password to the Tower for each day in the next three months is forwarded to him. The warrants for venison from the Royal Forests which date from the Middle Ages still come every year. The Lord Mayor used to receive four bucks every July and four does every November, the Sheriffs three bucks and three does each, and the Recorder, Chamberlain, Town Clerk, Common Serjeant and Remembrancer one buck and one doe each. The grant was suspended during the war but has been resumed since, albeit on a reduced scale, and each recipient gets one quarter buck in July and one quarter doe in November.

As the City's Chief Magistrate the Lord Mayor attends the Central Criminal Court for the ceremonial opening of the Court four times a year. He takes the central seat over which the Old Bailey Sword is hung, and this seat is otherwise left vacant. He also sits occasionally as a magistrate in the Mansion House Justice Room, but nowadays he has very limited time for this duty, and the Justice Room will shortly be closed.

All these traditional adjuncts of the mayoralty take up little of the lord mayor's time these days. More is spent on his numerous *ex officio* duties, as patron, chairman and trustee of many charities, hospitals and schools, notably the City of London School for Boys and that for Girls, and the City Freemen's School. He is also Governor of Christ's Hospital and Chancellor of the City University. These roles require his attendance at speech days, prize-givings and degree-givings. He is Trustee of the fabric of St Paul's Cathedral. As head of the City's own local government he summons and presides over the Court of Aldermen once a month and the Court of Common Council every three weeks. He summons the Liverymen twice a year to Common Hall, at midsummer for the election of the sheriffs and at Michaelmas for the election of the next lord mayor. He would also summon and preside over the ancient Court of Husting but this has not met since 1978. If the Lord Mayor is unable to be present on any of these occasions his place must be taken by an Alderman who has passed the Chair. He will be the *locum tenens*, and a warrant signed by the Lord Mayor is kept in the Town Clerk's office. It used to be kept by the Swordbearer in his fur hat, where he still keeps the key to the City Seal.

The Swordbearer is the first Esquire of the Lord Mayor's household. Together with the Common Cryer and Serjeant-at-Arms and the City Marshal he shares the duties of attendance on the Lord Mayor and the organization of his daily schedule. The Esquires work from an office in the Mansion House.

As the home and the office of the Lord Mayor, the Mansion House is a very busy place, with a large household headed by the lord mayor's Private Secretary and his Deputy. The Principal Assistant looks after the lord mayor's diary and there is a separate invitations office. There are secretarial staff for all these officers. The Steward, who lives in and supervises all private entertainments, is responsible for the wines and also the plate room, where a plate butler and two platemen care for the silver and gold-plated cups and salvers and keep the swords and maces in perfect condition. The Steward is also in charge of the lord mayor's robes and supervises the three footmen who attend him. The footmen and platemen can live in if they wish. Some do. There is a Hallkeeper in charge of the Walbrook entrance hall, who greets guests, and a Yeoman who acts as Toastmaster, sometimes stands in for one of the Esquires on ceremonial occasions and regularly shows parties of visitors round the Mansion House. There are four chauffeurs, two for the Lord Mayor and one for each of the Sheriffs. The Keeper of the Mansion House deals with day to day maintenance. The housekeeper runs the staff of maids, cleaners and cloakroom attendants. There are also separate security men and caterers on contract.

The Lord Mayor needs the Steward and footmen to assist with his robes. His outfit for the various functions is carefully prescribed. He has five different gowns. For most important City events, including the election and the Lord Mayor's Show, he wears his scarlet alderman's gown with a train added and a scarlet hood, known as the Cap of Dignity. For the sheriffs' election, the Admission and some other occasions he wears his violet alderman's gown. The black and gold state robe is worn at great banquets. There are two special robes connected with royalty. The reception robe of crimson velvet with an ermine cape is worn when the Lord Mayor receives the Queen or members of the Royal Family in the City. There is also a Coronation robe of rich crimson velvet. The last lord mayor to wear this was Sir Rupert de la Bère who attended the Coronation in 1953 and entertained the Queen and the Duke of Edinburgh at a Coronation luncheon in Guildhall. He was the last lord mayor to sit as a member of parliament during his year of office. It is perhaps an indication of how much more occupied lord mayors are today that this would now be out of the question.

The robes are not worn all day. Most of the time the Lord Mayor wears morning dress. During the day with the robes he wears 'Old Baileys': that is, black trousers and waistcoat with a lace jabot and ruffles at the wrists. 'Old Bailey' breeches, with black silk stockings and patent leather shoes are worn for white tie occasions. Court dress is similar but more elaborate. Whatever his dress the Lord Mayor wears his Jewel, or Badge of Office, on all formal occasions. This is a sardonyx cameo set in gold and carved with the arms of the City, with a garter of gold and dark blue enamel. The Jewel bears the City motto, *Domine Dirige Nos* in diamonds. Round the whole is a wreath of roses with thistle and shamrock intertwined, in gold set with diamonds. The present Jewel was made in 1802 and reset in 1866, replacing earlier Jewels of 1558 and 1607, which can be seen in portraits of early lord mayors. Sometimes the Lord Mayor wears the Jewel on a blue riband, but whenever he wears his Collar of SS links it is suspended from a portcullis at the centre. The collar was given to the lord mayors by Sir John Aleyn in 1545. It has twenty-eight ornate gold SS links joined by alternate enamel Tudor roses and gold knots. A replica has been made because the original Collar is now very fragile and is only occasionally worn.

There are five City Swords. That most commonly seen is the Sword of State which the Swordbearer carries before the Lord Mayor in processions. The 'Pearl' Sword (named from its pearl-studded scabbard) is carried by the Lord Mayor before the Queen when she attends a State function and is symbolically surrendered at Temple Bar. The last time this ceremony was performed was in 1977, when the Lord Mayor, Sir Robin Gillett, received the Queen in the City for a Guildhall luncheon to celebrate her Silver Jubilee. There is a 'Mourning' Sword and swords for the Old Bailey and the Mansion House Justice Room. Next to the Swordbearer in processions walks the Serjeant-at-Arms, bearing the great Mace. There are lighter travelling replicas of the Sword and Mace for the Lord Mayor's excursions abroad. The other City Mace is the Crystal Sceptre, which the Lord Mayor bears before the Sovereign at the Coronation. It is a crystal shaft 18 inches long with a gold jewelled head believed to date from the fifteenth century.

With all this panoply of robes and escort the Lord Mayor embarks upon his year as a major public figure. One of his most important functions will be, as it always has been, to entertain. His year begins with the grandest dinner of all, the Lord Mayor's Banquet, which nowadays is always held on the Monday following the Lord Mayor's Show. It is given by the Lord Mayor, who pays for half, and the two sheriffs, who share the remaining cost, in honour of his predecessor who is known as the late Lord Mayor. The latter is really the guest of honour, although most media attention is focused on the Prime Minister, who makes an important speech on Government policy. Turtle soup is no longer served, but the food and wine are first class, the lord mayor's procession enters to Handel's 'March' from *Scipio* and after the meal the Lord Mayor drinks to his guests with the Loving Cup which is traditionally circulated to all the guests. At the banquet, because of the numbers, several cups are passed round, filled with spiced wine, and the guests rise in their turn, three at a time. The person with the cup bows to his neighbour who lifts the cover with his right hand, and holds it while the other drinks. The third person protects his back. This custom is supposed to date back to the murder at Corfe Castle of King Edward the Martyr, who was slain while drinking. It is very popular at City feasts. After the speeches, by the Lord Mayor, the Prime Minister, the Archbishop of Canterbury and the late Lord Mayor there is dancing in the Crypt. It is the first of many great dinners the Lord Mayor will attend in Guildhall, which can accommodate about 700 guests. Some of these dinners will be for the reception of foreign heads of state, some for business companies or for organizations like the Guild of Freemen.

In the Egyptian Hall of the Mansion House, which holds about 300 people, the Lord Mayor gives several annual dinners. There are the banquets to the Masters and Prime Wardens of the Livery Companies, the Easter Banquet to the Diplomatic Corps, the Bishops' Dinner and the Judges' Dinner. On Plow Monday, the first Monday after Twelfth Night, there is a dinner for the Corporation staff, and there is the Aldermen's Dinner and the dinner for the Common Council and the other Governing Bodies of London. The last Mansion House banquet during the lord mayor's year is that given to the bankers in October, at which the Chancellor of the Exchequer makes a major speech on the economy. During the Christmas holidays there is a huge fancy dress party for children. As well as these official entertainments, hundreds of livery company and business dinners and lunches, as well as company and charity receptions take place in the Egyptian Hall. When the Lord Mayor is not giving or attending a function he entertains privately in his apartment on the second floor of the Mansion House. It is usual to invite a wide range of people from the City, from Parliament, from all parts of the United Kingdom and foreign and Commonwealth visitors. People come from the professions, from the arts and sciences, from the world of entertainment. The Lord Mayor hardly ever has a meal quietly at home, because he is invited to many more functions than he can possibly attend. He dines with most of the ninety-eight Livery Companies, either in a Company Hall or in the Mansion House. There are Ward Club luncheons, Corporation Committee dinners and functions of numerous business, charitable and professional bodies.

Throughout the year there are many church services which the Lord Mayor must attend. In St Paul's Cathedral the Lord Mayor has his own stall north of the Choir, opposite that of the Archbishop of Canterbury. On recent special occasions when the Queen has come to St Paul's, such as for example the wedding of the Prince and Princess of Wales, the Queen Mother's Eightieth Birthday celebration and the Thanksgiving Service at the end of the Falklands campaign, the Lord Mayor has borne the Pearl Sword before her up the steps and into the Cathedral. There are services for the City of London Schools, for the Soldiers', Sailors' and Airmen's Families Association, for the Old Contemptibles. There is the 'Chain Gang' service attended by mayors from all the London boroughs. There are services for the Festival of the Sons of the Clergy, for the Order of St John of Jerusalem and the City's own United Guilds Service.

In several of the City churches there are special annual services. In the Corporation church of St Lawrence Jewry, the Spital Sermon is preached on the day of the first Common Council after Easter. (This is a centuries-old tradition originating in the Priory of St Mary Spital, then held in various City churches until fixed at St Lawrence.) The Bridewell Sermon is preached every year in St Brides. At St Sepulchre, Christ's Hospital hold their annual St Matthew's Day service after which the pupils march through the City behind their band and are received by the Lord Mayor at Guildhall. Every April at St Andrew Undershaft the City historian, John Stow, is commemorated. A distinguished academic gives an address on the City's history and the Lord Mayor places a new quill pen in Stow's hand. In June a similar service is held at St Olave, Hart Street, for Samuel Pepys, and the Lord Mayor places a fresh wreath on the diarist's bust.

During the year there are some particularly colourful presentations to the Lord Mayor. In June he is given a single red rose by members of Tower Ward and parishioners of All Hallows, Barking. This was a quit rent originally imposed in 1381 on the wife of Sir Robert Knollys, who built a bridge from her house to a garden over the road, neglecting to ask the lord mayor's permission to do this. In October the Fruiterers' Company make their presentation of fruit, originating from a toll imposed by medieval mayors on fruit imported to the City, and are entertained to lunch by the Lord Mayor. Members of the Butchers' Company present a boar's head in January, a custom dating from the Middle Ages when they were granted the right to clean meat in the river.

There are many other traditional events in the City throughout the year, such as the Doggett Coat and Badge Race and the Vintners' and Dyers' Swan Upping on the river, the Beating of the Bounds of the adjoining parishes of St Peter ad Vincula in the Tower and All Hallows, Barking, the Trial of the Pyx, at which the Goldsmiths test the coinage, and the Quit Rents ceremony (described in Chapter 8). The Lord Mayor does not usually attend these.

Most of the rest of his time is taken up with the active business of a modern lord mayor. As the principal representative of the City he plays an important part in promoting good relations with businessmen all over the world. His position makes him an ideal promoter of British products. Although not in any way a government servant, but usually widely experienced in business affairs, he can and does assist the Government to make valuable and lasting contacts. Since he is non-party-political he is not tied to any one administration nor is he regarded as in any way partisan. Nowadays each lord mayor makes a number of overseas journeys, many at the specific request of the Government. This diplomatic role as an unofficial ambassador for Britain has developed considerably in recent years and is one of the most valuable activities of the mayoralty. Sir Alan Traill, lord mayor in 1984, visited China, Jakarta, Hong Kong, Mauritius, Bermuda, Abu Dhabi and Dubai as well as six European countries. Sir Greville Spratt (1987) went to Amman, Cyprus, Boston, Massachussetts, and Budapest. His long summer tour took him to Singapore, Kuala Lumpur, Brunei, Tokyo and Kyoto. In the autumn he visited the Low Countries. Equally important is the hospitality in the City to visiting heads of state. A banquet at Guildhall is an essential part of all State visits. Sir Allan Davis (1985) received the Emir of Qatar, King Juan Carlos of Spain and the President of the Federal Republic of Germany. Sir David Rowe-Ham (1986) received King Fahd of Saudi Arabia and the King of Morocco. The Lord Mayor is also busy in maintaining contacts with businessmen throughout the United Kingdom and he makes many visits to provincial towns and cities. He is concerned to forge links within the City with leading City financiers and industrialists. Sir Kenneth Cork started the Number One Committee, a group of city business experts who meet the Lord Mayor once a month to brief him about City matters.

What sort of person is chosen to undertake this demanding task? Although nominated by the Liverymen the Lord Mayor is elected by the aldermen from among their ranks, and they have the ultimate right to exclude anyone from their Court without giving any reason. Many a civic aspirant begins his career by getting elected to the Common Council. This enables him to learn about the working of the City and meet some of the people involved. He will have been elected at a Wardmote and may stand as candidate for the aldermanry of that or any other ward which becomes vacant. But if the Court of Aldermen decide he is not 'a fit and proper person and duly qualified for the office', they can reject him. The ward voters may return him three times. If the Aldermen reject him three times they can nominate their own choice. This power has been much criticized and contested. The test case was that of Michael Scales in 1831. He fought the Aldermen's refusal for several years and at each stage their position was upheld. Finally the case went to the House of Lords where the Court of Aldermen's right to the determination of an election as a court of exclusive jurisdiction was confirmed. Since then seven people have been refused, the last being in 1979 when the case was heard in the Divisional Court before Lord Widgery and Mr Justice Park, who gave judgment in favour of the Court of Aldermen.

There are those who regard this as unacceptable and for that and other reasons would still like to see the Corporation of London reformed, but the Government Commission into the City in 1960 decided to leave it unchanged. It decided that the City was an 'anomaly which should continue', and went on to state: 'Its wealth, its antiquity, the enormous part it has played in the history of the nation, its dignity, its traditions and its historical ceremonial make the City of London an institution of national importance.' In the 1970s, under the Labour Government, there was a movement to deal with the City but that too failed. Sir Robin Gillett, when lord mayor, made a particularly spirited defence of the City traditions.

Quite apart from the legal position, the Aldermen would claim that their experience makes them the best judges of the right sort of person to become lord mayor and the success of the mayoralty illustrates this. There has been a shadow on one lord mayor since the war. Denys Lowson, elected at the age of forty-four in 1950 and thus lord mayor in Festival of Britain year, was an exceptionally brilliant man. He was a gifted financier who made a fortune, and a man of great personal generosity who gave considerable sums to charities and a great deal of his time and energy to the support of various hospitals, the St John Ambulance Brigade and his five Livery companies. His year of office was very successful and included extensive travel overseas where he was widely fêted. It was some years later that he became involved in a discreditable deal in Unit Trusts, was exposed and served with an indictment. He was already a broken man and died a few weeks before the case was to be heard, so nothing was proved against him. He is the most recent lord mayor to appear in the *Dictionary of National Biography*.

Each lord mayor has his own interests and way of working, but all have in common great public spirit and devotion to duty. Their long apprenticeship in the service of the City, especially the year they spend as sheriff, gives them the necessary experience. They must be able to give up two full years out of their working lives, not usually consecutively, although sometimes the years are very close. It is often believed that candidates for the mayoralty must be uncommonly wealthy, but this is no longer the case. Lord mayors do have to be people of substantial means, about whose finances there is no question, because the year will be expensive and they will not be able to 'mind their own business'. The time-consuming duties of the modern mayoralty make it impossible for any of the leaders of finance and industry to consider the post. The actual amount spent varies from one individual to another and it is not practical to quote a single figure. The Corporation makes the Lord Mayor an annual allowance and pays for most of his travel and for official entertainments. It maintains the Mansion House and pays the staff. An accountant is appointed to advise the Lord Mayor during his year.

The personality of the Lord Mayor is very important. He must be someone who enjoys socializing, since that is what he is doing most of the time. He needs a certain public presence. For this the robes are a great help. He must be able to speak in public, for during the year he will have to make several speeches every day. Many lord mayors appoint a speechwriter to help with this task, but a few have a natural gift for speaking 'off the cuff', or like Sir Charles Trinder (1968) have a phenomenal memory. He has to possess great energy and stamina to take the unrelenting pressure of public engagements. The right person for the job will respond to the stimulus of being the centre of attention and of meeting people from all walks of life.

It used to be believed that lord mayors were rather old. As has been pointed out, this was not always so in the past, and certainly not in the early nineteenth century when there were several elected under forty years of age. However, in the first half of the twentieth century many lord mayors were in their late sixties and seventies. These days they are more likely to be around fifty, and anyway, as magistrates, aldermen must now retire at seventy. Sir Bernard Waley-Cohen, a distinguished lord mayor in 1960 was forty-six. Two in recent years, Sir Christopher Leaver in 1982 and Sir Anthony Jolliffe in 1983, were only forty-four when they took office.

Lord mayors hail from a wide area. Sir Leslie Boyce (1951) was an Australian who came to Balliol College, Oxford, as a Rhodes Scholar, was Member of Parliament for Gloucester from 1929 to 1945 and a director of the Gloucester Railway Carriage and Wagon Company. Sir Peter Gadsden (1979) was born in Canada, son of a clergyman who brought his family back to England when his children were very young. Sir Cuthbert Ackroyd (1955) came from Yorkshire, from a family who had been wool merchants for over 200 years. Sir James Miller (1964) was born in Edinburgh and was Lord Provost of that City in 1951.

Most lord mayors these days have a good start in life, the majority of the past twenty years having been to public school and Oxbridge. One or two have had military or naval training or have been partly educated abroad. An exception is Sir Robert Bellinger (1966). He left school at fourteen and started work as an office boy. He studied at evening classes at the Regent Street Polytechnic and rose to be chairman of Kinloch Provisions. He was a governor of the BBC after his year of office, from 1968 to 1976. Sir Christopher Leaver did not go to university and began his successful career in the wine trade as a milk roundsman.

Many lord mayors have made their own way into the City hierarchy, usually through the Court of Common Council, but there are several with family connections. Two mayoral families in particular stand out, the Truscotts and the Bowaters. The Truscotts came to London from Truro in the mid nineteenth century, when James Truscott set up a printing business and became a member of the Common Council. His son Francis was lord mayor in 1879. His son, George, was lord mayor in 1908 and was given the Honorary Freedom of the City in 1937 after fifty-five years service. Sir Denis Truscott (1957) is Sir George Truscott's nephew. The Bowater family have a long civic tradition with several Common Councilmen. The first member of the family to be lord mayor was Sir Thomas Vansittart Bowater (1913) who founded the Bowater Paper Corporation. He was followed in the mayoralty by his younger brother, Frank, many years later in 1938. Sir Frank Bowater's two sons both became lord mayor, Sir Noel in 1953 and Sir Ian in 1969. Sir Frederick Hoare was the first lord mayor from the banking family for over 200 years. Sir Peter Vanneck (1977) could look back to his great-great-great-great-grand-uncle, William Beckford. Sir Lindsay Ring's City catering firm, Ring and Brymer, took over the business of Samuel Birch, lord mayor in 1813. In the 1970s three lord mayors followed members of their family to the office. Sir Peter Studd (1970) followed his uncle, Sir John Kynaston Studd (1928). Sir Edward Howard (1971) followed his father, Sir Seymour Howard (1954), and Sir Robin Gillett (1976) followed his father, Sir Harold Gillett (1958). Sir Christopher Collett (1988) follows his grandfather, Charles Collett (1933) and uncle, Sir Frank Alexander (1944). Another uncle, Sir Kingsley Collett, was Chief Commoner in 1955.

Lord mayors today tend to be chartered accountants, stockbrokers or marketing men. Several have entered their family businesses. Some have set up on their own. Sir James Miller (1964) and Sir Gilbert Inglefield (1967) were both trained architects who went into engineering. Sir Ralph Perring (1962) founded the well-known furniture firm. Sir Bracewell Smith (1946) was an ex-teacher from Keighley who went into property deals and ended up chairman of the Ritz, the Carlton, the Park Lane Hotel and the Café Royal. Also in the hotel business is Sir Hugh Wontner (1973), son of an actor-manager. He is chairman of the Savoy Group, Catering Advisor to the Royal Household since 1938 and Clerk of the Royal Kitchens since 1953. Some have had distinguished military careers. Lord Mais (1972) is the only life peer to become lord mayor. He trained as a surveyor and engineer. He saw active service in the war in France, Persia and Normandy, was mentioned in despatches and awarded the OBE. His firm constructed the piers and pierheads for the Mulberry Harbours used for the Normandy landings, and was later involved in the reconstruction of Guildhall. Colonel Sir Greville Spratt (1987) joined the Coldstream Guards, served with the Arab Legion under Glubb Pasha and was ADC to the Queen from 1973 to 1978.

Someone with a completely different background is Dame Mary Donaldson, who was a nurse during the Second World War before she married John Donaldson, later to become the Master of the Rolls. She is the only woman who has so far made her way on to the Court of Aldermen and been elected sheriff and she was lord mayor in 1983. There were minor problems about dress, and a feminine version of 'Old Baileys' had to be devised, as well as a relaxation of the rules for frequent doffing of the mayoral hat. It was agreed that she should bow and not curtsy to the Queen. Otherwise Dame Mary was determined that the fact that she was a woman should make no difference to her mayoralty, and she had a very successful year of office.

One tradition of the mayoralty which is very much alive today is that of raising money for good causes. Each lord mayor uses his influence to raise very considerable sums, usually for specific charities which he has decided to support. A major fund was inaugurated by Sir Leslie Boyce in 1952 to commemorate King George VI, which provided a statue on Carlton House Terrace and set up schemes for a National Recreation Centre, new youth hostels and leadership training for young people, and clubs for old people. An example in the 1960s was Sir James Harman's appeal for cleaning St Paul's. These have tended to take the place of the great Mansion House disaster funds of the past, although these too are sometimes raised, as for example Lady Hoare's Thalidomide Appeal in 1961 and the appeal for the Moorgate Station disaster in 1975. Very recently people sent money for the victims of the King's Cross fire to the Mansion House. Recent lord mayor's charities have included Sir Allan Davis's British Foundation for Age Research and Sir Greville Spratt's three charities for children: Action Research for the Crippled Child, Great Ormond Street Wishing Well Appeal and the Lord Mayor Treloar College, which had also been supported by Sir Alan Traill.

Sir Anthony Jolliffe (1982) was determined to do something positive about unemployment. He set up the London section of 'Business in the Community', a partnership of major private companies working with the Government, voluntary organizations and representatives of the trade unions to promote active participation in training young people and promoting employment in communities all over the country. In 1988 this bore fruit in the first Dragon Awards to companies participating in the scheme. Sir Anthony is still closely involved in this work. Sir David Rowe-Ham supported the Prince's Youth Business Trust which aimed to help young unemployed people get started in business.

Past lord mayors, of whom at the time of writing there are twenty, are in demand for a huge number of public posts. Sir Peter Vanneck (1977) became a Member of the European Parliament. Sir Kenneth Cork (1978), as an insolvency law expert was closely involved with winding up the DeLorean Company. Sir Peter Gadsden is Chairman of the Britain Australia Bicentennial and was Founder Master of the Engineers'

Company. Sir Christopher Leaver is Chairman of the London Tourist Board.

Each lord mayor has a theme for his Show, often closely related to causes he wishes to promote. The Show is a splendid spectacle nowadays and draws huge crowds every year. By the late 1950s it was already so successful that on a weekday the disruption to traffic became quite unacceptable. Because of this the Corporation promoted legislation which resulted in an Act of Parliament in 1958, fixing the date of the Show from 1959 on the second Saturday in November. For the past thirty years the Show has provided a wonderful pageant for the thousands of people who come from all over the country and from abroad to see it. A full year of preparation is needed to organize a procession with over 150 different participating floats, bands, companies, military contingents. Together with the usual military bands, the Doggett Coat and Badge Men and the indispensable Pikemen and Musketeers of the Honourable Artillery Company, who form the Lord Mayor's personal escort, there are floats illustrating the Lord Mayor's theme, from businesses in the City and elsewhere, some having a particular association with the Lord Mayor. There are horse-drawn coaches for the twelve great Livery Companies, for the Lord Mayor's Livery Companies and a float from his ward. It is an indication of how today's Shows compare with the great age of the Lord Mayor's Show in the sixteenth and seventeenth centuries that the Elizabethan office of Pageantmaster was revived seventeen years ago.

The purpose of the procession is to accompany the Lord Mayor to the Royal Courts of Justice where he is presented to the Queen's Judges. Before this, Her Majesty's approval of his appointment will have been formally conveyed by the Lord Chancellor. In the six weeks between his election and his assumption of office the Lord Mayor Elect makes no public appearances. During October he goes quietly to Westminster accompanied by the Aldermen, the Sheriffs and the Recorder of London, where he is received by the Lord Chancellor. The Recorder introduces him, extolling his virtues, the Lord Chancellor signifies the Queen's pleasure at the citizens' choice, and everyone is regaled with cakes and hot spiced wine. Shortly after this the Sovereign's acceptance of the Lord Mayor Elect is announced. Nowadays it is customary for him to be awarded the GBE on that day.

On Lord Mayor's day the formal presentation to the Lord Chief Justice and the Judges of the Queen's Bench Division takes place in the Great Hall of the Royal Courts of Justice. The Recorder presents the Lord

Mayor, who swears that he will 'faithfully perform the duties of my office as Lord Mayor of the City of London'. The Recorder reads out a warrant declaring the citizens' choice and the Lord Chief Justice says to the Queen's Remembrancer, 'Let the warrant be recorded.' After this the Recorder invites the Judges to the Lord Mayor's Banquet and the Lord Chief Justice replies that some of them will have pleasure in attending. This is a pure formality, as it has already been established for weeks who will attend. The civic procession then goes to the Court of Appeal to pay a courtesy call on the Master of the Rolls and the Judges of Appeal and a similar invitation to the banquet is issued and accepted. After this the Lord Mayor rejoins his procession and rides back in triumph to the Mansion House through cheering crowds. It is his second day as lord mayor, because he actually took office the previous day.

12

ENDING AND BEGINNING

It is the second Friday in November. Everything is ready for the Lord Mayor's Show. The stands have been erected outside St Paul's, the programmes stacked, the floats prepared. The great state coach has emerged from the Museum of London, the Whitbread Shire horses have been groomed, their harnesses polished and burnished. Tomorrow it will be all sound and spectacle. Today it is quiet in Guildhall yard, although there is some stir. At the Mansion House the retiring Lord Mayor is entertaining his successor to lunch together with some members from both their Livery Companies, the Aldermen, the Sheriffs, the Recorder and the chief City officers. After lunch the Lord Mayor is the first to leave the house in state in his Rolls Royce with the Esquires and City officers. They proceed to Guildhall. The Lord Mayor Elect follows in his private car, attended by his chaplain. They meet in the Court of Aldermen, where the new Lord Mayor is formally introduced, and the retiring Lord Mayor takes his leave of the Court. A procession is formed, with the Lord Mayor, the Lord Mayor Elect, the Aldermen and the Sheriffs, all wearing their violet gowns and they go into the Hall.

In the centre of the Hall there is a large table round which are ranged a few rows of seats. The front row is for the Aldermen and City officers. Behind sit the wives, friends and relations of the participants and a few members of the public who have managed to obtain tickets. The retiring Lord Mayor sits at the head of the table with the Lord Mayor Elect on his left. The Recorder, the Senior Aldermen, the Town Clerk, the City

Comptroller, City Solicitor and the Remembrancer sit on the Lord Mayor's right; the Junior Aldermen, the Common Serjeant and the Chamberlain on the Lord Mayor's left. The Swordbearer and the Serjeant-at-Arms stand at the far end of the table facing the Lord Mayor. When all are seated the Serjeant-at-Arms comes forward with the Mace on his shoulder, bows three times, and stands with the Mace at rest. The Town Clerk then rises, bows three times and reads a short declaration which the Lord Mayor Elect, standing, repeats. These are the only words spoken at this otherwise silent ceremony. The Lord Mayor Elect signs a written version of his Declaration with a quill pen. At that point he becomes the new Lord Mayor. The outgoing Lord Mayor gives up his seat and they change places. The new Lord Mayor puts on his black tricorne hat.

Then the civic insignia are solemnly passed from the outgoing Lord Mayor to the incoming Lord Mayor. One by one the appropriate officers rise, make three reverences, advance with the symbols of office, present them to the old Lord Mayor who delivers them to the new Lord Mayor, bow three times and retire. Thus the Chamberlain presents the Crystal Sceptre, the Mayoral Seal and the City Purse, which are all handed by the old Lord Mayor to his successor, who places them on a velvet cushion in front of him. The Swordbearer presents the Sword. The Serjeant-at-Arms presents the Mace. These are too heavy to pass from hand to hand, so they are just touched by each Lord Mayor and then placed on the table. The Swordbearer presents the Collar of SS links and the Jewel on a velvet cushion. These are handed over to the Lord Mayor and then returned to him. The Principal Clerk to the Chamberlain comes forward, bowing, and recovers the Sceptre, Seal and Purse. The Swordbearer and the Serjeant-at-Arms take back the Sword and the Mace. The Comptroller and City Solicitor advance, bowing in the same way and present the Indenture for the City Plate and the Agreement for payment to the Lord Mayor of an allowance in lieu of all fees, which the Lord Mayor signs. He also signs the appointment of the Deputy City Gauger (a personal appointment by the Lord Mayor, now purely honorary), which the Remembrancer presents. The outgoing Lord Mayor hands over the keys of the City Seal and the Hospital Seal to the new Lord Mayor. All this takes some time, and is conducted in deep silence, only the measured footsteps echoing in the great Hall. Then the tension relaxes and all the Aldermen, Sheriffs and Officers advance to congratulate the Lord Mayor. After this he and the late Lord Mayor walk out, both wearing their hats, and are greeted by a fanfare from the State Trumpeters and the pealing of the bells of St

Lawrence Jewry. They both return to Mansion House in the Lord Mayor's car. There, with their wives, they have a cup of tea. Then the late Lord Mayor, who is packed and ready to go, briefly says goodbye to the staff and leaves without further ceremony. A new mayoral year has begun.

Appendix

LORD MAYORS OF THE CITY OF LONDON FROM 1189

The years given are those of election – the mayoralty extends now from November of one year to November of the next.

The letter W indicates the appointment or election of a Warden.

The figures in brackets indicate repetitions of any name in the list.

1189–1211	Henry FitzAilwyn	1253	Nicholas Bat
1212–14	Roger FitzAlan	1254–7	Ralph Hardel
1215	Serlo le Mercer	1258	William FitzRichard
1215	William Hardel	1259	John Gisors (2)
1216	James Alderman	1259–60	William FitzRichard (2)
1217	Salomon de Basing	1261–4	Thomas FitzThomas
1218–21	Serlo le Mercer (2)	1265	Hugh FitzOtho
1222–6	Richard Renger	1265	John Walerand (W)
1227–30	Roger le Duke		John de la Linde (W)
1231–7	Andrew Buckerel	1266	William FitzRichard (3) (W)
1238	Richard Renger (2)	1267	Alan la Zuche (W)
1239	William Joynier	1268	Thomas de Ippegrave (W)
1240	Gerard Bat	1268	Stephen de Eddeworth (W)
1240	Reginald de Bungheye	1269	Hugh FitzOtho (2) (W)
1241–3	Ralph Ashwy	1270	John Adrien
1244–5	Michael Tovy	1271–2	Walter Hervey
1246	John Gisors	1273	Henry le Waleys
1246	Peter FitzAlan	1274–80	Gregory de Rokesley
1247–8	Michael Tovy (2)	1281–3	Henry le Waleys (2)
1249	Roger FitzRoger	1284	Gregory de Rokesley (2)
1250	John Norman	1285–9	Ralph de Sandwich (W)
1251	Adam de Basing	1289	John le Breton (2)
1252	John Tulesan	1289–92	Ralph de Sandwich (2) (W)

1293–8	John le Breton (2) (W)	1362	Stephen Cavendisshe
1298	Henry le Waleys (3)	1363	John Nott
1299–1300	Elias Russell	1364–5	Adam de Bury
1301–07	John le Blund	1366	John Lovekyn (3)
1308	Nicholas de Farndone	1367	James Andreu
1309	Thomas Romeyn	1368	Simon de Mordone
1310	Richer de Refham	1369	John de Chichester
1311–12	John de Gisors	1370–1	John Bernes
1313	Nicholas de Farndone (2)	1372	John Pyel
1314	John de Gisors (2)	1373	Adam de Bury (2)
1315	Stephen de Abyndon	1374	William Walworth
1316–18	John de Wengrave	1375	John Warde
1319	Hamo de Chigwell	1376	Adam Stable
1320	Nicholas de Farndone (3)	1377	Nicholas Brembre
1321	Robert de Kendale (W)	1378	John Philipot
1321–2	Hamo de Chigwell (2)	1379	John Hadle
1323	Nicholas de Farndone (4)	1380	William Walworth (2)
1323–5	Hamo de Chigwell (3)	1381–2	John de Northampton
1326	Richard de Betoyne	1383–5	Sir Nicholas Brembre (2)
1327	Hamo de Chigwell (4)	1386–7	Nicholas Exton
1328	John de Grantham	1388	Sir Nicholas Twyford
1329	Simon Swanlond	1389	William Venour
1330–1	John de Pulteney	1390	Adam Bamme
1332	John de Prestone	1391	John Heende
1333	John de Pulteney (2)	1392	Sir Edward Dalyngrigge
1334–5	Reginald de Conduit		(W)
1336	John de Pulteney (3)	1392	Sir Baldwin Radyngton (W)
1337–8	Henry Darci	1392	William Staundon
1339–40	Andrew Aubrey	1393	John Hadle (2)
1341	John de Oxenford	1394	John Fresshe
1342	Simon Frauncis	1395	William More
1343–4	John Hamond	1396	Adam Bamme (2)
1345	Richard le Lacer	1397	Richard Whittington (1)
1346	Geoffrey de Wichingham	1397	Richard Whittington (2)
1347	Thomas Leggy	1398	Drew Barentyn
1348	John Lovekyn	1399	Thomas Knolles
1349	Walter Turke	1400	John Fraunceys
1350	Richard de Kislingbury	1401	John Shadworth
1351	Andrew Aubrey (2)	1402	John Walcote
1352–3	Adam Fraunceys	1403	William Askham
1354	Thomas Leggy (2)	1404	John Heende (2)
1355	Simon Frauncis (2)	1405	John Wodecok
1356	Henry Picard	1406	Richard Whittington (3)
1357	John de Stodeye	1407	William Staundon (2)
1358	John Lovekyn (2)	1408	Drugo Barentyn (2)
1359	Simon Dolseley	1409	Richard Merlawe
1360	John Wroth	1410	Thomas Knolles (2)
1361	John Pecche	1411	Robert Chichele

1412	William Walderne	1460	Richard Lee
1413	William Crowmere	1461	Hugh Wiche
1414	Thomas Fauconer	1462	Thomas Cooke
1415	Nicholas Wotton	1463	Matthew Philip
1416	Henry Barton	1464	Ralph Josselyn
1417	Richard Merlawe (2)	1465	Ralph Verney
1418	William Sevenoke	1466	John Yonge
1419	Richard Whittington (4)	1467	Thomas Oulegrave
1420	William Cauntbrigge	1468	William Taillour
1421	Robert Chichele (2)	1469	Richard Lee (2)
1422	William Walderne (2)	1470	John Stockton
1423	William Crowmere (2)	1471	William Edward
1424	John Michell	1472	Sir William Hampton
1425	John Coventre	1473	John Tate
1426	John Reynwell	1474	Robert Drope
1427	John Gedney	1475	Robert Bassett
1428	Henry Barton (2)	1476	Sir Ralph Josselyn (2)
1429	William Estfeld	1477	Humphrey Hayford
1430	Nicholas Wotton (2)	1478	Richard Gardyner
1431	John Welles	1479	Sir Bartholomew James
1432	John Perneys	1480	John Browne
1433	John Brokle	1481	William Haryot
1434	Robert Otele	1482	Edmund Shaa
1435	Henry Frowyk	1483	Robert Billesdon
1436	John Michell (2)	1484	Thomas Hill
1437	William Estfeld (2)	1485	Sir William Stokker
1438	Stephen Broun	1485	John Warde
1439	Robert Large	1485	Sir Hugh Bryce
1440	John Paddesle	1486	Henry Colet
1441	Robert Clopton	1487	William Horne
1442	John Hatherle	1488	Robert Tate
1443	Thomas Catworth	1489	William White
1444	Henry Frowyk (2)	1490	John Mathewe
1445	Simon Eyre	1491	Hugh Clopton
1446	John Olney	1492	William Martin
1447	John Gedney (2)	1493	Ralp Astry
1448	Stephen Broun (2)	1494	Richard Chawry
1449	Thomas Chalton	1495	Sir Henry Colet (2)
1450	Nicholas Wyfold	1496	John Tate
1451	William Gregory	1497	William Purchase
1452	Geoffrey Feldynge	1498	Sir John Percyvale
1453	John Norman	1499	Nicholas Ailwyn
1454	Stephen Forster	1500	William Remyngton
1455	William Marowe	1501	Sir John Shaa
1456	Thomas Canynges	1502	Bartholomew Rede
1457	Geoffrey Boleyn	1503	Sir William Capel
1458	Thomas Scott	1504	John Wynger
1459	William Hulyn	1505	Thomas Kneseworth

APPENDIX

1506	Sir Richard Haddon	1549	Sir Rowland Hill
1507	William Browne	1550	Andrew Judde
1508	Sir Lawrence Aylmer	1551	Richard Dobbis
1508	Stephen Jenyns	1552	George Barne
1509	Thomas Bradbury	1553	Thomas Whyte
1510	Sir William Capel (2)	1554	John Lyon
1510	Henry Kebyll	1555	William Garrarde
1511	Roger Achleley	1556	Thomas Offley
1512	William Copynger	1557	Thomas Curtes
1513	Sir Richard Haddon (2)	1558	Thomas Leigh
1513	William Browne	1559	William Hewet
1514	Sir John Tate (2)	1560	Sir William Chester
1514	George Monoux	1561	William Harper
1515	William Boteler	1562	Thomas Lodge
1516	John Rest	1563	John Whyte
1517	Thomas Exmewe	1564	Richard Malorye
1518	Thomas Mirfyn	1565	Richard Champyon
1519	James Yarford	1566	Christopher Draper
1520	John Brugge	1567	Roger Martyn
1521	John Milborne	1568	Thomas Rowe
1522	John Mundy	1569	Alexander Avenon
1523	Thomas Baldry	1570	Rowland Heyward
1524	William Bayley	1571	William Allen
1525	John Aleyn	1572	Lionel Duckett
1526	Sir Thomas Semer	1573	John Ryvers
1527	James Spencer	1574	James Hawes
1528	John Rudstone	1575	Ambrose Nicholas
1529	Ralph Dodmer	1576	John Langley
1530	Thomas Pargeter	1577	Thomas Ramsay
1531	Nicholas Lambarde	1578	Richard Pype
1532	Stephen Pecocke	1579	Nicholas Woodroffe
1533	Christopher Ascue	1580	John Branche
1534	Sir John Champneys	1581	James Harvye
1535	Sir John Aleyn (2)	1582	Thomas Blanke
1536	Ralph Warren	1583	Edward Osborne
1537	Sir Richard Gresham	1584	Thomas Pullyson
1538	William Forman	1585	Wolstan Dixie
1539	Sir William Hollyes	1586	George Barne
1540	William Roche	1587	George Bonde
1541	Michael Dormer	1588	Martin Calthorp
1542	John Cotes	1589	Richard Martin
1543	William Bowyer	1589	John Harte
1544	Sir Ralph Warren (2)	1590	John Allot
1544	William Laxton	1591	Sir Rowland Heyward (2)
1545	Sir Martin Bowes	1591	William Webbe
1546	Henry Huberthorn	1592	William Rowe
1547	Sir John Gresham	1593	Cuthbert Buckell
1548	Henry Amcotts	1594	Sir Richard Martin (2)

1594	John Spencer	1640	Edmund Wright
1595	Stephen Slanye	1641	Richard Gurney
1596	Thomas Skinner	1642	Isaac Penington
1596	Henry Billingsley	1643	Sir John Wollaston
1597	Richard Saltonstall	1644	Thomas Atkyn
1598	Stephen Soame	1645	Thomas Adams
1599	Nicholas Mosley	1646	Sir John Gayer
1600	William Ryder	1647	John Warner
1601	John Garrarde	1648	Abraham Reynardson
1602	Robert Lee	1649	Thomas Andrewes
1603	Sir Thomas Bennett	1649	Thomas Foot
1604	Sir Thomas Lowe	1650	Thomas Andrewes (2)
1605	Sir Leonard Halliday	1651	John Kendricke
1606	Sir John Watts	1652	John Fowke
1607	Sir Henry Rowe	1653	Thomas Vyner
1608	Sir Humphrey Weld	1654	Christopher Pack
1609	Sir Thomas Cambell	1655	John Dethick
1610	Sir William Craven	1656	Robert Tichborne
1611	Sir James Pemberton	1657	Richard Chiverton
1612	Sir John Swynnerton	1658	Sir John Ireton
1613	Sir Thomas Middleton	1659	Thomas Alleyn
1614	Sir Thomas Hayes	1660	Sir Richard Browne, Bt
1615	Sir John Jolles	1661	Sir John Frederick
1616	John Leman	1662	Sir John Robinson, Bt
1617	George Bolles	1663	Sir Anthony Bateman
1618	Sir Sebastian Harvey	1664	Sir John Lawrence
1619	Sir William Cokayne	1665	Sir Thomas Bludworth
1620	Sir Frances Jones	1666	Sir William Bolton
1621	Edward Barkham	1667	Sir William Peake
1622	Peter Probie	1668	Sir William Turner
1623	Martin Lumley	1669	Sir Samuel Starling
1624	John Gore	1670	Sir Richard Ford
1625	Allan Cotton	1671	Sir George Waterman
1626	Cuthbert Hacket	1672	Sir Robert Hanson
1627	Hugh Hammersley	1673	Sir William Hooker
1628	Richard Deane	1674	Sir Robert Vyner, Bt
1629	James Cambell	1675	Sir Joseph Sheldon
1630	Sir Robert Ducye, Bt	1676	Sir Thomas Davies
1631	George Whitmore	1677	Sir Francis Chaplin
1632	Nicholas Rainton	1678	Sir James Edwards
1633	Ralph Freeman	1679	Sir Robert Clayton
1634	Thomas Moulson	1680	Sir Patience Ward
1634	Robert Parkhurst	1681	Sir John Moore
1635	Christopher Clitherow	1682	Sir William Prichard
1636	Edward Bromfield	1683	Sir Henry Tulse
1637	Richard Ven	1684	Sir James Smyth
1638	Sir Morris Abbot	1685	Sir Robert Geffery
1639	Henry Garraway	1686	Sir John Peake

APPENDIX

1687	Sir John Shorter	1735	Sir John Williams
1688	Sir John Eyles	1736	Sir John Thompson
1688	Sir John Chapman	1737	Sir John Barnard
1689–90	Thomas Pilkington	1738	Micajah Perry
1691	Sir Thomas Stampe	1739	Sir John Salter
1692	Sir John Fleet	1740	Humphrey Parsons (2)
1693	Sir William Ashurst	1741	Daniel Lambert
1694	Sir Thomas Lane	1741	Sir Robert Godschall
1695	Sir John Houblon	1742	George Heathcote
1696	Sir Edward Clarke	1742	Robert Willimott
1697	Sir Humphrey Edwin	1743	Robert Westley
1698	Sir Francis Child	1744	Henry Marshall
1699	Sir Richard Levett	1745	Richard Hoare
1700	Sir Thomas Abney	1746	William Benn
1701	Sir William Gore	1747	Sir Robert Ladbroke
1702	Sir Samuel Dashwood	1748	Sir William Calvert
1703	Sir John Parsons	1749	Sir Samuel Pennant
1704	Sir Owen Buckingham	1750	John Blachford
1705	Sir Thomas Rawlinson	1750	Francis Cockayne
1706	Sir Robert Bedingfeld	1751	Thomas Winterbottom
1707	Sir William Withers	1752	Robert Alsop
1708	Sir Charles Duncombe	1752	Crisp Gascoyne
1709	Sir Samuel Garrard, Bt	1753	Edward Ironside
1710	Sir Gilbert Heathcote	1753	Thomas Rawlinson
1711	Sir Robert Beachcroft	1754	Stephen T. Janssen
1712	Sir Richard Hoare	1755	Slingsby Bethell
1713	Sir Samuel Stanier	1756	Marshe Dickinson
1714	Sir William Humfreys	1757	Sir Charles Asgill
1715	Sir Charles Peers	1758	Sir Richard Glyn
1716	Sir James Bateman	1759	Sir Thomas Chitty
1717	Sir William Lewen	1760	Sir Mathew Blakiston
1718	Sir John Ward	1761	Sir Samuel Fludyer, Bt
1719	Sir George Thorold, Bt	1762	William Beckford
1720	Sir John Fryer, Bt	1763	William Bridgen
1721	Sir William Stewart	1764	Sir William Stephenson
1722	Sir Gerard Conyers	1765	George Nelson
1723	Sir Peter Delmé	1766	Sir Robert Kite
1724	Sir George Merttins	1767	Thomas Harley
1725	Sir Francis Forbes	1768	Samuel Turner
1726	Sir John Eyles, Bt	1769	William Beckford (2)
1727	Sir Edward Becher	1770	Barlow Trecothick
1728	Sir Robert Baylis	1770	Brass Crosby
1729	Sir Robert Brocas	1771	William Nash
1730	Humphrey Parsons	1772	James Townsend
1731	Francis Child	1773	Frederick Bull
1732	John Barber	1774	John Wilkes
1733	Sir William Billers	1775	John Sawbridge
1734	Sir Edward Bellamy	1776	Sir Thomas Hallifax

1777	Sir James Esdaile	1826	Anthony Brown
1778	Samuel Plumbe	1827	Matthias Prime Lucas
1779	Brackley Kennett	1828	William Thompson
1780	Sir Watkin Lewes	1829	John Crowder
1781	William Plomer	1830–1	John Key
1782	Nathaniel Newnham	1832	Sir Peter Laurie
1783	Robert Peckham	1833	Charles Farebrother
1784	Richard Clark	1834	Henry Winchester
1785	Thomas Wright	1835	William Taylor Copeland
1786	Thomas Sainsbury	1836	Thomas Kelly
1787	John Burnell	1837	John Cowan
1788	William Gill	1838	Samuel Wilson
1789	William Pickett	1839	Sir Chapman Marshall
1790	John Boydell	1840	Thomas Johnson
1791	John Hopkins	1841	John Pirie
1792	Sir James Sanderson	1842	John Humphrey
1793	Paul le Mesurier	1843	William Magnay
1794	Thomas Skinner	1844	Michael Gibbs
1795	William Curtis	1845	John Johnson
1796	Brook Watson	1846	Sir George Carroll
1797	John Anderson	1847	John Kinnersley Hooper
1798	Sir Richard Glyn	1848	Sir James Duke
1799	Harvey Christian Combe	1849	Thomas Farncomb
1800	Sir William Staines	1850	John Musgrove
1801	Sir John Eamer	1851	William Hunter
1802	Charles Price	1852	Thomas Challis
1803	John Perring	1853	Thomas Sidney
1804	Peter Perchard	1854	Francis G. Moon
1805	James Shaw	1855	David Salomons
1806	Sir William Leighton	1856	Thomas Finnis
1807	John Ansley	1857	Sir Robert Carden
1808	Charles Flower	1858	David Wire
1809	Thomas Smith	1859	John Carter
1810	Joshua Smith	1860–1	William Cubitt
1811	Claudius Stephen Hunter	1862	William Rose
1812	George Scholey	1863	William Lawrence
1813	William Domville	1864	Warren Hale
1814	Samuel Birch	1865	Benjamin Phillips
1815–16	Matthew Wood	1866	Thomas Gabriel
1817	Christopher Smith	1867	William Allen
1818	John Atkins	1868	James Lawrence
1819	George Bridges	1869	Robert Besley
1820	John Thomas Thorp	1870	Thomas Dakin
1821	Christopher Magnay	1871	Sills Gibbons
1822	William Heygate	1872	Sir Sydney Waterlow
1823	Robert Waithman	1873	Andrew Lusk
1824	John Garratt	1874	David Stone
1825	William Venables	1875	William Cotton

APPENDIX

1876	Sir Thomas White	1923	Col. Sir Louis Newton
1877	Thomas Owden	1924	Sir Alfred Bower
1878	Sir Charles Whetham	1925	Sir William Pryke
1879	Sir Francis W. Truscott	1926	Sir George R. Blades, Bt
1880	William McArthur	1927	Sir Charles Batho
1881	John Ellis	1928	Sir John E. K. Studd
1882	Henry Knight	1929	Sir William Waterlow
1883	Robert Fowler	1930	Sir William P. Neal
1884	George Nottage	1931	Sir Maurice Jenks
1885	Robert Fowler (2)	1932	Sir Percy Greenaway
1885	John Staples	1933	Sir Charles Collett
1886	Sir Reginald Hanson	1934	Sir Stephen Killik
1887	Polydore de Keyser	1935	Sir Percy Vincent
1888	James Whitehead	1936	Sir George Broadbridge
1889	Sir Henry Isaacs	1937	Sir Harry Twyford
1890	Joseph Savory	1938	Maj. Sir Frank Bowater
1891	David Evans	1939	Sir William Coxen
1892	Stuart Knill	1940	Sir George Wilkinson
1893	George Tyler	1941	Lt. Col. Sir John Laurie
1894	Sir Joseph Renals	1942	Sir Samuel Joseph
1895	Sir Walter Wilkin	1943	Sir Frank Newson-Smith
1896	George Faudel-Phillips	1944	Sir Frank Alexander
1897	Lt. Col. Horatio Davies	1945	Sir Charles Davis
1898	Sir John Moore	1946	Sir Bracewell Smith
1899	Alfred Newton	1947	Sir Frederick Wells
1900	Frank Green	1948	Sir George Aylwen
1901	Sir Joseph Dimsdale	1949	Sir Frederick Rowland
1902	Sir Marcus Samuel	1950	Denys Lowson
1903	Sir James Ritchie	1951	Sir Leslie Boyce
1904	John Pound	1952	Sir Rupert De La Bère
1905	Walter Morgan	1953	Sir Noel V. Bowater, Bt
1906	Sir William Treloar	1954	H. W. Seymour Howard
1907	Sir John Bell	1955	Cuthbert L. Ackroyd
1908	Sir George Truscott	1956	Sir Cullum Welch
1909	Sir John Knill, Bt	1957	Sir Denis Truscott
1910	Sir Thomas V. Strong	1958	Sir Harold Gillett
1911	Sir Thomas B. Crosby	1959	Sir Edmund Stockdale
1912	Col. Sir David Burnett	1960	Sir Bernard Waley-Cohen
1913	Sir Thomas V. Bowater	1961	Sir Frederick Hoare
1914	Col. Sir Charles Johnston	1962	Sir Ralph Perring
1915	Col. Sir Charles Wakefield	1963	Sir James Harman
1916	Sir William Dunn	1964	Sir James Miller
1917	Charles Hanson	1965	Sir Lionel Denny
1918	Sir Horace Marshall	1966	Sir Robert Bellinger
1919	Sir Edward Cooper	1967	Sir Gilbert Inglefield
1920	James Roll	1968	Sir Charles Trinder
1921	Sir John Baddeley	1969	Lt. Col. Sir Ian F. Bowater
1922	Edward C. Moore	1970	Sir Peter Studd

MY LORD MAYOR

1971	Sir Edward Howard	1980	Sir Ronald Gardner-Thorpe
1972	The Rt. Hon. The Lord Mais	1981	Sir Christopher Leaver
		1982	Sir Anthony Jolliffe
1973	Sir Hugh Wontner	1983	Dame Mary Donaldson
1974	Sir Murray Fox	1984	Sir Alan Traill
1975	Sir Lindsay Ring	1985	Sir Allan Davis
1976	Sir Robin Gillett	1986	Sir David Rowe-Ham
1977	Sir Peter Vanneck	1987	Sir Greville Spratt
1978	Sir Kenneth Cork	1988	Sir Christopher Collett
1979	Sir Peter Gadsden		

SELECT BIBLIOGRAPHY

Sources for so many individuals and eight hundred years of City history range very widely and the following list contains only those I have found most useful. An essential introduction to the history of the City is R. R. Sharpe's *London and the Kingdom,* and for the early period up to the beginning of the seventeenth century John Stow's *Survey of London* is invaluable. The definitive work on the aldermen is A. B. Beaven's *The Aldermen of the City of London. The Dictionary of National Biography* covers the outstanding lord mayors, and those who were members of parliament are featured in the biographical sections of the *History of Parliament* (as yet incomplete). I have found the *Noble Collection* in the Guildhall Library Print Room and the Guildhall Record Office's *Biographical Details* very helpful. Obituaries of many lord mayors can be found in *The Gentleman's Magazine* and in *The Times.* Details of twentieth-century lord mayors are in the various volumes of *Who was Who* and in *Who's Who.*

Allen, W. F. *The Corporation of London: its Rights and Privileges,* London, 1858.
Ashton, R. *The City and the Court,* Cambridge University Press, 1979.
Baddeley, Sir John *The Guildhall,* Corporation of London, 1951.
   The Aldermen of Cripplegate, London, 1900.
Baker, T. *Medieval London,* Cassell, 1970.
Barron, C. 'Richard Whittington: The Man Behind the Myth'.
   Studies in London History, Hodder, 1969.
   'The Reign of Richard II', *Essays in Honour of May McKisack,* Athlone Press, 1971.
Beaven, A. B. *The Aldermen of the City of London,* 2 vols, Corporation of London, 1908–13.
Begbie, E. H. *Charles Cheers Wakefield,* Hodder, 1917.
Bergeron, D. M. *English Civic Pageantry, 1558–1642,* Edward Arnold, 1970.
Betts, J. *The Pageantry of London City,* Corporation of London, 1974.
Bird, R. *The Turbulent London of Richard II,* Longman, 1949.

Brooke, C. N. L. assisted by Mrs G. I. Keir *London 800–1216 The Shaping of a City,* Secker and Warburg, 1975.

Champness, W. H. *Sir John Champneys:* A Tudor Lord Mayor, manuscript Guildhall Library, 1951.

Clode, M. *The Early History of the Merchant Taylors,* L. Harrison, privately printed, 1888.

Cokayne, G. E. *Lord Mayors and Sheriffs of London 1601–1625,* London, Phillimore, 1897.

Crawford, A. *A History of the Vintners' Company,* Constable, 1977.

Dodd, A. H. 'Sir Thomas Middleton', *Elizabethan Government and Society,* Ed. Hurstfield, 1961.

Doolittle, I. *The City of London and its Livery Companies,* Dorchester, Gavin Press, 1982.

Eades, G. E. *Historic London,* Queen Anne Press, 1966.

Evelyn, J. *Diary of John Evelyn,* Oxford, Clarendon Press, 1955.

Fabyan *New Chronicles of England and France,* Ed. Ellis, 1811.

Fairholt, F. W. *Lord Mayors Pageants,* 2 vols, Percy Society, 1843–44.

Fell, R. C. *Passages from the private and official life of Thomas Kelly,* Groombridge, 1856.

Fiennes, C. *Journeys of Celia Fiennes,* Macdonald, 1982.

Fitzstephen, W. *Description of London* (see F. M. Stenton)

Flynn, J. S. *Sir Robert Fowler,* Hodder, 1893.

Foster, F. F. *The Politics of Stability,* Royal Historical Society, 1977.

Fox, C. A. 'Mr Moon the printseller of Threadneedle Street', *'Collectanea Londiniensia'. Studies presented to Ralph Merrifield,* London and Middlesex Archaeological Society, 1978.

Gairdner, J. *Historical Collections of a Citizen of London in the Fifteenth century* (also called 'Gregory's Chronicle') Camden Society.

   Three Fifteenth Century Chronicles, Camden Society.

George, M. D. *London Life in the Eighteenth Century,* Keegan Paul, 1925.

Girtin, T. H. *The Lord Mayor of London,* Oxford University Press, 1948.

Giuseppi, J. *History of the Bank of England,* Evans, 1966.

Gray, R. A. *A History of London,* Hutchinson, 1978.

Hibbert, C. *London, the Biography of a City,* Allen Lane, 1969.

Hickey, W. *Memoirs of William Hickey,* Ed. Alfred Spencer, London, Hurst, 1948.

Hoare, R. *A Journal of the Shrievalty of Richard Hoare 1740–41,* Bath, 1815.

Holmes, M. J. R. *Elizabethan London,* Cassell, 1969.

James, N. Brett *The Growth of Stuart London,* Allen and Unwin, 1935.

Jones, P. E. *Some London Civic Institutions,* London, Phillimore, 1946.

   'Whittington's Longhouse', *London Topographical Records,* Vol. 23 pp 27–34 plus plans, 1972.

Jordan, W. K. *The Charities of London 1480–1660,* Allen and Unwin, 1959.

Kent, W. T. G. *My Lord Mayor,* Jenkins, 1947.

   London Worthies, London, Phoenix House, 1948.

Knill, L. *The Mansion House,* Stanley Paul, 1937.

Lang, R. *London's Aldermen in Business,* Guildhall Miscellany, 1971.

Laurie, P. G. *Sir Peter Laurie: A Family Memoir,* Brentwood, privately printed, 1901.

Levin, J. *The Charter Controversy in the City of London,* Athlone Press, 1969.

Macaulay, T. B. *History of England,* Macmillan, 1913–15.

Machyn, H. *The Diary of Henry Machyn from 1550–1563,* Ed. John Gough Nichols, Camden Society, 1948.

Mackenzie, D. *Mayors and Alderman of Great Britain,* London, Clauston, 1935.

Malcolm, J. P. *Anecdotes of the manners and customs of London during the Eighteenth century,* Longman, 1811.

McKisack, M. 'London and the succession to the Crown during the Middle Ages', *Studies in Medieval history presented to F. M. Powicke*, 1948.

Masters, B. 'The Mayor's Household before 1600', *Studies in London History*, Hodder, 1969.

Masters, B. *The Chamberlain of the City of London*, Corporation of London, 1988.

Melton, F. T. *Sir Robert Clayton and the origins of English Deposit Banking*, Cambridge University Press, 1986.

Morton, B. N. *Americans in London*, Macdonald, 1988.

Myers, A. R. *London in the Age of Chaucer*, University of Oklahoma, 1974.

Newson, G. *American London*, Q Books, Kingston, Surrey, 1982.

Orridge, B. B. *Some account of the citizens of London and their rulers*, London, Tegg, 1867.

Owen, D. *The Government of Victorian London*, Cambridge, Massachusetts, Belknap Press, 1982.

Paget, J. T. *The Pageantry of Britain*, Michael Joseph, 1979.

Pearl, V. *London and the outbreak of the Puritan Revolution*, Oxford University Press, 1961.
  'Change and Stability in Seventeenth century London', *London Journal*, Vol. 5 No. 1, 1979.

Pepys, S. *The Diary of Samuel Pepys*, Ed. R. Latham and W. Matthews, Bell, 1970–73.

Perks, S. *History of the Mansion House*, Cambridge University Press, 1922.

Perry, M. *The Diary of Micajah Perry* (see W. Treloar)

Pulling, A. *Laws Customs etc. of the City and Port of London*, London, Bond, 1854.

Ramsay, G. D. *The City of London in international politics at the accession of Elizabeth Tudor*, Manchester University Press, 1975.

Reynolds, S. 'The Rulers of London in the Twelfth century', *History*, Vol. 1 vii, 1972.

Riley, H. T. *Chronicles of the Mayors and Sheriffs of London*, Trubner, 1863.
  Memorials of London and London Life, Longman, 1868.
  Trs. of the Liber Albus, the White Book of the City of London, 1868.

Rivington, C. *'Tyrant' The Story of John Barber*, 1988.
  'Sir Thomas Davies', *The Library*, Vol. III, September, 1981.

Robertson, D. *Chaucer's London*, Wiley, New York, 1968.

Round, J. H. *The Commune of London*, Westminster, 1899.

Rudé, G. F. E. *Hanoverian London*, Secker and Warburg, 1971.

Rye, W. B. *England as seen by foreigners in the days of Elizabeth and James*, 1865.

Sayer, T. L. *Gog, Magog and I*, London, Sampson Low, 1931.

Sayle, R. T. D. *Lord Mayors Pageants of the Merchant Taylors' Company*, London, privately printed, 1931.

Sharpe, R. R. *London and the Kingdom*, 3 vols, Longman, 1894.

Sheppard, F. H. W. *London 1808–1870, The Infernal Wen*, Secker and Warburg, 1971.

Smalley, G. W. *The Life of Sir Sydney H. Waterlow, Lord Mayor, Captain of Industry and Philanthropist*, Edward Arnold, 1909.

Stenton, F. M. *Norman London*, with a translation of William Fitzstephen's *Description of London*, Historical Association, 1934.

Stevenson, J. Ed. *London in the Age of Reform*, Blackwell, 1977.

Stockdale, E. *Ptolemy Tortoise*, Basingstoke, privately printed, 1978.

Stone, L. 'The Peer and the Alderman's daughter', *History Today*, Vol. II, 1961.

Stow, J. *Survey of London*, Kingsford Edition, 2 vols, Oxford University Press, 1971.

Summerson, J. *Georgian London*, Pelican, 1962.

Sutherland, L. S. 'The City of London and opposition to government 1768–1774', *The Creighton Lecture in History*, 1958.
  'The City of London and the Devonshire–Pitt Administration 1756–7', *The Raleigh Lecture in History*, 1960.

'The City in Eighteenth century politics', *Essays presented to S. L. Namier,* 1956.

Sutton, A. 'Sir Thomas Cook and his troubles', *Guildhall Studies in London History,* 1978.

'Richard III, the City of London and Southwark', *The Ricardian,* 1975.

Thomas, A. H. *Calendar of Plea and Memorial Rolls 1364–1381,* Cambridge University Press, 1926–61.

Thomas, A. H. and Thornley, I. D. Eds. *The Great Chronicle of London,* G. W. Jones, printer, 1938.

Thrupp, S. *The Merchant Class of Medieval London,* University of Chicago and Cambridge University Press, 1948.

Treloar, W. *Diary of a Lord Mayor including the Diary of Micajah Perry,* London, John Murray, 1920.

Wilkes and the City, John Murray, 1917.

Uffenbach, Z. C. *'London in 1710' The Travels of Z. C. von Uffenbach,* tr W. H. Quarrell and M. Mare, 1934.

Unwin, G. *The Guilds and Companies of London,* Frank Cass, 1963.

Venn, H. *Memoirs of the late Sir John Barnard,* London, privately printed, T. Hankey, 1885.

Walker, R. *Sir James Whitehead Lord Mayor Extraordinary,* typescript, Guildhall Library, 1987.

Webb, S. & B. *English Local Government. The Manor and the Borough,* Vol. 3, Longman, 1906–29.

Walsingham, *Historia Anglicana,* 2 vols, Rolls Series.

Weinstein, R. 'Sir John Leman: The Making of a Lord Mayor', *Proceedings of the Huguenot Society,* Vol. XXIV no. 4, 1986.

Welch, C. *Modern History of the City of London,* Blades East & Blades, 1896.

Williams, G. A. *Medieval London from Commune to Capital,* Athlone Press, 1970.

Withington, R. *English Pageantry,* 2 vols, Blom, New York, 1963.

Woodhead, J. R. *The Rulers of London 1660–1689,* London and Middlesex Archaeological Society, 1965.

Corporation of London Publications

Guildhall

Mansion House

City of London Official Guide

Statement as to the origin, constitution and functions of the Corporation of London 1974

Ceremonials of the Corporation of London, compiled by Raymond Smith, 1962.

City of London Select Booklist, by Donovan Dawe, 1972

The Remembrancia Analytical Index, E. J. Francis and Co., 1878

DEDICATIONS

Livery Companies and other companies

The Worshipful Company of Actuaries
The Worshipful Guild of Air Pilots and
Air Navigators
The Worshipful Society of Apothecaries of
London
The Worshipful Society of Arbitrators
The Worshipful Company of Bakers
The Worshipful Company of Barbers
The Worshipful Company of Barkers
The Worshipful Company of Basketmakers
The Worshipful Company of Blacksmiths
The Worshipful Company of Brewers
The Worshipful Company of Butchers
The Worshipful Company of Carmen
The Worshipful Company of Chartered
Secretaries and Administrators
The Worshipful Company of Chartered
Surveyors
The Worshipful Company of Clothworkers
The Company of Constructors
The Worshipful Company of Coopers
The Worshipful Company of Cordwainers
The Worshipful Company of Cutlers
The Worshipful Company of Dyers
The Worshipful Company of Engineers
The Worshipful Company of
Environmental Cleaners
The Worshipful Company of Farriers
The Worshipful Company of Feltmakers of
London
The Worshipful Company of Founders
The Worshipful Company of Framework
Knitters
The Worshipful Company of Fruiterers
The Worshipful Company of Fuellers
The Worshipful Company of Furniture
Makers
The Worshipful Company of Gardeners
The Worshipful Company of Glass Sellers
The Worshipful Company of Glaziers and
Painters of Glass

The Worshipful Company of Gold and
Silver Wyre Drawers
The Worshipful Company of Goldsmiths
The Worshipful Company of Gunmakers
The Worshipful Company of Haberdashers
The Worshipful Company of Horners
The Worshipful Company of Innholders
The Worshipful Company of Insurers
The Worshipful Company of Ironmongers
The Worshipful Company of Launderers
The Worshipful Company of Leathersellers
The Worshipful Company of
Lightmongers
The Worshipful Company of Loriners
The Worshipful Company of Marketors
The Worshipful Company of Masons
The Company of Merchants of the City of
Edinburgh
The Worshipful Company of Merchant
Taylors
The Worshipful Company of Musicians
The Worshipful Company of Painter-
Stainers
The Worshipful Company of Pewterers
The Worshipful Company of Plaisterers
The Worshipful Company of Plumbers
The Worshipful Company of Salters
The Worshipful Company of Scriveners
The Worshipful Company of Solicitors of
the City of London
The Worshipful Company of Spectacle
Makers
The Worshipful Company of Stationers
and Newspaper Makers
The Worshipful Company of Tin Plate
Workers alias Wire Workers
The Worshipful Company of Vintners
The Worshipful Company of Wax
Chandlers
The Worshipful Company of Weavers
The Worshipful Company of Woolmen

Masters, Prime Wardens and Upper Bailiff in 1989

W. John Alsford	The Worshipful Company of Farriers
Brian Atchley	The Worshipful Company of Coopers
Major Dennis Baker	The Worshipful Company of Carmen
John C. H. Baker	The Worshipful Company of Launderers
Mr R. H. Boissier	The Worshipful Company of Tin Plate Workers alias Wire Workers
B. L. M. Brew, TD	The Worshipful Company of Coachmakers and Coach-Harness Makers
Ian Richard Bush	The Worshipful Company of Lightmongers
Robin Cyril Chaventré, FCA	The Worshipful Company of Wax Chandlers
George R. B. Clarke	The Worshipful Company of Horners
Thomas O. D. Craig (Prime Warden)	The Worshipful Company of Basketmakers
Professor H. J. A. Dartnall, DSc, PhD, CChem, FRSC	The Worshipful Company of Spectacle Makers
Ian Frederick Davies	The Worshipful Company of Lightmongers
Harry F. Druce, FInstM, MInstPI	The Worshipful Company of Marketors
Lt.Col. Sir Vivian Dunn, KCVO, OBE, FRAM	The Worshipful Company of Musicians
E. J. P. Elliott	The Worshipful Company of Feltmakers of London
R. D. Emerson, MA, FCA	The Worshipful Company of Cordwainers
Ralph Gabriel, MA, CEng (Prime Warden)	The Worshipful Company of Blacksmiths
Reg Gill	The Worshipful Company of Horners
Mr D. J. K. Greggains	The Worshipful Company of Tin Plate Workers alias Wire Workers
Robert Henry Hamblin, MA, FCIS	The Worshipful Company of Wax Chandlers
Rear Admiral P. G. Hammersley, CB, OBE	The Worshipful Company of Engineers
Robert Hardy, CBE	The Worshipful Company of Bowyers
Derek P. C. Harris	The Worshipful Company of Tobacco Pipe Makers and Tobacco Blenders
D. G. Hope-Mason	The Worshipful Company of Fruiterers
Vice Admiral Sir John Lea, KBE	The Worshipful Company of Plumbers
Robert John Leighton, TD	The Worshipful Company of Stationers and Newspaper Makers
John G. Lightowler	The Worshipful Company of Painter-Stainers
Raymond Lister, MA (Prime Warden)	The Worshipful Company of Blacksmiths
V. C. M. Lister	The Worshipful Company of Leathersellers
John Bassett Lumsden	The Worshipful Company of Wheelwrights
Michael MacLagan, CVO, FSA, Richmond Herald	The Worshipful Company of Scriveners
Geoffrey Wyndham Marshall	The Worshipful Company of Pattenmakers
Michael C. Martin Esq, CEng, CBIM, MIProdE	The Worshipful Company of Framework Knitters
Mr P. E. Moody, CBE, FIA	The Worshipful Company of Actuaries

DEDICATIONS

Peter G. Nathan, MA — The Worshipful Company of Gold and Silver Wyre Drawers

Colonel F. G. Neild — The Worshipful Society of Apothecaries of London

Graham R. Newman Esq (Prime Warden) — The Worshipful Company of Shipwrights

Ronald H. Peet, CBE, MA, FIA — The Worshipful Company of Insurers

Douglas M. Read — The Worshipful Company of Scientific Instrument Makers

John Reid, RIBA, PPCSD — The Worshipful Company of Chartered Architects

Dennis Roberts, BSc(Econ), FCIS — The Worshipful Company of Chartered Secretaries and Administrators

Doctor John Scorey — The Worshipful Company of Woolmen

John Harry Scrutton, FRICS — The Worshipful Company of Barbers

John Charles Smethers, FCA, JP — The Worshipful Company of Barbers

Robert Steel, CBE — The Worshipful Company of Chartered Surveyors

Fred S. Stringer Esq, BSc, FRIN, CEng, FRAeS — The Worshipful Guild of Air Pilots and Air Navigators

Ronald E. Sylvester — The Worshipful Company of Builders Merchants

Charles Henderson Tidbury — The Worshipful Company of Brewers

Maurice Vinter — The Worshipful Company of Builders Merchants

John S. Walker-Arnott — The Worshipful Company of Loriners

Jack L. Wallworth — The Worshipful Company of Feltmakers of London

M. A. C. Winterton, TD (Upper Bailiff) — The Worshipful Company of Weavers

Carl Aarvold
His Honour Judge J. S. R.
    Abdela, TD, QC
Conrad Abrahams
Keith Abrahams
Julian Dyke Acland
Dr Douglas Ian Acres,
    CBE, JP, DL
Alfred W. D. Adams
Mrs Jennifer Adams
William Henry Adams
Nicholas R. Adlam
John J. Adler
Ian Agnew
Arthur John Ainsley
Ewart Ingham Akeroyd
F. M. L. Akeroyd, BSc,
    CEng, MICE, FIHT,
    FIAT
Edith J. Albert, BA, MSc
V. L. Albert, FFA
Robert W. Alderton
John Aldington
Sir Alex Alexander
Sir Charles G. Alexander,
    BT
Richard Alexander
The Lady Alexander of
    Weedon
Philip F. Allday, FCA
Donald W. S. Alloway
Arthur Peter Cullerne Allt
Mrs Jenny M. Alsford
Richard Alston
Lionel P. Altman, CBE
G. Anthony Alton
Oswald E. Ames
Nicholas and Wendy Amey
Dr A. J. Amos, OBE
Derek Amos
A. A. J. Anderson, OBE
David M. Anderson
Robert Anderson
Alan C. F. Andrews
Stanley G. Angell
Francis Brittain Angier
Marcus Annesley
John Anthony, BSc

Anthony W. J. Appleton,
    BEd, FRICS, FCIOB
Dr W. J. Appleyard
S. Christopher Apps
Samuel Dougan Apsley
Francis George Martin
    Archbold
Francis Norman Archbold
G. W. F. (Bill) Archer,
    MBE
Harold Francis Archer
Peter Arkell
Geoffrey Flockton
    Armitage
Colonel W. E. I.
    Armstrong, OBE, TD,
    DL
Lord Armstrong of
    Ilminster
David Samuel Arno
John Charles Arno
D. P. J. Arnold Esq
P. A. Arnold Esq
Alex J. Arthur
Harold M. Arthur
Captain W. Ashby
Neil Ashley
Michael Henry Richardson
    Astbury
Anthony Alec Astor
E. F. Atkins
Major General Sir Leonard
    Atkinson, KBE
Alistair C. Attwood
S. Caroline Attwood
Thomas J. Attwood
Buchan of Auchmacoy
Maurice Frank Avent
Walter S. Avery
Captain J. S. L. Ayre

Robin P. Back
Revd Canon Martin
    Baddeley
Sidney R. Badley-Horner
Anthony F. Bagley
Alexander Richard Wynn
    Bailey

John A. Bailey
James Stuart Bain
Genetta Mary Baird
Miles St Clair Baird
Stewart Baird
The Reverend Donald
    Baker
Mr Henry Edmeades Baker,
    MA, CEng, FIEE, MICE
J. D. Baker, JP, FCA
Louise Baker
Peter Baker
Richard S. Baker
Ronald Charles Baker
Terrence Edward Baker,
    FCIB, MBIM
Tony Baldry, MP
A. Allen Baldwin
Edward Bales
The Earl of Balfour, JP
Richard Creighton Balfour,
    MBE, DHM
D. H. Ball
Geoffrey Ball
Ian Strickland Ball
Aubrey Ballinger
Walter Balmford
Constance May Bamford
George Cooper Banks
Trevor John Banks
James Michael Edward
    Bannister
Michael Bannister
Robert Michael Charles
    Bannister
Frederick P. Barber
Nicholas P. Barber
Henry George Barbour
Robert David Barbour
Clifford Barclay
James Phiminster Barclay
Timothy H. Barclay
Richard H. Barden
F. Roy Barker
Thomas Lloyd Barker
Captain W. J. Barker
Colonel William Barker
A. W. Barnes

F. W. J. Barnes Esq, MBE,
LLB(LOND)
John Barnes Esq,
LLB(LOND)
Peter W. Barnes
Ronald J. Barnes, FCIS
Rose and Kenneth Barnes
Mrs David Barnett
David Barnett
Philip H. Barnett
Rory Barnett
Stanley G. Barnett, CBE,
DL
Mrs Sylvia Barnett, OBE
Stuart Alan Barr
Dr Dennis Barrett, CBE,
DSc, FBHI
Donald Howard Barrett
James W. Barrett, JP
Stephen Barrett
Anthony C. Barrett Greene
Captain Michael Barrow,
DSO Royal Navy
Peter W. Barrows
John Bartlett
Donald Leonard Barwick
Charles Eric Bateman
Lieutenant Colonel G. B.
Bateman, OBE, Queens
Bob Bath
Sir John Batten, KCVO,
MD, FRCP
Michael H. Batterbury,
FRICS
Robin S. Battersby
Group Captain R. P. Batty,
OBE
John A. Baty
Morris J. Baty
John H. Baxter, RD*
Geoffrey Alfred Bayman
Esq
Giles William Kirwan Beale
Wing Commander Roland
Beamont, CBE, DSO*,
DFC*, DL, FRAeS
Lt. Col. R. Wyn Beasley,
RNZAMC, OBE
Edward V. Beaton
Hon Richard Beaumont

Colin Frederick Beaumont-
Edmonds, MC
Richard J. Beaven
Richard Theodore Beck
Esq, FSA, FRIBA,
FRSA, MRTPI
Mr B. D. K. Becker
Basil G. C. Becker, VRD
Patricia A. Beecham
Mrs Elise Beedle
Captain Eric Beetham
Peter J. Begent
Roy H. Begley
David P. Bell
R. D. A. Bell
Michael John Bellis
Wing Commander D. I.
Benham, OBE, DFC and
Bar, AFC
Edward Wright Bennett
John Bennett
Mr and Mrs Malcolm
Bennett
R. S. Bennett
Ronald R. Bennie
Sir Christopher Benson
David Bentata
Frederick John Bentley,
LCG
Yasha Beresiner, LLB
Victor Berger
Francis J. Bergin
Maxwell J. Bernard, FBCO
Ian P. Bethwaite
Clifford C. Beverly
John Shelley Bevington
Peter Michael Bickford-
Smith
Nicholas Rushton Spencer
Bickham
Alderman Hugh Bidwell
Edward G. C. Bing, FCIS,
FSCA
John Anthony Francis
Binny
Brian F. Bird
F. G. Bird
Harvey M. Bird
P. G. Bird Esq, TD
Ronald A. H. Bird

Roy William Bird, MBE
Arthur Birkett-Robinson
Peter L. Biroum-Smith,
FCII, AIAA
Dr R. J. Birts, MBBS
Helen Biscoe-Taylor
Jennifer Biscoe-Taylor
Michael F. Biscoe-Taylor
Lieutenant A. T. Bishop,
Royal Navy
Jack S. Bishop
John W. Bishop
Maurice J. Blaber
Edward J. Black
Thomas C. Black
Captain Gerald W.
Blackburn
Elizabeth Blackman
Charles Anthony Walter
Blackwell
James Hamilton Blackwood
David A. Blaikie
Jack G. Blandford
Cyril Blausten, JP, FSVA
Michael Blayney
Paul Bleaney
R. J. Blincow
Mr Sheriff Simon Block
G. W. G. Bloore
Fiona R. Bluck
Charles Piers Bluett
James Edward Nutcombe
Bluett
Stuart A. Blyth
Norman Robert Boakes
Valerie Anne Boakes
John Edward Boden
John A. Boddy
Brian Bodycombe, MBE,
FBIM
Richard P. Boggon Esq,
MA, MChir, FRCS
Martin S. Boissier
Philip Bollom
Ernest L. Bond, BEM,
MInstM
Arthur G. R. Bone, CStJ,
AE
William George David
Bone

George William Boner
Jurat M. W. Bonn
Michael C. M. Boon
David Laurence Booth
Brian P. Boreham
Clement Borrie
M. A. (John) Bosman
Thomas F. K. Boucher
Martyn H. Bougourd
Lt.Col. Peter W. S. Boult,
TD
Harold Kenneth Boulter
William S. Boulter
Kenneth Frederic Boustred
Helen Mary Boutall
Raymond Owen Bowden
Mr J. Charles R. Bowman
Peter Bowring
C. C. W. Box-Grainger
John Bradbeer
Walter Reginald (Rex)
Bradburn
Roger N. Bradley
Ron F. Bradley
R. G. Bradshaw Esq
Captain T. M. Bramble
Alan Bramley Esq
Stanley R. Brand
Dr Alan P. Bray
Arthur R. Bray
Terry Brean
Dr O. B. Brears, OBE
Captain Mansel Raymond
Bremberg
Michael Brent
Geoffrey Plimsoll Shaw
Brewer
Ian D. Brewster
Bridewell Royal Hospital
Paul Bridges
Frank Briggs
John Briggs
N. A. Briggs
W. J. Briggs
John Richard Bright
Michael Bright
Ronald S. Bright
Dr A. Daly Briscoe
Richard S. Bristowe
Dr Mark G. Britton

Robin Shedden Broadhurst
Michael John Cleeve
Brocklehurst
Jack Brookfield, OBE
John A. Brooks
Richard Brooman
Alan R. Brown
Dr Anthony G. Brown
Lt.Col. Basil Hector Brown,
OBE
Deputy David Tyrrell
Brown
Donald Brown
Jonathan Brown
Keith Brown
Keith William Brown
Michael Brown
Peter Eric Brown
Sir Raymond Brown
Anthony Gore Browne
John Browne, MP
Dr Christopher E.
Brownsdon
B. S. T. Bruce
Ian Donald Bruce, TD, MA,
LLM
Sir Douglas Bruce-Gardner,
Bt
Dr Rupert Bruce-Mitford
D. Victor Bryant
Douglas Ronald Bryden
William James Bryen
Mr Michael Richard
Toraville Bryer Ash
Vice Admiral Sir Peter
Buchanan, KBE
Ernest J. W. Buckler, FCIB
A. J. H. Buckley
P. Anthony Bull
Sir Walter Edward Avenon
Bull, KCVO
Barnaby Burgess
Edmund Burgess
Elizabeth Mary Burgess
Ian Burn
Mr J. G. Burnell
George Kenneth Burness
Carey Paul Burnett, TD
John Merrick Burrell
Alan Burrough, CBE

A. David Burton
George E. Burton
Gerald Burton
Raymond M. Burton, MA
Stanley H. Burton
M. A. Burtonshaw
John E. Bury, MA
James Augustus Bushman
Bruce Lionel Butcher
Arthur Butler
Mr Christopher Butler
Mr Michael Butler
Sir Richard Butler
J. C. F. B. Byllam-Barnes

Peter E. Cadbury
Group Captain H. L.
Calder-Jones, OBE
Captain Kenneth E. Camp
Audrey Campbell
K. L. G. Campbell, Hon
CGIA
Marilyn and Bruce
Campbell
Anthony Canham
Stanely George Cannon
Billy Carbutt
O. Carew
Dennis Charles Peter Carey
Hans Carlsson
Angus M. E. Carmichael
Keith Stanley Carmichael
Sir Andrew H. Carnwath,
KCVO, DL
Leonard John Carpenter
Captain George Harold
Carr
Richard Carr
Michael Carr-Archer
W. David Carrington, JP
Arthur A. Carter
A. S. Carter
E. B. Carter
H. E. Carter
Derrick Carter-Clout
Juliet Cartwright
Brenda Mary Cass
Thomas Graham Castle,
MBE
Nicholas J. Cater

Paul R. Cater
Philip T. Cater
Gordon V. Catford
Benson F. Catt, JP, FCA, CC
Leslie H. Catt, CEng, FIEE
Anthony G. Cavan
Francis Joseph Cave
Nicholas Cawdron
Raymond P. St G. Cazalet
J. D. Cazes, DFC
Margaret R. Chadd
Michael John Chalcraft
Terence James Chalcraft
Derek Chalk
Peter A. Chalkley
Norman Chalmers, FCA
Alderman John Chalstrey
W. R. F. Chamberlain
Wing Commander E. Chambers, MBE, AE
Mark L. Chambers Esq
Peter Bertram Chambers
Philip H. Champness
Barbara Chandler
P. R. Chandler
Hubert George Chapman
Captain John Chapman
Kenneth Chapman, MB, ChB(Edin), FRCOG, FRACOG, MMSA
Michael William Chapman
Donald George Charity
C. Robert Chatterton
Captain Lawrence C. Chegwidden, MAP
David Chivers
Frank Roy Christian
Steven Roy Christian
Lt.Col. D. J. Christie, CBE, ERD, DL (deceased)
Peter J. Chuck
A. E. Church
Mr Alan Church
John-David Nikolas Ciclitira, LLB, AKC
Norman M. Civval
Lt.Col. B. D. H. Clark, MC, GM
Clifford A. L. Clark

David B. Clark
Mrs Inez Clark (in memory of R.F.C.)
James Henry Clark
John F. B. Clark
Roy Clark
Commander Victor Clark, RN
Agnes Joyce Clarke (née Coventry)
J. D. H. Clarke, Esq, BEM
James Henry Clarke, CEng, FRINA, FIMarE, FCMS
Ronald W. Clarke
Stanley W. Clarke
Thomas and Victoria Clarke
Lt.Col. Geoffrey Ellis Clarkson, TD
John R. Clayton, CBE
William Clayton
David Brian Clement
David M. Clement
Robert D. Clephane
C. J. Cleugh
Jack Andrew Clifford
Francis W. Clinton
Robert E. Clisby
John Main Clissold
Reginald Allan Clough
Timothy James Erskine Clough
John Favell Coales
Dr Gerald Anthony Cockcroft
Maurice Douglas Cocking
W. Trevor Cocks
Robert W. Codling
Mr Guido Coen
Julian A. Cohen
Leslie Samuel Cohen
Michael A. Cohen
Nicola A. Cohen
Commander C. E. Colbourn, RN, DSO, BA
Charles Colburn
Christopher Gordon Colclough, MA Cantab
Sir Colin Cole, KCVO, TD, BCL, MA, FSA, CC
H. H. Judge Richard Cole

Mr Norman Stanley Cole
Captain R. J. Cole, DSC, RD
Mr and Mrs Mark Cole
Westerman A. Cole
John Cecil Coles
Ronald Jeffery Coles
Alastair J. C. Collett
Alexandra L. C. Collett
Angus C. C. Collett
Alderman Sir Christopher Collett, GBE, MA
Rod and Sue Collier
Anthony H. Collins
Ernest James Collins, MBE
H. A. Collinson
Thomas Amner Colvill
Barry Kenneth Colman
Kenneth Colman
Alistair I. Colston
Ian E. Colston, JP, DL
Oliver Colthurst
Bill Comber
Ivor Compton
P. R. C. Coni, OBE, QC
Edward Arthur Connell
Dr C. K. Connolly, TD, MA, FRCP
Group Captain John Hurn Constable
Cdr. W. G. Constantine, RD**, RNR
Diana Natalie Conway
Robert Clive Conway
Rosita Conway
Professor Adrian M. Cook
Albert I. Cook
Lt.Col. C. P. P. Cook
Commodore Harry Home Cook
Charles R. Home Cook
Leonard Miall Cook
Ralph Wallace Cook, MBE, JP
Raymond Dennis Cook
Chris and Yvonne Cooke
Captain Claude Brendon Cooke
Captain C. H. D. Cooke-Priest, Royal Navy

John W. Coomber
Michael Henshaw Coombes
The Coopers' Company and
Coborn School
Alan H. Cope
George Stanley Cope, OLJ,
CEng
William J. T. Copeland
Michael Colin Copsey
Dr Ian Corall
Dennis George Corble
John H. Cordle
Sir Kenneth Cork, GBE,
DLitt
Mr Alderman Roger Cork
John James Louis Corkill
W. Douglas Corkish
Neil Corkish
Ewan C. B. Corlett, OBE,
MA, PhD, FEng
Peter E. Cornish
Charles Legh Shuldham
Cornwall-Legh
Thomas S. Corrigan
John H. Cossins, CBE
Antony Coster
Peter L. Coster, JP
David Cottrell
Dr Colin J. Coulson-
Thomas
Lea P. Cousins
Raymond J. R. Cousins
Deputy Edwina Coven,
CBE, JP, DL
Allan M. Covey
John Leslie Huxley Cowan
A. S. T. Cowell
Gordon Edward Cowlett,
TEng (CEI)
Caroline Victoria Cowper,
LLB, ACII
Aubrey J. Cox
Donald Charles Cox
Geoffrey A. Cox
Dr R. A. F. Cox, FRCP,
FFOM
Dr Stuart James Cox, JP,
MB, BCh, BAO
Anthony Crabbe
John Julius Crace

Terry Cracknell
Nigel C. Craddock
W. Aleck Craddock, LVO
Robert A. Crafter
John M. Craig
Alexander Cranbrook
Peter Charles Crane Esq
Mr William F. C. Crane
Frank Craven
Stanley Douglas Crawford
P. H. Cresswell
Edward J. Crinage
Douglas Allan Crockatt,
OBE, RD, JP, DL
J. L. Crockatt, JP, LLB,
FRSA
Peter Crofts
David Robert Crome
Graham Crompton
Francis H. Cropp
Louise Croset
William James Croser
Roland William Cross
Sir Leonard Crossland
Leslie J. Croston
Derek C. H. Crouch
Bernard Crymble
Dr Gavin Anthony Cullen,
FRCVS
Albert Doughty Cullum,
MM
Barbara M. Culverhouse
John R. Cunningham
Sir John Curle, KCVO,
CMG
Kenneth Sidney Curlewis
Graham Curley
V. H. P. Currie-Cathey
H. Philip Curtis
Kingsley W. Curtis
Nikki Curtis
Lewis A. Curtis
Robert Bruce Adcock
Cushman
P. J. Custis, CBE

Alastair Dacre Lacy
Richard Dennis Casserley
Dallimore

James Matthew Percy
Dalton
William Dalton, FRICS,
FIAS, FCIArb
Justin Dawson Damer
Philip L. Daniel, KSG,
KCHS
Philip Harry Daniels
Alec M. Dann
Mathew T. Dansey
Terence J. Dansey
Geoffrey Darby
John O. R. Darby
Edward Darvell
Murray Edward Darvell
John Darwin
Cyril F. Dashwood
Anthony W. C. Davey
R. J. C. Davey
Leonard E. Davidge
William H. Davidson
Alastair Gordon Davie
Anthony W. Davies
Brian Davies
Brian R. Davies
Derek L. Davies
G. Michael Davies
Dr M. E. Davies
Mervyn Davies
Norman Davies
Robert R. Davies
Albert Davis
Bernard Roland Davis
Charles George Davis
Cyril Kenneth Davis
Herbert Edmund Davis
Leslie C. S. Davis
Martyn P. Davis
Michael D. Davis
Simon N. Davis
William F. Davis
Christopher Davson
Henry Tallents Davy, MA
(Oxon)
Mr P. F. Davy
John R. Dawes
Howard Edwyn Day
John Rupert Deacon Esq,
LMCSA, MBBS
Alex W. Deakin, TD

John W. Deal
Michael Debenham
Emanual Dee
J. A. de Grey-Warter Esq
G. P. S. Delisle
Carl S. den Brinker
Terence A. G. Dendy
H. Wynne Denman
Gordon H. Denney
Barry E. Dennis
Delwyn D. Dennis, OBE
Leonard V. G. Dennis, JP
Wing Commander Arthur
 Charles Henry Denny
Dr A. A. Denton
Elkan de Power
Raphael D. de Sola
Paul L. de Weck
Kenneth Francis Dibben
Peter Vernon Dickins
B. C. Dixie
Michael Trevor Dixon
Roger Dixon
Mr Peter T. Doe
David Macfarlane Doig
Geoffrey Dollimore, CBE
Richard A. Domb
James T. Donald
Professor John D.
 Donaldson
Dame Mary Donaldson,
 GBE, DSc (Hon)
Peter K. Donaldson
Wing Commander Edmund
 Donovan, OBE, DFC,
 RAF (retd.)
Robin P. Doran
R. A. Dorman
Captain D. A. Dornom,
 RD*
Mrs J. E. Douglas
Sir Robert Douglas, OBE
Dr Arthur Percy Douglas-
 Jones
John Keith Dowell
David Edward Dowlen
Mitchell L. E. Dowlen
John C. Downer
Desmond Draper
J. A. Draper

Harry H. Draycott
John W. Drenker
Miss Anna K. Drew,
 BPharm
Sir Arthur Drew, KCB
Dr C. D. M. Drew, MRCP
Derek Colin Drew
Harry E. Drew Esq, CB
Peter R. L. Drew, OBE
Lt.Gen. Sir Robert Drew,
 KCB, CBE, KSEJ, FRCP
C. R. Driver
Mrs Valerie R. Drummond
David Ducat
Fernand Andre Duchezeau
Peter Duffield
John Edwin Duggan
Lt.Col. David A. B. Duke,
 TD
Robert A. Duncan
John Dunham
A. A. Dunitz, JP, CC
James L. Dunkley
Air Marshal Sir Patrick
 Dunn, KBE, CB, DFC,
 FRAeS, RAF (Retd.)
Richard M. Dunne
Mr Mark Robert Dunnett
Mr Robert Walter Dunnett
Viscount Dunrossil
Douglas Francis Dunstan
Derek Dutton
Isobel Dworetksy
Ralph A. D. Dymond
Walter J. Dymott, MBE,
 FCA

Edmund John Keble
 Montriou de Longchamp
 Eagles
Eric S. Earl
Eugene Roderick Earland
Bertram David East
East India, Devonshire,
 Sports and Public
 Schools Club
Joe Eaton
G. H. Edmunds, FCA,
 ACMA
Richard John Edmunds

Arthur Edwards, FWRI,
 FCIT
Frank W. Edwards, CBE
Gordon Edwards
Gordon Frank Edwards
John Edwards
Leslie James Edwards
Captain R. C. Edwards
R. D. K. Edwards
R. F. T. Edwards, FInstM
Elwyn Eilledge
Kenneth F. Einfeld
S. J. S. Eley
W. Harvey Elias, JP
The Venerable Peter
 Charles Eliot
Harold Leeming Ellershaw
William E. L. Ellery
Marvin Ellin
N. E. Elliott
Trevor Elliott
Beverley Charles Ellis
Francis Henry Ellis
Howard R. Ellis, JP
Sir Ronald and Lady Ellis
Captain Oliver Elsom
Christopher John Elvy
David R. J. Elvy, BSc
 (Econ) Hons
David Acfield Emms
Donald Ensom
Albert Francis 'Bob' Ensor
Robert John Ensor
Sir Geoffrey Errington, Bt
Alfred Essex
Alan Essex-Crosby
Peter Esslemont
John E. Evan-Cook, JP
Clifford Evans
Dudley Montague Evans
Edward John Evans, MB,
 BS, DCH
Hugh Alexander Evans
J. A. L. Evans
John W. Evans
Oliver Evans
Peter Nixon Evanson
Vincent Everard
R. A. Everest
John V. Everritt

Leslie Evershed-Martin
Allen Exley, OBE, FRSA, FCSD
Noel W. Eyers

S. Alan Fabes
Howard Fair, FCA
Edward A. Fairburn
Kenneth Faircloth
Alistair Julian Russell Fairclough
Ian Walter Fairclough
Philip Fairclough, OBE
John Godfrey Fairer
G. H. A. Falkus, armiger, FCIOB
Alastair Farley
Geoffrey R. D. Farr
Sydney P. Farr
M. C. Farrar-Bell
William J. Farrelly, KCSG
Peter Farrer, MC
Daphne Farrier
Roy Farrier
Michael Farrow
Bruce Farthing Esq, MA, CC
Robert E. Faulkner
Anthony W. Fay
Frederick Henry Fearn
Daniel Fearon
Basil H. F. Fehr, CBE
Michael Feld
John A. Fell
Wilfred Fell
Alan F. Felstead
John William Fenmor-Collins
Leonard A. Fernee
Percy Albert Ferris
Michael Wogan Festing
M. A. O'B ffrench Blake
The Reverend Barry Palmer Palmer Ffynché
Miss Linda Anne Ficker, BSc, MB, BS, FRCS
Ronald Francis Walter Ficker Esq
C. E. Fiddian-Green

George W. Field
Guy Field
The Duke of Fife
Mrs Timothy Finch
Ernest R. A. Findlay
Major R. G. Findlay-Shirras
Andrew J. Finlayson
David J. Finlayson
John H. Finlayson, FRICS, FRVA
Kenneth John Innes Finlayson Esq, MB, BS London
Michael J. Finlayson
Paul D. J. Finlayson
Stuart J. Finlayson
John P. Finney
S. P. A. Fiorentini
C. A. Firmin, MBE
Carl Fisher, Dip Arch, FRIBA
James Fisher
Michael Howe Fisher
Dr P. J. Fisher, BSc, PhD, FRSA
Patrick J. Fisher
Geoffrey R. Fisk, FRCS
Neil H. L. Fitton
Rodney C. A. FitzGerald
Eric Flack
John Ernest Flaherty
Roger William Flaherty
Bertram Flatters
Victor Fleming, FIAL, Hon GSM
Roger Flemington Esq, FCIB
Jack N. A. Fletcher
Kenneth Fletcher
Deputy Sir David Floyd Ewin, LVO, OBE
Thomas Foley, DipM, FBIM, FIMC, FRGS, FRSA, KtT
Arthur Francis Forbes
Derek F. K. Forbes, FLIA
James Forbes
Professor Emeritus Sir Hugh Ford
David A. Fordham

Mr William Edward Fordham (Bill)
John E. J. Foreman
Stephen John Forman
His Honour Judge Giles Forrester
Gerald Forsberg, OBE
Frederick Dennis Bulwer Forster
John R. Forward
D. Alan Foster
Derek Foster
R. W. J. Foster
William Robert Brudenell Foster
William Foulds
Captain G. Fowkes
A. E. Fowler
Alan B. Fox
Albert Robert Fox, FRIBA
Cyril G. Fox, FRSH, FCIArb.
A. J. Frankenberg
Dr A. W. Frankland
Raoul Franklin
Patrick Franklin-Adams
Charles Edward Frappell, CC
Hazel Elizabeth Frappell
David Freedman
Marcus Freedman
Roland Freeman
Geoffrey Ernest French
James H. French
John French, D. L.
Peter R. French, RD, FRCS
W. J. L. French
T. W. Fripp
Colin F. Frizzell
Anne and Gerald Frizelle
Jack Coverdale Froom
George F. C. Fudge
Gilbert T. Fuge, OBE
Keith Saxon Fullwood
Clara A. Furness
Robin H. Furniss

John Gadd, CBE
Elizabeth Gadsden

DEDICATIONS

Alderman Sir Peter
  Gadsden, GBE, AC
Mr W. F. P. Gammie
Clifford N. Gandy
Ian D. Gardiner
Maurice Soanes Gardner
Robert William Gardner
Grahame McDonald
  Garland
Frank H. Garner
J. Edward Garner
John Garner
Gerald Archer Garnett
Bernard William Garrett
D. P. Garrett
Councillor John Richard
  Garrett
Simon T. Garrett Esq
Captain Ronald Frederick
  Garrod
Stanley A. Gates
Donald Geddes
Gerald Geddes
Joyce Geddes
George M. Gee, FRSA,
  JP
Mr P. D. M. Gell
A. D. Genet, FBIM
B. L. Genet, FInst, BM
E. A. Genet, MCIT
The Revd. George E.
  Gerrard, FCIS, SBStJ,
  TEM
Roy David Gibaud
Captain Ian Gibb
Eric L. Gibbard
David Gibbes
Robert Gibbins
The Hon Sir David
  Gibbons, KBE, JP
George Cuthbert Gibbons
George Gibbs
Michael W. Gibbs
Debee Gibson
Joe Gibson
B. M. Gilbart-Smith
Geoffrey Reginald Gilbert
Robert V. Gill
Jack Gillam
James Scott Gilliatt

His Honour Bernard B.
  Gillis, QC
Philip Girle
Stella Muriel Girling
William John Glanville
John S. Glanvill-Smith
Dr Noel Glanvill-Smith
Denis Glass
George Glass
Viscount Glenapp
Dr Richard B. Glover
Dr Alan Glyn, ERD, MP
Ronald Edward Goacher,
  CEng
Dr J. W. Goadby
Peter Frank Godfrey
Norris M. Goddard, FCA
John Godley
Robert Gold, FCA, CC
Pamela Goldberg
Gavin Golder
Gerald Golder
Ian Golder
John B. Goldsmith
Walter K. Goldsmith
Norman N. Goldwater Esq,
  MBE
James Stuart Golfar
John Stuart Golfar
Nicholas David Golfar
Christopher W. Gomm Esq
G. H. Ross Goobey
Francis Goodall
Raymond B. Goodchild
John Herbert Goodger
Joseph Henry Goodhart
M. H. Goodhart
Alfred J. Gooding, OBE
Robert M. S. Goodsall
Albert William Goodwin
Julie Goodwin
Colin G. Gordon-Smith
J. C. W. Gorse
Brian Goswell
Dr Richard Sherwin
  Gothard
Audrey Gough
George Gough, FRICS
Harold Gould, OBE, JP,
  DL, FCA

Pauline M. Gould
Mr Paul Gourmand
Peter J. Grafham
Stanley Grafham
George William Graham
Alderman Michael Graham
S. Grahame-Ross
Felix W. Grain
Reginald Ernest Grainge
Peter Granger Esq
D. E. Grant Esq
Simon Grant-Rennick Esq
John Gratwick Esq, OBE
David William Gravell
Francis C. Graves, OBE,
  DL, FRICS
John R. H. Graveson
Roy W. Gravestock
Professor T. Cecil Gray,
  CBE, KCSG, JP
Philip M. J. Gray
Robin Gray
Arthur E. C. Green, MBE,
  TD, DL, FRICS
Arthur H. Green, ISO, CStJ
George Richard Green, MC
Gerald John Green
John Robert Green
Keith Mackenzie Green
Richard C. Green
Richard M. C. Green
Sir Derek Greenaway, BT,
  CBE, TD, DL, JP
Geoffrey F. Greenhalgh
Dick Greenwood
Fiona J. Gregory
James D. Gregory
W. A. Gregory, DFC
V. S. Greig
Major General Nigel St
  George Gribbon, OBE
John Griffith
John Griffith
Arthur Lasenby Griffiths
E. Llewellyn Griffiths
Frank Llewellyn Griffiths
John Griffiths, CMG, QC
Roger Griffiths
Mr W. H. Griffiths, MA
William Maximillian Griggs

George John Grimes
John Grindall
Major General John
  Groom, CB, CBE, FBIM
Professor Peter
  Grootenhuis, DSc,
  FCGI, FEng
Noel A. Grout
Walter Dunbar Watkins
  Grubb
Robert H. Gudgeon
Rex Guillaume
H. Edward Gumbel
Arthur Geoffrey Stewart
  Gumersall
Paul W. Gunn
C. P. Gunner
D. B. Gunner
Major Norman Gunton, JP,
  MIEnvSc, MBIM, ACIS,
  FCIArb
John Barton Guy

David C. F. Haggis
John Randal Haigh
C. MacIntyre Hailey-Ives
M. G. M. Haines
Alan V. Hall
Arthur H. Hall
Lt.Col. Austin Patrick Hall,
  TD RE(V)
C. Gordon R. Hall
Jack Hall
Leonard Hall
Norman L. Hall
Albert Hallam
Roy Graham Hallett
Peter A. H. Halliday
Andrew G. S. Hamilton
Gerald Stafford Hamilton
A. Hamilton Hamilton-
  Hopkins, KCLJ
David B. Hammerson
Peter S. Hammerson
Mrs Sue Hammerson, OBE
Stephen Keith Hammerton
Audrey M. Hammond
Wilfred C. Hammond,
  MBE, JP, FCIS, FRSA
David Hamp-Gopsill

Roland Edgar Spillar
  Hampton
D. Grahame Handley
Geoffrey Hankins
Harold Rich Hansen Esq
The Lord Hanson, Robert
  Hanson and Brook
  Hanson
Leslie R. Harborne
Alan Hardcastle
Mr Miles Hardie
Ernest G. Harding
Norman H. Harding, CC
Laurence C. Hardy
Christopher Peter Hare
Bertie Edmund Harper
H. E. (Ted) Harper
John Henry Harper
Kenneth Robin Harper
Laurance Harper
Robert C. H. Harrap
Brian N. Harris
Gilbert Eric Whiteford
  Harris
Dr H. R. Harris
Joe H. Harris
David Harrison
Douglas Michael Harrison
Richard Harrison
Anthony J. Hart, DSC, JP
Dr F. Dudley Hart
Colin Anthony Hart Esq
John Hart
Mr and Mrs John G. M.
  Hart
Edward Hartill
Sir Frank Hartley, CBE
Anthony Charles Hartwell
Eric Hartwell, CBE
Keith Alan Hartwell, BSc
John E. Harvey
Professor Michael G.
  Harvey
David E. W. Harvie
J. Keith Harwood, OBE
Glenn Michael Hasker
Martin Edward Hasker
Eric R. Hassall
A. F. R. Hatfield
J. A. E. Hathrell, OBE

Professor William Martin
  Hattersley
Alex Haussmann
Mr John Hauxwell, FInst,
  BM
J. R. Havers-Strong, FRCS,
  FCOphth
Kenneth R. Haward
Peter N. Haward, FBHI
John A. Hawkins
L. T. S. Hawkins
R. I. Hawtin
Robert Gordon Haxforth
Doctor David Hay
Nicholas David Hayes
Ronald Wilton Hayes
Walter Hayes
Christopher Frank Hayman
Jean and Derek Haynes
W. S. Haynes
Anthony Hayward
Thomas Charles Stanley
  Haywood
The Rt Hon Lord
  Hazlerigg, MG, DL, TD
Eric H. Head, TD, FCA
John D. Heal, FCIOB
Francis J. R. Heaps
Roger J. B. Heasman
Ken Heather
Ralph Hedderwick
Laura Rebecca Isabel
  Hempsall
Anthony C. Hemy, RIBA
Derek C. Hemy
Michael B. Henderson
Michael Henderson-Begg
Michael A. W. Hendry
Nicholas Hendy
Robin Hendy
Lt.Col. R. L Henson, MBE
Gordon George Mactavish
  Hepburn
T. S. Herring
Harold John Hesketh
Michael Hesketh-Prichard
Dr D. G. Hessayon
Norman Joseph Hewitt
Richard Thornton Hewitt,
  OBE, MA

Aubrey T. Heyer
Catherine Heyer
Christopher Heyer
A. L. Heymann, MBE
Geoffrey Heywood
Stuart Hibberdine
Mr Roy Hibbin
James W. Hickman
John Hickman
P. N. Hickman Esq.
G. J. R. Hickmott, MBE,
    FCII, FCIArb
Robert William Hicks
Thomas Peter Hicks
Terence William Higgins
Tom W. Higgs
Allan Highfield
Dr David Finnemore Hill
David R. Hill
E. W. F. Hill
Ian M. Hill
Julian Hill
Colonel L. J. L. Hill, MC
    (retd.)
Monty Hiller
David Hill-Kelly
Sidney Hillman
R. A. Hills
Derek G. Hilton
Matthew S. P. Hinckley Esq
C. E. Hindson
John Hine
Royston G. Hine
Foster O. Hipperson
Lord Hirshfield of Holborn
Frank Ronald Hitchins
J. Michael Hoare
Harold Hobbs
George V. Hodges
Thomas E. S. Hodgson
Wilfrid B. Hodgson
D. H. Hodson Esq
David M. Holland
Michael R. Hoffman
Thomas Dinsdale Hogg,
    FRICS, FCIArb
John S. Holden
Sir Derrick Holden-Brown
Captain Kenneth F. R.
    Holding, FNI

Frank R. D. Holland
Frank W. Holland, MBE,
    FIMIT
Major Stanley Holland, TD,
    JP, FBSC, RA
Godfrey V. Holliday
Thomas Henry Hollings,
    FRICS
Jonathan Robert Holloway
Marlowe A. J. Holloway
Paul George Holloway
Richard Guy Holloway
Colin Holman, JP
Bernard Alfred Holmes, FC
Peter Holmes
Stanley C. Holmes, MBE,
    TD
Stewart Holmes
Dr Roger A. Hood
B. A. Holroyd
Arthur Holt, IEng, MIBE
S. John Holt
Bill Honey, FCA, FCIS
Alan Hood
Lt. Cdr. A. H. E. Hood, RN
    (retd.)
Mr D. M. A. Hook, MA,
    FEng
Paul J. B. Hooper
Deputy H. W. S. Horlock,
    MA
John Ewen Troup Horne
John N. Horne
Alan A. Horsford
Lt. Cdr. A. C. Horsley, MC,
    MRIN-RINR
Dr A. R. Horwell
John Leonard Hough
Brian A. Houghton
Peter How
Clifford Stanley Howard
Graham R. H. Howard
Mr J. F. Howard
John Howard
Captain John A. Howard
Oliver Crewdson Howard
Robin S. Howard
Ian Howat, FRICS
Charles Keith Howe
H. Eric Howells

Lord Howie of Troon
Commander H. Derek
    Howse, MBE, DSC, RN
Professor Thomas Hoyes
Frederick W. Hoyles
Jack Hubbard
Mr Les Hubbard, FBCO
Malcolm Hubble, JP
Gordon Huck
D. H. Hudson Esq
Peter E. Hudson, FCA
Richard Hudson
Revd Dr Gordon Huelin
Rodney P. Huggins
David Treharne Hughes
E. W. Hughes
John Hamilton Hughes
Leslie T. D. Hughes, C de G
Michael G. E. Hughes
Morris Hughes
Barry Hulin
Roger F. Humm
Commander A. D. Hunt,
    RD*, RNR (retd.)
D. E. J. Hunt, DSC and Bar
Harry Clifford Hunt
Kenneth Bernard Huntbatch
James M. Hunter
Mr Basil Hurrell
Kenneth Hurst-Brown
Ken Hurt
Ian S. Hutcheson
Stuart J. G. Hutchinson
Russell Hutchons
Keith Hutton
Geoffrey Hyde
Kenneth Hylton-Smith
Anthony James Hyne

Major Derrick Ide-Smith
Peter C. F. Imison
Gordon M. Infield
Norman T. Ingham
David Richard Bonner
    Ingmire
Sir Gilbert Inglefield
Peter McDonald Ingram
Dr R. C. Ingrey-Senn
William Innes, OBE
Evan Innes

Frank E. Ireland
David J. G. Ireson
Barry Irving
Edward Isaacs
J. P. Ivens

Bernard G. L. Jackman
Anthony John Jackson,
   OBE
Barry T. Jackson
Edward A. Jackson
Ian Jackson
John Maxwell Jackson
Kenneth C. Jackson
Leonard Ring Jackson
L. St. J. T. Jackson
Air Vice Marshal Sir Ralph
   Jackson
Major Richard J. Jackson,
   TD, HAC
Richard T. Jackson
William S. Jackson
Michael Jacobs
Ronnie Jacobson
Mohammed Jalie
Derek W. James
Captain Jeremy James
Captain J. H. James
Dr Ursula James
Peter Frederick Jameson
Dr J. Jancar
Dr Boaz A. Jarrett
John Jarvie
Michael Henry Vickery
   Jeans
Clifford W. Jeapes
Barry John Jefferies
John Jeffery
Derek J. Jeffrey, FBIM,
   FRGS, FRSA, KtT
Colin J. Jeffries, MBE
K. A. G. Jeffries, FCA
A. Philip Jenkins
Geoffrey P. Jenkinson
Nigel P. Jenkinson
Victor J. Jenner, JP, FBIM
C. Robert Jennings, FPRI,
   FRSA
Jørn Munch Jensen
Leon Jessel, MBE, JP

C. N. M. Joannides
Bowbrick John
Brian Pryce Johnson
David Johnson
Derek Anthony Norman
   Johnson
Murray Johnson
Rex Johnson
Roger and Dinah Johnson
David Johnston
Dr Roy D. Johnston
Albert George Joiner
Sir Anthony Jolliffe, GBE
Robert St John Jolliffe
Brian R. Jones
Captain Eric Jones
Dr Gwilym Murray Jones,
   OBE, MBE (Mil),
   FRCGP
James Anthony Jones
John Avery Jones
Peter Boam Jones
Ralph Godfrey Jones
Richard Harding Jones
Roderick Alan Jones
Raymond C. Jorden
Hugh Joscelyne, JP
Hugh Mortimer Joseph,
   CBE, Hons CGIA,
   FInstPS, FRSA
Jack Michael Joseph
Peter Thomas Joyce
Roger L. Judd
Stanley G. S. Judd

M. L. Kaczmarek
William Howlett Kelleher,
   MD
Charles H. Keeler, OBE
Christopher Anthony
   Gedge Keeling
Maureen W. F. Kellett
Mrs Carole Kelly, JP
Clive R. Kelly
Ian Kelly
Clive Kendall
George Langton Kendall
John Maxwell Kennedy
Nigel A. Kennedy
Roy W. Kenzie

Martin Kepple
Michael J. Kerr
Julian W. Keyes
Bernard Kilkenny
T. L. Kind, ARICS
Charles Albert King
Frederick John James King
Geoffrey King
Geoffrey Thomas King
Jack N. King
Joseph King
Peter King
Tony King
Austin Kingwell
Laurence Kinney
Ronald Kinsey of Kinsey
Michael A. Kirk
David Mackenzie Kirke-
   Smith
Alex Kirkwood
Mary E. Kirwan
Revd Benjamin Edward
   Knight
H. V. Knight, MBE, FCA
Kenneth Mackenzie Knight
Leslie William Knott
Keith Knowles
Dr Lance M. J. Kramer,
   TD, MA, PhD, CBiol,
   FIBiol
Christopher S. G. Kurkjian
Susan Ellen Kuruber
O. S. Kverndal
David William Edgar Kyle

Philippe F. Lacamp
Victor W. Lacey-Walker
Edward G. M. Lachlan-
   Cope Esq
Leslie T. Lack
John W. Lake
Nell Lam
Denis A. Lamb
Major O. F. Lambert, CBE
Peter Lambert
Anthony Eric Lambkin
Alan Lamboll
Peter N. Lamprell-Jarrett,
   KCSG
John M. Lancaster

Max Lander
Raymond Percy Lane
Michael F. Lang
Ronald Arthur Lang
Sean L. Lang
A. D. G. Langmead, TD, CC
S. H. A. Lapidus
Sqn. Ldr. E. Paul Lash, AFC
H. L. Lassen
Christopher John France Latham
Dr Colin R. Lattimore, JP
Neil L. T. Laundon
Major John E. C. Laurie
Peter Colet Laurie
Barry T. M. Law
Christopher Lawrence
David E. Lawrance
Harold N. Lawrence, TD
Murray Lawrence
Hugh Robert Lawrence-Swan, MInst, TT
Philip Lawrence-Swan, MInst, TT
Valerie May Lawrence-Swan, MInst, TT
Geoffrey C. H. Lawson
J. P. L. Laycock
Cyril G. Lea
J. R. F. Leach
The Hon. Leslie Leathers
Captain A. A. Ledger, retd., (Late RA(T))
Colin James Lee
G. A. Lee
Ronald A. G. Lee, RDP, FRPS, L
Ronald Arthur Lee
Hugh L. Leedham-Green Esq, MA (Oxon)
John Richard Lees-Jones
George Ivor Leftley
Patrick Legge
James H. Leicester
Volker Leichsering
Morris Leigh, PhD (Hons)
Dr Frances E. A. Leishman
David W. Leith

Bryan Norman Lenygon, MA, LLB, FCA, FCIS, ATII
Roy Le Poidevin
Peter Lerwill
His Honour G. F. Leslie, MA
Mr Michael Lester
Alan Lettin
Timothy P. Levy
Jack Lewin
A. James W. Lewis, JP
Bernard Lewis
Dr Brian Lewis
Clifford John Lewis, FIA
Ewan A. G. Lewis
E. R. Charles Lewis
John R. S. Lewis
Lawrence David Lewis
Redge Lewis
G. E. Liardet
Mr John W. Libby
Israel Mayer Librach
Clive William Lidstone
Leslie Limer
Andrew M. Lindley
David Harry Lindop
David Lindsay, JP
Reginald H. Line, ChEng, FIProdE
Oscar Arthur Lines
Peter J. Lines
James Alfred Linfield
James Frederick Link, RSS
Roger Linscott Lintern
David Churchill Linton
Kenneth F. Lipscomb
R. L. Lisney
Mr Hyman Liss
John P. List
Roland Lister
D. J. Little
John R. Little
Graeme A. Living
F. Leslie Living
B. J. Livingston
Timothy Charles Llewellyn
Angus Lloyd
Reginald H. Lloyd
Robert D. Lloyd

F. R. Loader, FCA, JDipMA, FCMA, FCIS
Sir Leslie Loader, CBE
Charles Loats
John M. Lock
Brian Locke
Henry S. Lockhart
Major L. H. Lockley, FRICS
Marty Lockney
John Lindsay Logue
Dr D. E. London
Kenneth A. Long
Peter Longfield
E. Iain Longman
O. E. Longshaw
Colonel Thomas Lord, CBE, ERD, TD
Joe Loss, LVO, OBE
A. G. Mark Loveday
Mark A. Loveday
Mervyn Allport Loverock
Miss Alison Joanna Low
Ernest Low
William Kenneth Lowe
M. J. Lowther
Sir Ian Lowson, BT
Dr Aubrey K. Lucas
Bernard George Budden Lucas
Prebendary Dick Lucas
Edwin Raymond Luckham-Down
Melvyn Raymond Luckham-Down
Edwin William Ludlow
Richard W. P. Luff
G. H. Luffingham, MB, BS, MRCGP
George E. Lunt
Jeffrey Edward Lush
B. E. H. Lynch
James Lynch
Patrick Lynch
A. Henry Lyons
D. H. Lyons
Mr A. St G. Lyster

A. W. MacCaw Esq
Peter Duncan MacCorkindale

Patrick J. O'Farrell, FCIS, MBIM
Captain Paul A. Ogden
Antony R. O'Hagan Esq, TD
John Older
Charles Frederick Oliver
Alderman J. M. Y. Oliver
Rodney John Oliver
Martin Burgess Olley
Neville Olsberg
Wilfred Olsen, FCA, ACIS
Matthew Henry Oram
Dermot Peter O'Reilly
Kevin Joseph O'Reilly
Peter G. Orpin
Dr Robin Orr
Robin Orr, CBE
H. John Osborne
Trevor Osborne
John Conor O'Sullivan
Maurice Oswald-Jones
John W. Ottaway
George Owen, FCIS, FCMA
Charles A. Owens
John Richard Owen-Ward

Brigadier John Packard
C. Neville Packett Esq, MBE, KStJ, JP
Alan Charles Padgham
J. A. M. Padley-Smith
John M. F. Padovan
Ivan Page-Ratcliff
Leonard Pagliero, OBE
David V. Palmer
Derek H. Palmer
Colonel K. W. Nicholls Palmer, OBE, KStJ, ERD, TD
Major-General Sir Michael Palmer, KCVO
Beryl M. Palmier
Terence M. Pamplin
Gordon D. Pannell
J. S. Park
John C. G. Parker
Leonard John Parker
Leslie Cyril Frederick Parker

Robert Stewart Parker, MA
Dr Stephen Barry Parker
Thomas Parkinson, MD, FRCP
Hugh Charles Parkman
Stanley C. Parrish, JP
George J. Parrott
Alan Parry
Kenneth E. Parry
Michael Parry
D. J. Parry-Crooke
Arthur E. L. Parsons
Dr D. L. T. Parsons
Mrs Joyce Parsons, JP
Raymond Arthur Parsons
John A. Parton
Richard Michael Patey
Harley M. Patrick
John Patrick
Francis C. Paul
George F. Paulley
Roland Paxton
Aaron G. Payne
George D. Payne
Michael Payne
Lt.Col. Robert A. Payne, KStJ, JP
Roger L. Payton
Colin Richard Kirwan Peal
A. H. Pearce
Michael J. Pearce
Alan Fordham Pearcy
Donald B. Pearse
Harry Pearse
Jill Anne Pearse
Richard J. C. Pearson
Richard W. R. Pearson
Sarah C. Pearson
James Pellerin
Mr John W. Pendleton
David Frederick Penn
Captain Richard Somerset Pennefather, RN (retd.)
Ronald F. Penney, FCA
David M. Pennington
The Hon David Pennock
Captain D. M. Penrose, TD
Jack Owen Pentelow
Geoffrey Perfect, JP
E. G. Perkins

Michael John Perkins
Sidney Alfred Perkins
Laurence Permutt
Daphne Perrett
Anthony Perry
Dr Ian C. Perry
John H. Perry
Leonard Perry
Bruce Anthony Peskin
William Peterkin
Barrie Peters
Michael Narramore Peterson
Sir Daniel Pettit
Ray Pettitt
Lorraine Pevreall
George Arthur Walter Phelps
John F. Phillips, CBE, OStJ, QC
Mrs Mary E. Phillips, ACIS
Dr A. Holmes Pickering, JP
Maurice E. Pickering
Victor Albert Edward Pickett
Geoffrey W. Pickin
Antony Robert Pierce
L. G. Pierson
His Honour Judge Pigot, QC
Dr Gordon Arthur William Pike
Richard E. L. Pile
Gordon W. Pingstone
David M. Pinkham
Patrick Pirie-Gordon
Peter Bright Harold Piper, CBE, FCIB
F. H. Pitcher
Mr James Pitcher
David Pitts
Gordon Sedgwick Planner, MBE
Mr Adrian Platt
Alan Rowland Pledge
George Charles Pledger
Paul Podolsky
Charles Leslie Pollard
Nigel Edward Pollard, IEng, MILE

DEDICATIONS

Rebecca S. Pollard
Vivien and Christopher
Pollard
Norman Travers Pollitt
Adrian J. Pontin
Peter J. T. Poole
John Poore
Walden Porter
Simon Pott
C. Victor Potter
Norman C. Poultney
John Keith Lytton Powell
Christopher Powell-Brett
Ian W. Powley
Quentin Prebble
James K. Prentice Esq
Mrs Denise S. Presland
Derek William Methven
Pretty
Brian T. G. Prevost
Christopher J. S. Price
Philip Martin Price
B. J. Prichard Esq, LLB
Barry W. Pride
Steven C. G. Pritchard
David H. Probert
Gordon Procter
Arthur Caradoc Prothero
Allan F. Prouten, CEng,
FRINA, FIMarE
Leonard Prouten
Sir David Pryke, Bart
James Henry Pull, CEng,
FIMechE, MIMarE,
MRINA, MConsE
Denis Purcell
Alfred Purse
A. J. R. Purssell
Colonel J. F. E. Pye, OStJ,
FCIT, FSCA,
AInstMechE
Geoffrey F. Pygall
Andrew James Pyke
Jeffrey D. Pywell

Peter Quaile, JP, FCII

Peter William Racey
Dr Maurice Rackow
Patrick V. Radford

Donald Ellis Raley
John C. Ramsden, CBE
Robert C. M. Rankin
Paul Rann
Karra Venkateswara Rao
Henry David Raschen
Brian Rawles
E. H. Rawlings
Stanley Ray
Anthony Arthur Rayner
Derek Rayner
Peter Rayner
John J. Redman, CA
Richard Redmayne
Christopher John Reed
B. St G. A. Reed, CBE, MC,
DL
Deputy J. L. Reed, MBE,
MA
Jonathan Austin Reed
R. J. Reed
T. G. Reeday
Joan Frances Rees
Mary Elizabeth Rees
Professor Linford Rees,
CBE
David R. Reeve
Gavin S. Reeve
Peter J. Reeves
Leary Reginald
Frank Rehder
Jim Reichgelt
David Reid, FCA
Sir Robert Reid, CBE
P. A. Revell-Smith
Brian Edwin Albert
Reynolds
Peter Reynolds
David Richards
Ivor B. Richards
John F. Richardson, PhD
Dr Harry R. C. Riches
Gary Richmond
Brian Rider
J. A. Ridge
H. D. Ridgeon
Captain John Ivens Rigby
Christopher Rimmer
R. H. G. Ring
Dr Albert H. Rinsler

Alan Rippon
Peter Allan Rippon
The Rt. Hon. The Lord
Rippon of Hexham, PC,
QC
(Thomas) Norman Ritchie
Charles Arthur Rivington
Christopher T. Rivington
Peter Richard Roast (Jnr)
William H. Robbins
Denis H. Roberts
D. Gwilym M. Roberts
John H. P. Roberts
Martin Welch Roberts
Peter D. T. Roberts
Donald James Robertson
Don Robinson
Geoffrey H. Robinson
Captain J. B. Robinson,
AFC and Bar
Hon. Maurice Robson, FCA
Clive Roffe, JP
Christopher Michael
Catesby Rogers
David John Rogers
Klaus Roitsch
John A. Roll Pickering
Andrew Rooke
Anthony Rooke
Helen Rooke
Sir Denis Rooke, CBE,
FRS, FEMS
George Arthur Rooley
Gerald R. Rose
John Ross
William Moffat Ross-
Wilson
Miles E. Rotherham
Claire E. Rowan
James A. R. Rowan
William G. Rowan
David Rowden
Kenneth Rowe
Alderman Sir David Rowe-
Ham, GBE
Roger H. Rowell
Reginald S. Rowland
Geoffrey Rowley
Newton Hayward Rowson
Royal Automobile Club

Norman Patrick Royal
Norman Royce
Professor R. D. Rubens
R. Stephen Rubin
Maurice Rundle Esq.
Captain A. G. Russell
Clive S. Russell
Dr Jeremy Russell
Joseph Dennis Russell-
  Gaunt
Brian Ruston
R. R. C. Ryall, FRSA
Kenneth Ryden, MC, DL,
  FRICS, FRSP(E)
Marjorie Olive Ryder
William J. Ryder

Colin F. Sach
John Saffery
Dr Arthur M. Sage
Mr Richard A. Sage
The Earl of St Aldwyn, PC,
  GBE, TD, DL
Sebastian B. Salama
Dr Robert William Salmon
Robin S. Salvesen
Captain C. B. Sanders, CBE,
  RNR
Brigadier C. D. Sanders
Richard J. Saner
Peter H. Santley-Dilley
Mr Donald Saunders,
  FBCO, FBOA, HD
Frank Saunders
Deputy Richard Saunders
Russell Saunders
Robert C. Savage, FCIS
H. John J. Savery
Mr Kenneth Sawford
G. M. Sayer
Stephen T. Sayer
J. B. H. Scanlon
R. G. Schloerb
Irving Schnider
J. H. B. Schroder
Peter John Schryver
Karl Schubert
Professor Jon W. Scopes
Peter G. Scopes
Dr John Scorey

Lt.Col. Sir James Scott, Bt
Raymond Copas Scott
Thomas Seager Berry
Richard Leonard Seaman
Norman Searle
James Sedcole
Christopher E. Sedgwick,
  JP, FCA
William M. Seeman
Baron Sewter
Eric H. Sexton
Gerald E. C. Sexton
Joan E. C. Sexton
Christian Seymour
Winifred Seymour
E. R. T. Shaerf
Paul Shaerf
David M. Shalit, CC
Sir William Shapland
William Crowley Sharman
James A. Sharples
Leonard A. Sharpless
Frank Shaw, CEng,
  FIMechE, Hon
  FIMechIE
J. Bryan Shaw
Captain John Shaw
John George Shaw
Philip Shelbourne
Jeremy J. Sheldon
Norman G. Sheldon
Richard S. R. Sheldon
P. G. Shelley
Robert P. Shepherd, JP
Roland W. Shepherd
Mr and Mrs Robin Sherlock
Eustace P. G. Sherrard
Nathaniel Edward
  Carwardine Sherwood
C. R. G. Shewell-Cooper
Deputy Alfred Burnett
  Shindler, FCIArb
Phyllis Netta Shindler
Peter Ashley Shipton
Albert John William
  Shirley, OBE
Paul E. Shirville
S. R. R. Sholl, MA (Oxon)
Clifford Harry Short
Ernest John Shurvinton

F. N. Shuttleworth
Romano Sidoli
R. Martin Silber
John M. Silbermann, OBE,
  FCIT, FRSA
Mrs Anne C. Arnold Silk
Mrs Marjorie Silk
Henry Silver
Ronald E. Silvester
Royston Charles Silvester
Peter A. Sim
James Albert Simmons
Keith Edward Simmons
Ronald Simmons
Stephen James Simmons
R. M. Simmonds
Vernon Churchill Simmonds
Peter Simonis
Caroline Simpson
R. Neil Sinclair
Dr Francis A. Singer
J. M. Singer
Mrs Margaret Singer
Hugh Sinnett
Hugh Dudley Sinnett
Jack Lufkin Garland Skeet
G. B. Skelston
Skilbeck Holding Company
Colonel B. G. Skinner
Sir Benjamin Slade, Bt
Derek Harrison Slade, JP
Lt.Col. Hector Slade,
  MBE, TD
Norman Whittard Slatter
Mr A. E. B. Smale
Mr Stanley George Smart
Alan G. Smith
Albert Donald Smith
Arthur Smith
Barrie E. Smith
Brian A. Smith
C. J. S. Smith
Cyril L. Smith
Frank Smith
Frederick George Smith
Gordon Walkerley Smith
Humphry M. Smith, OBE
Ivo Smith, MA, MChir,
  FRCS
J. M. Lewin Smith

Leslie E. Smith, JP
Lt.Col. L. H. Smith, OBE, TD, DL
Dr N. Brian Smith, CBE
Richard Mann Smith
Ronald E. E. Smith
Terence W. Smith
Lt.Col. William Alexander Malcolm Smith, TD, BA, MB, ChB, DOMS (Eng)
Christopher Smyth
Anthony Hugh Snodgrass
Michael E. Snow
Peter Ben Snow
John W. Solomon
Richard Somers, JP, FCA
Harvey M. Soning
John Southgate
W. F. W. Southwood
Frank Spanner
John Spanner, TD, CC
P. G. Sparks
Derek T. Sparrow, MA
Eric W. Sparrow
Ronald F. Spears
Maurice Louis Spector
George Raymond Speed
Brian Howard Spencer
Percy Gordon Spencer
Willian B. Spencer
William R. Spencer
Francis Spencer-Cotton
Michael C. B. Spens
T. C. Spicer Esq, JP
S. E. A. Spong
Alderman Sir Greville Spratt, GBE, TD, DL, DLitt
D. Robert Spray, BA, FCA
Carole Eileen Spriggs
Colin A. Springate
Ernest S. Springate
H. John Spurrier
Leonard Edwin Stace
Christopher M. Stacey
J. A. L. Stacey
John P. Stacey, TD, FRCIS
Thomas R. Stacey
John Anthony Stafford, OBE, CEng, FIProdE

Peter M. Stafford
Brian J. Stanfield
Kenneth Alan Staniland
Arthur Holbrow Stanton
Captain Eric Starling, FRMetSoc, MRAcS
Graham F. R. Starns
Martin Starr
Admiral Sir William Staveley, GCB
James W. Stead
Cyril Steed
Sir David Steel
F. W. Stephens & Co.
John W. Stephens
Peter J. Stephens
Stanley F. Stephens
Leon Sterling
Sir Sigmund Sternberg, JP, OH, KCSG
A. C. Stevens
Laura Stevens
Peter E. Stevens
Francis Malcolm Stevenson
Graham L. Steventon
M. de M. A. Stewart
R. M. I. Stewart
Malcolm D. Stirling
Marie and Gerald Stitcher
Mr Vernon N. Stockton
Michael C. Stoddart
Peter L. B. Stoddart
Captain David Alexander Stokes, OBE
Geoffrey S. Stokes
M. Veronica Stokes
Lt.Col. L. E. W. Stokes-Roberts
S. W. H. Stone
Kenneth P. W. Stoneley
C. H. W. Storer
John G. F. Stoy
A. L. Strachan, CBE, BSc, FRICS
H. Muir Stratford
John Strickland
John Strickland-Goodall, RI, RBA
Jonathan Strong
Andrew Stroud

Sir Peter Studd, GBE, KCVO, MA, DSc, DL
William John Sturdy
Simon H. Sturge
Peter Anthony Sturgess
Aubrey l'Anson Styles
Barry J. Styles, FICS
Roger W. Suddards
His Honour Edward Sutcliffe, QC
Dan W. Sutherland
S. Sutherland Pilch
Alan Sutton
Derek Sutton
Geoffrey W. Swaffield
Noel E. B. Swan
Bill Swanson
Cyril Sweett
O. M. W. Swingland, QC
Peter R. Swinnerton
William R. Sylvester
Brian Charles Symonds, ACII, APMI
Joseph William Symonds

Gavin Nicholas Tait
John Francis Tait
Robert Lindsey Tallack
Heather Tate
Mr John Richard Tattersall
Basil Taylor
Brian R. Taylor
C. K. B. Taylor, TD
Clifford Charles Taylor
Doris Alice Taylor
Ms Eileen Taylor
Frank Taylor, FCA, FCIS
J. A. F. Taylor, TD
Mr and Mrs Jeremy Taylor
John Taylor
John Peter Taylor
John William Ransom Taylor
Mr Julian Taylor
Keith Millard Taylor
Lee A. Taylor
Maxwell Taylor
Maxwell E. Taylor
Noel E. H. Taylor
Roger Taylor

Dr John G. Teall
James F. Tearle
Captain Maurice Tenger
Robert H. A. Terry
Govindsinh Thakore
Michael James Theakston
George Peter Theobald
David George Thomas
David W. Thomas
Handel Thomas
Lilian Irene Myfanwy
  Thomas, LIB
Martyn Price Thomas
David Thompson
D. M. Thompson
Gerald F. M. P. Thompson
H. R. P. Thompson
I. M. Thompson
James W. M. Thompson,
  JP
Professor Raymond
  Thompson, CBE, FEng
Raymond F. Thompson,
  CEng, FIMechE
Richard A. Thompson
Roy J. D. Thompson, FCA
Sheila and Kenneth
  Thompson
A. B. Thomson, FRICS,
  FCIArb
Clive Thomson, JP
Lt.Col. J. C. Thomson,
  MBE, TD, JP, DL
James P. S. Thomson, DM,
  MS, FRCS
Malcolm George William
  Thomson
Mr Gordon Thorburn
Sir Gerald Thorley
Napier Thorne
Alec W. Thornhill
Christopher Cholmondeley
  Thornton
Douglas H. Thornton
James D. Thornton
Adèle Loraine Thorpe
John G. Thorpe
Captain J. S. Thorpe
Richard Thorpe
Tiphook Plc

Trevor John Tiplady
Robert Marsh Tipping
Roy Tiley
Dr The Hon Alexander H.
  Todd
George A. Todd, CA
Helena Tolvanen
E. A. Tomazos
Ivan Tomlin, JP, PPCIOB
John W. Tompkins,
  DipArch (Hons), RIBA
David R. Tong, ARIBA
  FFB
Dr Peter Tooley
Ian J. S. Tosh
G. Harold R. Towers
Sqn Ldr Peter Towsey,
  BCOM, FCA
B. E. Toye
Alderman Sir Alan Traill,
  GBE, MA
James Roberton Train
Mrs Elizabeth Tranter
Richard Tranter
Kenneth Mathewson Travis
J. G. Tregoning Esq
Mrs O. D. Trentham
D. F. A. Trewby
E. Trillwood,OBE
N. J. Trillwood
Sir Charles Trinder, GBE,
  Kt, KStJ
Group Captain John W.
  Tritton, AFC
Silvino S. Trompetto, MBE
Donald Troup
Mark Edwin Tubbs
Sidney Edward Ernest
  Tuck
Sir Edward Tuckwell,
  KCVO
Group Captain H. M. H.
  Tudor, DFC, AFC, RAF
  (retd.)
Colonel Greville Tufnell
Captain M. N. Tufnell,
  CVO, DSC, Royal Navy
Derek Tullett
F. J. Turnbull
Nigel V. Turnbull

Alan Turner
C. Brian G. Turner
David J. Turner
Ernest Harry Turner
Karen Turner
Noël H. P. Turner
Michael W. Turton
Sylvia I. M. Tutt
John Ian Tweedie-Smith
Raymond William Twiddle
Major General Sir Leslie
  Tyler, KBE, CB

T. M. A. Upfill-Brown
Robert Upsdell, JP
Eric Upton-Kemp, TD,
  FRICS
David Richard Uren
Robert Mark Uren
T. R. Usher
Merlin Usher-Smith

Peter Valpy Esq
J. A. Vander-Spiegel
Neville D. Vandyk
Digby Vane
Donald Vanhegan
Air Cdre. The Hon Sir Peter
  Vanneck, MEP
Charles Keith Vartan,
  FRCS, FRCOG
Robert John Vaughan
Philip H. Venning
Richard Vergette
Miss S. J. V. Verner
His Honour Judge Verney
James L. Vernon
Dr J. P. Vestey, BM, MRCP
Joy Viall, JP
John Arthur Vickers
Peter John Viggers
Bertie W. Vigrass, OBE,
  VRD
Ronald A. Vincent
John Vinnicombe, MA,
  MChir, FRCS
Dr Jur Jürg W. Vogel
Rainer Vogt

DEDICATIONS

Thomas S. Waddell
R. W. Waggett
Roy E. L. Wagstaff
Lt.Col. C. D. Wain, MBE,
TD, DL
Michael S. T. Waite
Martyn R. Wakefield
Raymond L. Wakeham
Sir John Wakeley, Bt, FRCS
H. Richard Walduck
Stephen H. Walduck
Thomas H. Walduck
Alderman Christopher
Walford
Alec Vesey Walker
Anthony John Walker
Douglas M. Walker
Grant Walker
Major H. J. Walker, DSO
Iain B. Walker
Brigadier J. D. Walker, OBE
K. L. Walker
Louis David Walker
Dr T. M. Walker
Hugh H. Walker-Arnott
John S. Walker-Arnott
Major Sir Patrice Wall, MC,
VRD, RM (retd.)
Nevile G. Wallace
Maurice E. Wallage
Edward W. Wallaker
Percy G. Waller
C. J. Walliker
Martin William Arnold
Wallis Esq
Eldred Wright Walls
William Walrond
Jack B. Walsby
E. S. Walton
Brian Warburton
B. K. Ward
Mr C. R. P. Ward
P. J. Ward
Lt. Cdr. Geoffrey Wardle,
MBE, RN
Stuart J. H. Waring
J. Michael Warner
Simon Paul Warner
H. J. W. Warrell
Michael Raymond Warren

Colonel Ralph Warren
Brian W. Waters
Claire E. Wates
David Wallace Wates
Hugh R. Wates
Edward Watkins
Captain Horace Watkins,
MN
John Watkinson
Dr Duncan Watney
Sarah and David Watney
Alexander George Watson
Christopher David Watson
Robert J. Watson
Ronald Watts
Arthur Reginald Waylett
Len Weaver
Clifford F. J. Webb
Edward James Webb
John V. Webb
Mr M. H. S. Webber
John A. Wedgwood, CBE
William Ernest Weetman
John Weir
William Weir
Sir John Welch, Bt
Lt. Cdr. I. R. Wellesley-
Harding, RN
Francis Charles Wells
John R. Wells
Keith A. Wells
Richard Wells
James E. Welsby
David Hartley West
George Philip West
Peter Hartley West
E. J. Westnedge, OBE
Alec Weston
Rear Admiral C. A. W.
Weston, CB
John Steven Wharton
Wilfred Hartley Wharton,
JP
Marlene and David G.
Whatley
W. Norman Wheat, MBE,
BSc
Ivison S. Wheatley, MA
Jack Wheeler
John A. C. Wheeler

Thomas Whipham
J. Brian Whitaker
Sam Whitbread
Montague C. J. Whitby
Mr Eric White
Mr James W. White,
MGDS, LDS, RCSEng,
CC
John White
John Kingsley White, TD
Lewis White
Norman A. White
Thomas Haydn Whitehouse
Henry V. White-Smith
Captain Denis T. Whitham
Harold O. Whiting
Richard Whittington, MC
Nigel Roy Whitwell
Benjamin J. Wickham
D. E. Wickham, MA,
ARHistS
J. E. A. Wickham, MS, BSc,
FRCS
Stephen P. Wickham
Captain D. B. Wilkie
Charles Maldwyn Wilkin
Edward Wilkinson
R. P. A. Willan
Robert M. Willan
W. F. Willats
Arthur Charles Willcocks
Ronald E. B. Willcox
Vernon and Rosina Willey
Alan P. Williams
Bryn Williams
Lieutenant Commander
David Williams, FNI,
Royal Navy
Frank Williams
Geoffrey M. J. Williams,
MA, FEng, FICE,
FIStructE
Hugh Curzon Williams
John and Kay Williams and
Children
John R. Williams
Kenneth Lindsley Williams
Ray Williams
Professor Robert C. G.
Williams, OBE

W. Charles Williams
Captain D.. K. Williamson
D. Williams-Thomas
E. B. Williams-Thomas
J. S. Williams-Thomas
Squadron Leader Charles H.
  Willis, AFC, AE
Nicholas Wills
John Wilmshurst
Sir Anthony Wilson
Bryan C. Wilson
C. Thelma Wilson
Frank Peter Wilson
Lt.Col. H. R. G. Wilson
James Ryland Wilson
John J. H. Wilson Esq,
  OBE
Robert H. Wilson
Geoffrey Windsor-Lewis
Peter S. Winfield
Thomas Frank Winkworth
Paul Winner
Dr Henry Winsley-Stolz
Michael Hugh Winterborn,
  FRCP
Nicholas R. Winterton, MP
Robert Cameron Wiseman
John C. Wittich
Francis E. B. Witts

H. A. Woellwarth
Laurie S. Wolder
Herbert Wolman Esq
Barbara Wood
Miss Joan Wood
John Edward Wood, OBE
Malcolm Wood
Richard Wood
Anthony Russell Bethune
  Woodd
John Page Woodger
Brian Woodifield
Barry M. Woodman
Dr P. W. R. Woodruff
Robert Woodward
Leslie P. Woolf
Robert MacDonald
  Woollard
C. D. Wootton-Woolley,
  CBE, MM, LLD(Hon)
L. A. Worham
Peter F. Worlidge
Roger P. M. Wormal
Peter Roydon Wormell Esq
Francis Edward Worsley
Frederick Maynard Wraight
E. Alan Wright
Keith G. Wright
Keith Godfrey Wright

P. R. S. Wright
Peter Wright
John L. Wybrew
John Wykes
A. P. Wyman

Peter G. Yarranton
Sir Eric Yarrow
Captain Peter Thomas
  Yeandle
Frank W. Yeomans
Richard David Yeomans
Richard Youell
Arthur Young
George C. Young
Alderman Neil Young
Nicholas E. Young
Peter L. Young
Ronald Young
Thomas Young, OBE
William C. Young, MA,
  FIOP
David Keith Youngman

Michael Philip Zaidner
I. Arnold Ziff
Michael André Zuckerman

INDEX

Abbot, Sir Morris 83, 86
Abdul Aziz, Sultan of Turkey 152
Abney, Sir Thomas 101, 103
Ackroyd, Sir Cuthbert 174
Acton, Sir William 84
Adam, Robert 102
Adams, Thomas 87, 88–9
Adrien, John 13
Alexander II, Tsar of Russia 153
Alexander, Sir Frank 175
Aleyn, Sir John 56, 168
Allen, William Ferneley 152
Alleyn, Thomas 89
Allot, John 61
Althorp, Lord (John Charles Spencer) 140
Amadas, Robert 53
Amcotts, Henry 50
Anderson, John William 133
Andrewes, Thomas 88
Anne, Queen 104, 105, 109
Asgill, Sir Charles 116
Ashurst, Sir William 100
Askew, Anne 54
Askham, William 28
Astry, Ralp 45
Atkyn, Thomas 84, 87
Attwood, Thomas 140
Audley, Hugh 94
Aylmer, Sir Lawrence 52

Baddeley, Sir John 163
Baker, Richard 68
Baker, Timothy 32
Bamme, Adam 26, 27
Barber, John 106, 109
Barentyn, Drew 27–8
Barker, John 157
Barkham, Edward 81–2, 104
Barnard, Sir John 107, 109, 110, 111, 112,
    113, 115, 116–17
Barne, George (mayor 1552) 49, 57
Barne, George (mayor 1586) 49
Bat, Gerard 12
Bateman, Sir Anthony 89
Bateman, Sir James 101, 107
Becher, Sir Edward 108
Beckford, William 116, 119–20, 122–3, 175
Belknap, Sir Robert 23
Bellinger, Sir Robert 174
Bennett, Sir Thomas 75, 81
Berry, Joseph 116
Billers, Sir William 110
Billesden, Robert 43
Billingsley, Henry 49, 59, 60
Birch, Samuel 136, 175
Blachford, John 114
Blades, Sir George 160
Blanchard, Robert 101
Blanke, John 50

INDEX

de Bury, Adam 20, 21
de Chigwell, Hamo 17, 18
de Cotun, John 17
de Farndone, Nicholas 16
de Gisors, John 16–17
de Keyser, Polydore 156–7, 158
de Kirkeby, John 15
de la Bère, Sir Rupert 167
de Montfort, Simon 13
de Northampton, John 23, 25, 26, 27
de Norton, Geoffrey 16
de Pulteney, John 19
de Refham, Richer 16
de Rokesley, Gregory 14, 15, 158
de Sandwich, Ralph 16
de Wengrave, John 17
Dee, John 60
Dekker, Thomas 32, 72, 78
Dethick, John 88, 89
Dickens, Charles 144
Dimsdale, Sir Joseph 160
Disraeli, Benjamin 154
Dixie, Wolstan 49, 59–60, 62, 69
Dobbis, Richard 63
Dodmer, Ralph 48–9
Donaldson, Dame Mary 4, 175–6
Donne, John 80
Draper, Christopher 49
Dryden, John 94
Ducket, Lionel 52
Dudley, Edmund 51, 52
Duell, William 113
Duke, Sir James 147–8
Duncombe, Sir Charles 103–4

Edward I, King 13, 14–16, 18
Edward II, King 16–18
Edward III, King 18–22
Edward IV, King 34–5, 36–7, 45
Edward VI, King 57
Edwards, Sir James 93
Edwin, Sir Humphrey 102–3
Eleanor of Provence (wife of Henry III) 11
Elizabeth I, Queen 53, 58, 59–65, 68, 75–6
Elizabeth II, Queen 168, 170
Elizabeth, Queen of Bohemia 78
Ellis, John Whittaker 155
Empson, Sir Richard 51, 52
Esdaile, Sir James 126–7
Essex, Robert Devereux, 2nd Earl of 60

Estfeld, William 34, 44
Evans, David 158–9
Evelyn, John 72, 89, 91, 95
Exton, Nicholas 26
Eyles, Sir John (mayor 1688) 97
Eyles, Sir John (mayor 1726) 107–8
Eyre, Simon 31–2

Fahd, King of Saudi Arabia 171
Farncomb, Thomas 148
Fauconer, Thomas 33, 44, 45
Faudel-Phillips, George 151, 159, 163
Ferrers, George 57
Fiennes, Celia 73–4
Fitch, Ralph 59
FitzAilwyn, Henry 10, 158
FitzAlan, Roger 10
Fitzmary, Simon 12
FitzOsbert, William 10
FitzRichard, William 12
Fitzstephen, William 9
FitzThedmar, Arnald 9, 13
FitzThomas 12–13
Fitzwaryn, Alice 29
Fludyer, Sir Samuel 119
Foot, Thomas 88
Forster, Stephen 44
Fowke, John 88
Fowler, Robert 154, 155, 156
Fox, Charles James 129
Frederick, Sir John 89, 90
Freeman, Ralph 82
Froissart, Jean 27
Frowicke, Henry 14
Fryer, Sir John 107
Fuad II, King of Egypt 163

Gabriel, Thomas 151–2, 153
Gadsden, Sir Peter 174, 176–7
Gardiner, Sir Thomas 83
Garrard, Sir Samuel 104
Garrarde, John 49, 104
Garrarde, William 49, 57
Garraway, Sir Henry 72, 83–4, 86
Garraway, Sir William 83
Gascoyne, Crisp 115–16
Gaveston, Piers 16
Gayer, Sir John 84, 87
Geffery, Sir Robert 97
George I, King 105–7, 109

221

INDEX

Shaw, Sir James 134–5, 137
Shorter, Sir John 97
Sidney, Thomas 149
Skeggs, Edward 52
Skinner, Thomas 60, 132
Smith, Sir Bracewell 175
Smith, Joshua Jonathan 134, 136
Smith, Thomas 136
Soame, Stephen 64
Soames, Thomas 84
Soulsby, William 160
Spencer, Elizabeth 60–1
Spencer, Sir John 43, 60–1
Spode, Josiah 144
Spratt, Sir Greville 171, 175, 176
Stable, Adam 22
Staines, Sir William 134
Stanier, Sir Samuel 105
Staper, Richard 59
Stapleton, Bishop Walter 17
Starling, Sir Samuel 92
Staundon, William 27
Stockton, John 35, 36
Stokker, Sir William 36, 61
Stone, David 154
Stone, Lawrence 61
Stow, John 53, 67–8, 75
Stow, Thomas 53
Strafford, Thomas, 1st Earl of 84–5
Strong, Sir Thomas Vesey 160, 161
Stuart, Charles Edward (Bonnie Prince Charlie) 114–15
Studd, Sir J. E. Kynaston 163, 175
Studd, Sir Peter 175
Summerson, Sir John 92
Swynnerton, Sir John 77–8

Taillour, William 36
Taylor, Sir Robert 116
Thompson, William 139
Thorp, John Thomas 136, 138, 139
Tichborne, Robert 88, 89
Toms, W. H. 131
Tooke, Horne 123
Townsend, James 119, 125
Townshend, 2nd Viscount 107
Traill, Sir Alan 171, 176
Trecothick, Barlow 123–4
Treloar, Sir William 160–1, 163
Trinder, Sir Charles 173

Trott, Martha 94–5
Trustcott, Sir Denis 174
Truscott, Sir Francis W. 174
Truscott, Sir George Wyatt 162, 174
Truscott, James 174
Turner, Sir William 92–3, 164
Twyford, Sir Nicholas 23, 25, 26
Tyler, Walter 25

Uffenbach, Conrad Von 104–5

Vanneck, Sir Peter 175, 176
Venour, William 23, 26
Verney, Ralph 35, 36
Victoria, Queen 145, 155, 157
Villiers, Barbara 101
Vincent, Sir Percy 163
Vyner, Sir Robert 92, 93–4
Vyner, Thomas 88, 89, 93

Waithman, Robert 136, 138–9
Wakefield, Sir Charles 160, 161–2, 163
Waley-Cohen, Sir Bernard 174
Walpole, Sir Robert 104, 106, 107, 108,
    109–10, 114
Walsingham, Thomas 25–6
Walton, Isaac 64
Walworth, William 20, 23, 24–5
Ward, Sir John 96, 100, 107
Ward, Sir Patience 95, 96, 100, 139
Warner, John 87
Warren, Sir Ralph 56
Waterlow, Sir Sydney 153, 154
Watson, Brook 133
Watts, Sir Isaac 103
Watts, Sir John 77
Webb, Sidney *and* Beatrice 143
Webb, William 69
Webbe, William 49
Webster, John 71
Weld, Sir Humphrey 77
Welles, John 31, 34
Wellington, Arthur, 1st Duke of 135–6,
    138, 139
Wheeler, Elizabeth 101
Whitehead, James 157–8
Whitmore, Sir George 90
Whittington, Richard 27, 28–30, 40, 41, 43,
    158
Whittington, Sir William 28

INDEX